Proclaim Peace

Proclaim Peace

Christian

Pacifism

from

Unexpected

Quarters

EDITED BY

THERON F. SCHLABACH AND RICHARD T. HUGHES

Introduction by Shirley Hershey Showalter

UNIVERSITY OF ILLINOIS PRESS   URBANA AND CHICAGO

This book is printed on acid-free paper.

The editors are grateful to Dr. William S. Banowsky, former president of Pepperdine University, who facilitated the funding that helped to make this volume possible.

Library of Congress Cataloging-in-Publication Data

Proclaim peace : Christian pacifism from unexpected quarters / edited by
 Theron F. Schlabach and Richard T. Hughes ; introduction by Shirley
 Hershey Showalter.
    p.   cm.
  Includes bibliographical references (p.   ) and index.
  ISBN 0-252-02262-9 (cloth : acid-free paper). — ISBN 0-252-06588-3
 (pbk. : acid-free paper).
  1. Pacifism—Religious aspects—Christianity—History. 2. Pacifism—
United States—History. 3. United States—Church history. I. Schlabach,
Theron F. II. Hughes, Richard T. (Richard Thomas), 1943– .
BT736.6.P76   1997
261.8'73'0973—dc20   96-10069
                                       CIP

CONTENTS

Contributors

Index

PREFACE

Richard T. Hughes

Is the study of pacifism in history worthwhile if academicians have not established its normative value for themselves? Can they treat it simply as a historical story? If historians do not interact with pacifism and let it engage them, can they treat the subject authentically?
—*Charles Chatfield*

This book contains essays by several Christian historians who have engaged the pacifist tradition from a variety of Christian perspectives. With few exceptions the authors participate in Christian traditions that are not generally identified as peace churches but that have seriously engaged the pacifist witness at various levels and at various times in their histories. The fact that these historians care deeply about the pacifist witness and that most of them write about that witness in the context of their own traditions imbues these essays with the quality of engagement and interaction for which Professor Chatfield has called.

Most, if not all, of these authors are deeply sympathetic to the pacifist heritage. Some, such as Ronald Wells, write from a just-war framework, albeit with just-war interpretations quite supportive of pacifism. William Marty is the only author who seriously questions the legitimacy of the pacifist witness. Indeed Marty forthrightly indicts the liberal Protestant variety of pacifism that was strong between World Wars I and II. Nonetheless his essay fits this book, both because Marty comments on a tradition of Christian pacifism outside the historic peace churches and because the essay rounds out a conversation with other authors of the volume.

Marty's essay—which offers a critique much like that of the prominent midcentury Protestant theologian Reinhold Niebuhr—explores the views of Christians who adopted pacifism as a strategy for winning global peace. In Marty's view their movement was doomed to failure because its pacifism robbed it of any real ability to exercise political power in a world that respects violence and threats of violence. In his own words, "A politically engaged pacifism, by its commitment to pacifism, undermines the very strategies it proposes for avoiding war." As a result, Marty concludes, "The new pacifism helped to produce invasions, war, conquests, and the deaths of some tens of millions."

Those are charges that anyone concerned with peace and justice must take seriously. How would Christians who espouse an absolute pacifism respond?

The essays that follow shed light on that question. Indeed, in several of the traditions considered here, two normative visions surface time and again. One vision looks to the apostolic church as the standard for Christian behavior and as a foundation for the pacifist witness. This theme emerges in varying degrees of intensity in the essays on the Churches of Christ, the Church of God (Anderson, Indiana), the Assemblies of God, and the Church of God in Christ. Murray Dempster perhaps spoke for all these traditions when he wrote that the early Assemblies of God understood pacifism as "the moral sign of a restored New Testament Apostolic faith."

The second vision appeals to an eschatological understanding of reality. With this vision believers avidly long for a time when God's rule on this earth will be complete. More to the point, they reject the norms of the "principalities and powers of this present age" when those norms fail to conform to their understanding of the kingdom of God. Instead they conform their lives to that kingdom, which they anticipate will finally triumph over all the earth.

One finds this sort of eschatological vision especially among the Seventh-day Adventists, who, as George Knight has noted, "imbibed their view of government from the great, panoramic prophecies of Daniel and the Book of Revelation." And Patricia McNeal informs us that the statement by virtue of which "the American Catholic peace movement was born" rested on distinctly eschatological foundations. In that statement a midwestern Catholic radical named Paul Hanley Furfey based pacifism squarely "on the Christian's calling to a kingdom of love and peace, which takes precedence over one's calling to obey the state." Developing that idea, Furfey then "called for a return to the eschatological pacifist vision of the early saints and church fathers." Although the essays do not always spell out this vision, it is common knowledge that a strong eschatological vision also informed the Churches of Christ, the Church of God, the Latter-day Saints, and a variety of pentecostal traditions, especially in their earliest years.

Perhaps none of the authors here articulates the eschatological vision and its relevance for the pacifist ethic more cogently than does Leonard Allen in his response to the essays on the Churches of Christ and the Church of God. "The Christian ethic," Allen argues, "is grounded in a bold eschatological claim—the claim that in Jesus' death and resurrection the 'powers' of this present age have been disarmed and defeated. . . . Knowing this, the disciple can follow Jesus in all things, even in those things that seem to be utterly impractical and unworkable to those who do not know what Christians know. The Christian way of nonresistance and nonviolence is grounded in just such an eschatological claim."

Skeptics might well dismiss these two visions—the vision of Christian beginnings and the final triumph of the kingdom of God—as sheer escapism, nothing more. Those who affirm these visions understand them in a very different way, however. For them the apostolic age and the eschatological kingdom of God are sacred epochs that bracket history and time and thereby offer indispensable supports that sustain an alternate vision of reality. In turn that alternate vision of reality sustains an ethic radically different from the norms that sanction violence and war.

In spite of these supports, it is striking how quickly the pacifist tradition crumbled in many of the traditions considered here, especially during wartime. For the Churches of Christ and the Assemblies of God, the pacifist tradition unraveled especially during World War I. For the Church of God, the collapse occurred especially during World War II. For the Church of God in Christ, collapse was evident during World War II and virtually complete by the time of the Vietnam War.

The loss of an eschatological or a restorationist perspective is a fundamental reason for such collapse. In addition, the stories told in this book reveal again and again the failure of these churches to develop a *tradition* of pacifism sustained by meaningful *narrative*. For example, Murray Dempster has noted that the Assemblies of God and World War I were born in the same year. In that light, he observes, "before they had an opportunity to cultivate a pacifist *tradition*, . . . history had overtaken them and the nation's patriotic war spirit had invaded the house, never to leave."

Merle Strege argues that the Church of God also failed to develop a meaningful pacifist tradition or any kind of narrative by which that tradition could be shared with succeeding generations. "Without the narratives of a peace church," Strege argues, "it is difficult to sustain pacifist commitments in the face of a powerful nationalist ideology."

On the other hand, the Churches of Christ developed a strong pacifist witness in the early nineteenth century, even though that witness declined as the century wore on and virtually collapsed during World War I. Michael Casey argues that the collapse of that witness rested in part on the rationalism and biblicism of the Churches of Christ, which virtually precluded narrative. In that tradition, Casey notes, "one's own prejudices, emotions, and experiences are to be hidden and kept out of sight in studying the Bible and Christianity; there is no legitimate place for experience or personal narrative. Consequently no stories of COs are told in church or in Bible study. When narrative, history, and tradition are devalued, events and experiences quickly recede in the collective memory."

Ironically one could argue that many of these Bible-based, sectarian movements missed the narrative in the Bible itself. As Chatfield reminds us, "Pacifists without a peace church heritage . . . return to the Bible precisely because the Bible at least offers a story: principle validated in experience."

Furthermore, time after time, according to these essays, communities of faith that began with a strong pacifist ethic abandoned that ethic in the interest of a distinctly American virtue: the freedom to choose. This pattern sets them in contrast to heirs of the sixteenth-century Anabaptists. One might well conclude that the American religious traditions treated in this book lacked the characteristic that perhaps was more responsible than any other factor for the persistence of pacifism among groups with roots in Anabaptism. That characteristic is a serious ecclesiastical discipline that nourished resistance to the values of the larger culture.

Although particular wars took their toll on the pacifist witness of certain traditions, it is important to observe that those same wars both sustained and helped to create a pacifist witness in other contexts. As Theodore Kornweibel has pointed out, the Church of God in Christ, a largely African-American community of faith, is a notable case in point. Although the federal government and its various agencies placed that community under intense pressure to conform to the militarism demanded during World War I, the community refused to collapse. At the same time, having been rejected from the mainstream of American life because of the color of their skin, they knew that equal opportunity in the United States was closed to them regardless of the stand they took on violence and war.

Similarly the Roman Catholic church illustrates the virtual creation of a strong pacifist witness in the context of a war that helped to undermine that witness in other communities of faith. As Patricia McNeal points out, the American Catholic church underwent significant transformation during the Vietnam era. Prior to Vatican II Dorothy Day's *Catholic Worker,* with its Catholic Worker movement, was the single force that "kept the Catholic pacifist witness alive" in the United States. But, McNeal observes, Vatican II "implicitly . . . undermined the theory of the just war," which had long informed the Catholic tradition. Perhaps because Vatican II coincided with the Vietnam War, a pacifist tradition that had been stirring in American Catholicism since the mid-1930s now blossomed into full flower. McNeal notes that by 1969, "in absolute numbers the Catholic church had more COs than did any other religious body." Perhaps more important, "for the first time in U.S. history the American Catholic hierarchy declared that conscientious objectors, even selective conscientious objectors, have a basis for their position in modern Catholic teaching."

Finally, many of the stories in this volume tell of profound ambiguity regarding war and peace, even if the ambiguity surfaced in different traditions in different ways.

In the first place, the Latter-day Saints represent a tradition in which ambiguity was part and parcel of the church's theology from the outset. The community stood for peace but finally drew the sword in self-defense. As Joseph Smith affirmed, "We are for peace, and we intend to have it, if we have to fight for it."

In the second place, ambiguity characterized other traditions, since the leaders on the one hand and rank and file on the other were split on questions of war and peace. Perhaps no denomination illustrates this characteristic more graphically than the Assemblies of God. Although many journal articles from that group reflect a pronounced commitment to pacifism during the denomination's earliest years, those articles—according to Dempster—reflect the commitment of leaders, not of members. Therefore many articles exhibit "a definite advocacy character. Their goal was to persuade, not to describe an established denominational position."

Finally, ambiguity also surfaced in churches that traditionally had subscribed to just-war theory. For example, based on that theory the

United Methodist church rejected war in principle while supporting the government's war efforts. Therefore many Methodist young people learned that war is unacceptable and yet received little or no support from their church when they claimed conscientious objector status.

Likewise a vocal group of "neo-Calvinists" influenced by Reformed church–reformer Abraham Kuyper challenged the traditional just-war position of the Christian Reformed Church. These Kuyper followers spoke out especially in the context of the Vietnam War. In 1977 their church responded with an important synodical pronouncement, "Ethical Decisions about War." As Ronald A. Wells has noted, this report made "a pacifist response to war a . . . legitimate stance for Reformed Christians." Later, however, when the Gulf War broke out, leaders of the Christian Reformed tradition fell back on the old just-war theory. As Wells explains, pacifists in that communion, feeling estranged, asked their church, "What good is it to have a good position on war if, when the test comes, it does not issue in good behavior?"

All in all, the essays in this book reflect serious engagement with the pacifist witness on the part of a diverse group of Christian denominations. They also reveal the importance of narrative, tradition, and strong theological supports for keeping that witness alive. Finally, however, they reveal how difficult it is to sustain that witness in the democratic culture of the United States, especially in times of national mobilization for war.

Proclaim Peace

INTRODUCTION

Shirley Hershey Showalter

If one is interested in achieving a degree of justice and order in the world, then one must be willing, if necessary, to resist armed aggression with force.
—William R. Marty

Christians through the centuries have believed that even in suffering and through the seeming triumph of evil, God is present. They have believed that the God who triumphed over evil through innocent suffering and death on the cross triumphs in history, even while evil humans still kill innocent ones. With that faith, some Christians decide that they need not join those who hurt and kill in order to help their God.
—Ted Koontz

I thank God for the persecution. "For all that live godly must suffer persecution."
—Bishop Charles Harrison Mason, of the Church of God in Christ, as quoted by Theodore Kornweibel Jr.

Many readers of this book will not be pacifists. Nor will they identify with all the varieties of religious experience—Pentecostal, Churches of Christ, Church of God, Church of God in Christ, Mormon, Adventist, liberal Protestant, Methodist, Roman Catholic, and Christian Reformed—on which this book draws. Perhaps they will know or agree with none of them. Why then read this book? The three epigraphs correspond to three important reasons: (1) to understand competing Christian views of war, their origins, and their particular trajectories inside

different churches; (2) to recognize the role of personal and biblical stories, images, and songs in creating a Christian pacifist tradition; and (3)
to observe the importance of willingness to suffer as a central issue of
Christian pacifism.

The issue of how Christian churches in America have defined themselves around questions of war and peace illustrates the paradoxical
nature of Christianity itself, for pacifism assumes strength in weakness.
When the church increases in numbers, wealth, and attachments to the
culture, pacifism declines. Nonetheless, pacifism can spring up within
or return to large denominations also, usually as a minority of a denomination's members begin to become active for social justice. Today the
numbers of pacifists among Catholics and liberal Protestants are growing. Among Churches of Christ, Adventists, Mormons, and Assemblies
of God, however, only remnants of once-vibrant pacifist traditions remain.

It seems that pacifism never dies but often fades away. To recall two
phrases from the 1960s, the answer to the question, "What if they gave
a war and no one came?" is still "blowin' in the wind."

COMPETING VIEWS OF WAR

If one is interested in achieving a degree of justice and order in the world,
then one must be willing, if necessary, to resist armed aggression with force.
—William R. Marty

An outsider to pacifism may wish to begin with Professor William R.
Marty's passionate and cogent critique of the liberal Protestant, "engaged," twentieth-century version. Marty's analysis not only injects some
honest skepticism into a group of essays generally sympathetic to
pacifism, but it also illustrates why "realism" and just-war theories are
much more popular than pacifism. Such theories conform better not
only to the human and national instinct for self-defense but also to re-
alpolitik ideas of justice and order. In this book Ted Koontz points out
that realism has no better record of preventing war than does pacifism,
yet he grants that it is hard to argue with Marty's critique on its own
terms. Marty contends that, by opposing preparedness and all sanctions,
men like the Fellowship of Reconciliation's Kirby Page and *Christian
Century* editor Charles Morrison actually extended and worsened the
violence of the eventual and probably inevitable march of Adolf Hitler.
Thus Marty can argue that by trying to make pacifism effective, liberal

Protestants accomplished just the opposite: they expanded the scope of violence.

Of course Marty is in the good company of Reinhold Niebuhr, the noted theologian who championed hard-headed "realism" over soft-minded pacifism, particularly liberal pacifism. In 1961, in an introduction to a reprint of philosopher William James's classic *The Varieties of Religious Experience* (1902), Niebuhr rejected James's optimism partly because he rejected James's views about war. In an understatement of his objection to James's search for a "moral equivalent" for violence, he called James's formula "a rather too simple road to a warless world."[1] Explaining his own position, Niebuhr focused on the collective destiny of the human race, using some of his favorite language: "perplexities," "anxiety," "catastrophe," and "just relations in the increasing intricacies of a technical civilization." In 1961 Niebuhr thought that James's ideas were very dated: "Living after two world wars and in the midst of a nuclear dilemma, we are bound to take the problem of the meaning of history more seriously than James did."[2]

Thirty-four years later Americans have not become more optimistic about peace, but many have become more interested in preventing war. Catholics, especially, find the threat of nuclear war to be the one convincing reason that pacifism is desirable and that just-war theories are inadequate. In 1962, however, just one year before the Second Vatican Council, Niebuhr could not have predicted that Pope John XXIII would create an entirely new Catholic attitude toward all war in a nuclear age through his encyclical *Pacem in Terris*. Nor would he have guessed that in 1983 the American Council of Bishops would declare that pacifists in the Roman Catholic church have support in church doctrine. Patricia McNeal's essay in this book carefully details the changes in the official doctrine of the Catholic church.

Although leaders of many Protestant and Catholic churches are pursuing peace on an even broader scale than they did in the 1930s, the fact remains that in the last American test of the strength of that commitment—the Persian Gulf War of 1991—few clergy and even fewer laymembers actively opposed America's action. All through this century the interest in peace was strong between wars but then shifted dramatically, as if by Pavlovian conditioning, once the president sent in troops or Congress declared war. During war a thin layer of nonsectarian pacifism frequently gives way to deeply entrenched just-war theory and habits of obeying the state.

Charles Chatfield's overview essay at the beginning of this book explains why, at least between wars, pacifism can coexist with American patriotism. The religious dreams of creating a "city on the hill" or a "holy experiment," plus George Washington's and Thomas Jefferson's wise isolationism, provided a historical justification for social reformer Jane Addams's argument in 1917 that "peace is patriotic." Chatfield locates Addams and other "friends of peace" in early twentieth-century America within a tradition of internationalism that started in 1815 with citizens' action groups in the United States, Europe, Russia, and Japan, and he describes their attitude toward their own countries as "patriotism without walls." He credits these groups with many accomplishments, from the Kellogg-Briand Pact of 1928, to the establishment of international nongovernmental organizations (NGOs) as peacemaking ventures in poor countries, to the creation of many domestic organizations designed to relieve hunger and human suffering. To be sure, Chatfield does not explain why this kind of patriotism will inevitably win if the nation as a whole sees pacifism and patriotism as being in conflict. Nevertheless, he describes the development of a sense of global interdependence as essential to a contemporary American identity: "Americans will mature in that kind of patriotism insofar as they nurture that type of pacifism." Chatfield thus admires the very people whom Marty chastises.

As a Mennonite pacifist, I sympathize with Chatfield's "friends of peace." As an American studies scholar, however, I, along with respondent Ted Koontz, share some of Marty's and Niebuhr's skepticism about the efficacy of engaged pacifism even while I prefer it to militarism. Sometimes—indeed, often—pacifism does not achieve its goals. To at least one kind of religious mind in America, however, efficacy matters less than faithfulness.

THE ROLE OF STORIES, IMAGES, AND SONGS

Christians through the centuries have believed that even in suffering and through the seeming triumph of evil, God is present. They have believed that the God who triumphed over evil through innocent suffering and death on the cross triumphs in history, even while evil humans still kill innocent ones. With that faith, some Christians decide that they need not join those who hurt and kill in order to help their God.
—Ted Koontz

For the reader who sympathizes with pacifism or who is at least fascinated by its survival, the preceding words from the conclusion of Ted

Koontz's response to William R. Marty and S. Ronald Parks hold a key to one of the most intriguing questions regarding all the essays in this volume. What factors sustain pacifism within American Christian churches, and what factors cause it to fade away? Although the historic peace churches—including, among others, Quakers, Mennonites, Brethren, Amish, and Hutterites—are *not* the subject of this volume, they shadow it. That is because, on this subject, they are in effect a control group. What keeps a counterintuitive and countercultural tradition alive in one group and lets it die out in another? Surely the causes must be many, yet a number of the authors of these essays (Chatfield and Strege especially) hint at one important distinction: peace churches have a theology that allows, even privileges, lived faith rather than propositional faith. When lives change through faith, people tell their stories to one another. As a community tells its stories, it develops a tradition capable of adaptation to each generation's circumstances.

For example, a well-nurtured Mennonite should be able to tell the story of Dirk Willems, a Dutchman who paused in 1569 to rescue his would-be captor while attempting to escape his execution for the crime of being an Anabaptist.[3] Willems pulled his pursuer, a palace prison guard, out of frigid water after the man had broken through thin ice on a castle moat. Thereupon Willems was recaptured and eventually burned at the stake. The 4,000 Anabaptists who died for their faith were not all so heroic, but the fact that the *Martyrs' Mirror* (1660) mesmerized generations with its conflict-filled, inspiring, and sometimes gory tales did more for Mennonite identity than did theological treatises. Historian John S. Oyer has written that "next to the Bible and some hymnals," the *Martyrs' Mirror* was (and, in some cases, is) "the most important literary possession of Mennonite families."[4]

The story of the *Martyrs' Mirror*'s relation to Mennonite pacifism during the American Revolution is instructive. Originally the tome was written in Dutch, whereas the first American Mennonite communities spoke German. On the eve of the French and Indian War, Mennonites wanted the stories to be put into German, especially for the sake of their youth, as political tensions within the colonies increased. By 1748–49 they had gotten a scholar and the press at the Ephrata Cloister in Pennsylvania to translate the stories and print 1,300 copies of the 1,512-page compilation.[5] The stories that Mennonites absorbed from the *Martyrs' Mirror* are a strong explanation of why Mennonites maintained their pacifism during the American Revolution.

Stories seem to be valued within Christian traditions in inverse proportion to emphasis on rationalism or teleology. Churches that place strong emphasis on a learned clergy, systematic theology, or orthodoxy seem to have difficulty sustaining pacifism. Michael Casey, of Pepperdine University, concludes in his Churches of Christ essay that those congregations' "Baconian Enlightenment heritage," which emphasized rationality and excluded experience and personal narrative, had prevented pacifism from taking root: "When narrative, history, and tradition are devalued, events and experiences quickly recede in the collective memory."[6]

Likewise, Ronald Wells traces the result of the 1977 "Ethical Decisions" report on war within the Christian Reformed Church. A new biblical hermeneutic resulted in a document Wells describes as "a landmark in the social teaching of the Christian Reformed Church." This closely reasoned statement did not declare the Bible to be an unequivocally pacifist book, but it did recognize a progression in the Bible toward peace and away from war. It also questioned the authority of the state in cases of unjust war, and it created a process by which the church should attempt to discern whether a particular war is just or unjust, even while giving support to those who might dissent from the church's conclusion. The rational basis for support of a pacifist minority (or even a majority) was in place, but Wells laments that it was not used in the Persian Gulf War. The document passed the Calvinist test of justification for pacifism but could not pass the test of experience. When orthodoxy means more than orthopraxy, more than the search for the right way to live, then the church's energy goes toward sustaining right belief, which may not always make its way into practice. When orthopraxy influences orthodoxy, doctrine cannot flourish unless biblical interpretation and stories of the faith call it forth and sustain it.

Orthopraxy requires help from a community of the like-minded. Its method of belief is deontological, rooted in moral obligation and commitment, rather than teleological, focused on the design and purpose of nature. Communities seeking to be the church use pictures, stories, and other folk art forms to nourish conviction. Both highly educated and minimally educated pacifists use narratives, sometimes consciously, sometimes not. Pacifist writers have a special role to play in the development of contemporary communities. As Richard Bernstein has said of twentieth-century Yiddish writers, they mix "old and new in a new cultural creation."[7]

The best way to illustrate the connection between narrative, community, and pacifism is to examine a poem. Among Mennonites a renaissance in the arts is beginning in the United States; in Canada such a renaissance has been flourishing for more than three decades. One young U.S. poet, Julia Kasdorf, whose ancestry includes both Mennonites and Amish, lends a vigorous voice within the fledgling renaissance in the United States. Her use of narrative sometimes lovingly subverts or overtly challenges the tradition from which she sprang. Her life connects the old sectarian pacifism to a newer liberal Protestant pacifism, so that not surprisingly she becomes most lyric about her Mennonite and Amish tradition when it points to peace. Her poem "Uncle" is included in her first book, which won the Agnes Lynch Starrett Poetry Prize in 1991:

At nine I knew what Jesus would do
if he got C.O. just for being born
Mennonite. He'd go anyway, like you.

In the name of peace, he'd race
an ambulance through the screaming streets
of Saigon. He'd grow a moustache to show
he wasn't a soldier—a speck
on the camera lens, Grandpa insisted.

He'd take a generator to a village
in the hills where golden children
would run behind him yelling, "Mother Fucker."

He'd thrust brilliant green blades
of rice into the fields where men's legs
and the torsos of water buffaloes exploded
when plows struck bombs in the mud.

When the planes returned, he'd load
whomever he could into the only car,
drive to a refugee camp, and there give up
at last, as you gave up bearing that war
on your tall, blond body.

Lost across the continents for months,
you returned to us, the uncle of someone else,
gaunt as a corpse, pale and haunted.
And when you could barely finish
a child's portion at Howard Johnson's,
that was the only miracle I could grasp.[8]

This poem shows us an incarnational way of knowing.[9] A child has a tall, blond uncle who does not accept an easy conscientious objection

(CO) alternative to the Vietnam War. Instead he does what the child thinks Jesus would do—he goes to the place of war and tries to make peace. The poem's narrative draws much of its authority from its connections to the parables Jesus told and the life he lived. The child must know a lot of Bible stories already to imagine Jesus in Saigon. By the fifth stanza the child no longer simply imagines Jesus doing what her uncle has done. She totally conflates the two beings into one, speaking as though to Jesus: "and there give up / at last, as you gave up bearing that war / on your tall, blond body."

An anthropologist looking at this poem might call it "thick description" of a deeply interconnected community. Every person in the poem other than Jesus and the Vietnamese is a blood relative of the child, who is learning in the same way that village children learn the world over— from kin and from elders. The poem ends with a striking image. The uncle's shrunken stomach, unable to digest an adult portion, is a physical emblem of how he bears his suffering in the body. His smallness in size bespeaks largeness of spirit to a child who has heard that to enter the kingdom of heaven, adults must become children again (Mark 10:15). The fantastic stories the nine-year-old has read or heard from the Bible, and perhaps from the *Martyrs' Mirror,* leave the world of the mind and enter her spirit through her body as she observes his body. She witnesses a eucharist. Food and drink become the blood and body of Christ.

Kasdorf's poem focuses on a courageous individual who comes out of a particular community and then re-enters it. The uncle "got C.O. just for being born / Mennonite," but instead of accepting an alternative to war arranged before his birth, he searched actively for a test of his own conviction. He exceeded the minimal pacifist standard of his separated community.

The uncle's "engaged" form of pacifism builds a bridge between the two kinds of traditions historians explore in this collection. Like ethicist Ted Koontz, Julia Kasdorf stands between a separated community and the idea of the autonomous individual. The poem "Uncle" moves between these two ways of being. Echoing Koontz, one might say that the uncle in Kasdorf's poem has tried to help his God but has discovered that he cannot. He has neither ended war nor created peace. He has returned home more broken than triumphant. As he sits in a restaurant surrounded by family, he exhibits what the Anabaptists called *Gelassenheit,* meaning "yieldedness." Thus the poem, having begun with an active individual leaving both community and nation to contribute to peace and test his own limits, moves to a chastened person who cannot explain rationally what has happened to him. More important than words, however, is his presence and his return to "us," the people from which he came. The story happens for the sake of the child. She will take his moment of pain and transform it into a poem, adding her witness to his. Behind both their stories lie centuries of other stories they must make new again for the old story to continue.

This book of historical essays offers several narrative gems that potentially are as powerful as "Uncle." Thus one of the best contributions this collection makes to American religious history is the restoration of pacifist stories in places where we would hardly expect to find them. Most of these stories were lost or deemphasized as churches veered away from pacifism. Grant Underwood of the religion department of Brigham Young University tells the story from the Book of Mormon about Lamanites who buried their swords and refused to fight. When attacked, they "praised God even in the very act of perishing under the sword." On that day over a thousand of their attackers converted to Christ. A story like this one makes pacifism accessible to a Mormon, even though the official doctrines of the church may not encourage it.

THE ROLE OF SUFFERING

I thank God for the persecution. "For all that live
godly must suffer persecution."
—*Bishop Charles Harrison Mason, of the Church of God*
in Christ, as quoted by Theodore Kornweibel Jr.

Bishop Charles Mason's words come from another recovered story about praising God in the act of suffering. Since pacifism during war is much more difficult than pacifism in peace, pacifist stories often focus on grace under wartime pressure.

Had Charles Mason been born a decade earlier than 1866, he would have been a slave, as his parents had been. His Missionary Baptist upbringing and his own deeply spiritual nature led him into a revival ministry in 1893, with emphasis on personal conversion and sanctification. Mason visited the "Azusa Street" Pentecostal revival in Los Angeles and returned to Memphis, Tennessee, with a new mission: to spread to others the "third blessing" he had received. In 1907 Mason became the Chief Apostle of the Church of God in Christ, a small sect comprising mostly black sharecroppers and urban mill hands in the South and Southwest. Like other early pentecostals, Mason took the gospel teachings on peace literally. He urged his followers to follow the example of Jesus and refuse to shed human blood, including killing in war.

World War I brought Mason into a major conflict with federal authorities who refused to believe that the bishop and his church members were genuine conscientious objectors. Hatred and fear created a terrible climate for all conscientious objectors in this war, but black COs were doubly suspect. Mason escaped any physical harm in the 1918 investigation into his beliefs and practices. The cases against him in Paris, Texas, and Jackson, Mississippi, were dropped. Testimony he gave years later puts Mason squarely into the Christian pacifist tradition:

> The Holy Ghost through me was teaching men to look to God, for he is their only help. I told them not to trust in the power of the United States, England, France or Germany, but to trust in God. The enemy (the devil) tried to hinder me from preaching the unadulterated word of God. He plotted against me and had the white people to arrest me and put me in jail for several days. I thank God for the persecution. "For all that live godly must suffer persecution." (2 Tim. 3:12) (see Kornweibel's essay, chap. 3)

The Church of God in Christ has in its history a worthy forebear to Martin Luther King Jr. By reclaiming Mason's voice, Kornweibel offers us more than pacifist history. He also documents interracial harmony within the church—for example, the exchange of the "holy kiss" between a white man and a black man—an interracial harmony that was as threatening to outsiders as was pacifism. Kornweibel's essay should spur other church historians and African-American historians to consider closely why restorationist revivalist movements often succeed at breaking down racial, gender, and even class boundaries at the beginning but soon revert to the old divisions. What is the connection between early pacifism in many of these churches and the practice of greater equality within the church? Could a restoration of pacifism where it once existed lead to a restoration of greater equality, especially if there is historical evidence that it too once existed?

A related question should challenge historians and future biographers of Martin Luther King Jr. We all know how important Gandhi and Thoreau were to King's brand of engaged nonviolence. If there was one Bishop Mason, however, how many more might there have been, and might King himself have known about some of them? Are there more African-American Christian pacifists whom historians have not yet recovered, and could they have helped to prepare the way for the civil rights movement?

Bishop Mason's statement is important not only in relation to larger connections to African-American nonviolence it may hold. It is important also because Mason's joy in suffering echoes familiar, if strange-sounding, voices—the New Testament's Paul and Silas singing in prison, Christian martyrs laughing and praising God as flames licked their robes, and Martin Luther King Jr. soaring to the mountaintop even as he stood ready to accept death. Mason understood the most profound power pacifism offers. Instead of staying mired in questions of local conflict, the person who draws on faith for pacifism searches for a "mountaintop"—a better place to see God's cosmic design and to remember God's promises. Aided by a restorationist ideal or a vision of a peaceable kingdom, the religious pacifist trusts that the ultimate answers to human conflicts lie in God's hands and in God's time.

Perhaps no issue separates contemporary pacifists more than the question of suffering. To left-leaning Christians, 2 Timothy 3:12, with its implication that suffering is avengeable only in the afterlife or in God's own time, in this life sounds like the "opiate of the people." Feminists within Christian pacifism have critiqued the church for allowing this doctrine (and even exploiting it) to support an abusive patriarchy. Mary Daly's claim that "the way of the cross" is not the way for women[10] has spurred much interest in doctrines of the atonement among feminist theologians. Some are concluding that "Christianity is an abusive religion that glorifies suffering."[11]

That charge has merit to the extent that the church has denied, acquiesced in, or covered up the suffering of its own people at the hands of its own people. Pacifists are no more immune to racism and sexism, for example, than are other Christians. Probably there are a lot more stories of pacifist women, and of African Americans, Hispanic Americans, Native Americans, and Asian Americans, yet to be recovered. When we find them, surely we can expect to find new insight about the meaning of suffering within Christian pacifism.

Glorification of suffering for the sake of suffering is not pacifism but masochism. To profit from convincing someone else to suffer is to exploit. Yet Bishop Mason's willingness to suffer was also the source of his own empowerment. He saw himself as a servant, yes—but not as the servant of white people. The devil was telling them what to do. He was the servant of the Holy Ghost, and his life was therefore like the uncle's life in Julia Kasdorf's poem—it was a living lesson. The Bible had offered him so many narratives and precepts confirming the rightness of his choice that he felt secure in his suffering. In a postmodern world scholars might say that the bishop was constructing his own knowledge. But they could never make that statement with the bishop's approval.

• • •

The editors of this volume hope to disturb the comfortable in any tradition. Pacifists need the challenge of the realist and just-war theologians. Liberal pacifists can learn from the consistency of sectarians. Sectarians should not allow their emphasis on suffering to prevent them from working for justice. Rationalists must acknowledge the power of the heart, of the body, and of memory. The experience-oriented storytellers can use the help of more systematic thinkers in interpreting their stories.

Thus a collection of anomalous examples may accomplish for American religious history what pacifism itself has done for the church—testify to the value of looking at the world from another point of view.

NOTES

1. Reinhold Niebuhr, introduction to William James, *The Varieties of Religious Experience* (New York: Collier, 1961), 8.

2. Ibid.

3. Readers who connect into the World Wide Web can read the story of Dirk Willems by going to the *Mennonite Quarterly Review* home page at the Goshen College web site: http://www.goshen.edu.

4. John S. Oyer, *The Mennonite Encyclopedia*, s.v. "Suffering" (Scottdale, Pa.: Herald, 1990).

5. Richard K. MacMaster, *Land, Piety, Peoplehood: The Establishment of Mennonite Communities in America 1683–1790*, The Mennonite Experience in America, ed. Theron F. Schlabach, vol. 1 (Scottdale, Pa.: Herald, 1985), 144.

6. This observation conforms to the strong emphasis on narrative in contemporary theology and among theological educators. Henri J. M. Nouwen, expanding on Elie Wiesel's statement that "God made man because he loves stories," explains some of stories' power in his book *The Living Reminder: Service and Prayer in Memory of Jesus Christ* (New York: Seabury, 1977): "The rabbis guide their people with stories; ministers usually guide with ideas and theories. We need to become storytellers again, and so multiply our ministry by calling around us the great witnesses who in different ways offer guidance to our doubting hearts" (65). Nouwen continues, "One of the remarkable qualities of the story is that it creates space. We can dwell in a story, walk around, and find our own place. The story confronts but does not oppress; the story inspires but does not manipulate. The story invites us to an encounter, a dialog, mutual sharing" (65–66).

7. Richard Bernstein, "Tevye and Other Comforts in a Crumbling World," *New York Times*, July 21, 1995, C26.

8. Julia Kasdorf, "Uncle," in *Sleeping Preacher* (Pittsburgh: University of Pittsburgh Press, 1992), 27. © 1992. Reprinted by permission of the University of Pittsburgh Press.

9. The work of Parker Palmer, especially his *To Know As We Are Known: A Spirituality of Education* (New York: Harper and Row, 1983), is quite relevant here. Just as theology that leaves no room for experience cannot sustain pacifism, education that leaves no room for experience closes off the heart, one of learning's most vital sources. A small group of teachers today is beginning to recover a spiritual base in education, partly by encouraging students to connect the subject of the classroom to the subject of their lives. See John D. Lawry, "*Caritas* in the Classroom: The Opening of the American Student's Heart," *College Teaching* 38, no. 3 (Summer 1990): 83–87. Both pacifism and the "spirituality movement" within education thrive on narrative.

In his essay Lawry includes a summary of the work of English anthropologist Colin Turnbull, whose book *The Human Cycle* (New York: Simon and Schuster, 1983) focuses on the educational practices of Mbuti and Ituri peoples of central Africa. Turnbull once tried to explain to Ituri elders that in England, activities associated with rites of initiation are instituted by young people themselves. Turnbull's account concludes, "'Did you have no teachers?' they asked. Then when I told them that our teachers were not kinsmen or friends, or even known to our families, and that they only taught our minds and trained our bodies in sports and games and didn't teach our hearts or spirit, they understood, I think, why we seem as cold to them as we do" (Turnbull quoted in Lawry, "*Caritas*," 84).

10. Mary Daly, *Beyond God the Father* (Boston: Beacon, 1973), 71–80.

11. Joanne Carlson Brown and Rebecca Parker, "For God So Loved the World?" in Joanne Carlson Brown and Carole R. Bohn, eds., *Christianity, Patriarchy, and Abuse*, 1–30 (New York: Pilgrim, 1989), 26.

I

ℐℰ

PACIFISM AND PATRIOTISM

A Basic Theme in U.S. History

ℐℰ

Charles Chatfield

Together, patriotism and pacifism are a basic theme in U.S. history. Labels raise the issue of truth in packaging, however. Patriotism and pacifism mean quite different things to various people, and each of those two labels has changed its connotations over time. As for pacifism, in their most general senses the terms *pacifism* and *pacifists* refer to a movement of people who initially called themselves simply "Friends of Peace."

The one exception to this broader definition is the oldest and most complete form of pacifism—sectarian nonresistance—which involves total renunciation of war along with some degree of withdrawal from society and the creation of nonresistant communities. Some examples are the medieval Waldenses and the fifteenth-century Czech Brethren, the Swiss Brethren of the 1527 Schleitheim Confession, the Mennonites who traversed Europe and emigrated to North America, and, less clearly, the Quakers. Such groups are surely friends of peace, but the broad term *pacifists* has included others as well.

The broader stream of pacifism has engaged patriotism quite directly. As historian Peter Brock has observed, "the age of global warfare has demanded a basic rethinking of the issues of peace and war for . . . pacifists, and indeed for humankind as a whole."[1] In fact the need to rethink became pressing also for patriots.

One political cartoon of 1916, during the Great War, presented Uncle Sam trying to ride both a war-horse and a dove of peace.[2] During that election year Woodrow Wilson campaigned on the slogan "He kept us out of war"—but also on a platform to increase the navy and the army. The cartoon presented American patriotism as more or less straddling war and peace, militarism and pacifism. In fact both war and peace are woven into the fabric of our patriotism.

Patriotism is at least a basic love and loyalty for a homeland. It is a sign that "when you scratch a man you touch loyalty."[3] Patriotism is an ancient feeling, older than the nation-state, and indicates that in some measure each person is defined by community. It is loyalty to the ideals and institutions of a community. Josiah Royce called it "the willing and practical and thorough-going devotion of a person to a cause."[4] William James wanted the nation to be something "that one feels honored by belonging to."[5]

What a people are honored by belonging to, what they are loyal to, is what defines them as a people. A people's particular kind of patriotism derives from their national story and in turn defines their national identity. For Americans, much of that story and identity has to do with war, but much of it also has to do with peace. Thus a basic theme in American history is not patriotism *or* pacifism but rather patriotism *and* pacifism.

This conjunction is true not only for Americans, however. Consider four posters from the 1983 *Kirchentag,* or church festival, held in Dresden, in what was then East Germany. The first poster image portrayed a seed borne on the wind and carried the *Kirchentag* theme: "Vertrauen wagen, damit wir leben können" (dare to trust, so that we may live). Explicitly the theme asserted that festival participants dared to trust their biblical faith so that they might have life in Christ. Implicitly it meant, "We Christians in East Germany dare to trust biblical faith beyond communist ideology, dare to trust church leadership beyond the state, and dare to trust ourselves beyond our detractors—so that we may live as fully as possible in this communist state and beyond its walls." Trust is the seed of hope.

For the same festival a group working on the problems faced by Christian children in East German public schools created a second image. In it were two persons, each confined within a bottle and unable to reach a hammer lying between the two jars. A child who felt separated and alienated from others of her age drew the picture. The child was bottled up as a Christian, while the other was isolated as a communist, and neither could break out to the other. A third image suggested a more complex role. It had eyes looking out of (or into) a keyhole: the Christian's role is to look out on a hostile community that, in turn, is looking in watchfully.

Finally, a fourth *Kirchentag* poster depicted, above a cross, a white dove sitting on a (communist-) red high-tension wire. This image announced the role of the Christian as a witness to peace. It is a role that leaves the Christian vulnerable.

In all four posters Christian faith preserves and conveys an alternative vision in political culture. Similarly, pacifism also preserves and conveys an alternate vision in American political culture. That fact deserves some thought.

. . .

On Good Friday 1917 the U. S. government chose war. Six weeks later America's most respected woman, Jane Addams, addressed the City Club of Chicago. She titled her talk "Patriotism and Pacifists in War Time." What kind of patriotism, and what kind of pacifism, did she have in mind?

At fifty-seven Jane Addams was the first citizen of Chicago, the city where she had launched the settlement house movement and campaigned for other reforms. Scarcely six months after the outbreak of war in Europe, she had presided over an international gathering of women in Holland and carried their appeal for peace to European capitals and also to President Woodrow Wilson. When she returned, Chicago honored her. Public respect for pacifists had begun to erode as the United States plunged into the war, and so Addams reminded her fellow citizens that pacifism is a special calling of patriotism. Said she:

American pacifists believe . . . that the United States was especially qualified by her own particular experience to take the leadership in a peaceful organization of the world. . . . America had come to stand . . . for the principle of federal government and for a supreme tribunal whose decisions were binding upon sovereign states.

We pacifists hoped that the United States might [extend] federation and . . . peaceful adjudication . . . in the wider and more difficult field of international relationships.

Can the pacifists of today be accused of selfishness when they urge upon the United States not isolation, not indifference to moral issues and to the fate of liberty and democracy, but a strenuous endeavor to lead all nations of the earth into an organized international life worthy of civilized men?[6]

These words of Jane Addams ring with a familiar pride of country. They resound with the idea that the United States has a mission to be a beacon to the nations for peace and justice—an idea as old as John Winthrop's Puritan city on the hill, William Penn's holy experiment in Pennsylvania, Woodrow Wilson's "war to end war," Franklin Roosevelt's Four Freedoms, or George Bush's new world order (whatever that meant). When Jane Addams linked peace with national ideals, she was playing an old tune. She also identified peace with national interest. George Washington, John Adams, and Thomas Jefferson had all avoided war at great cost to their own popularity, she observed, but in the best interests of the country. Addams's message was clear: peace is patriotic.

Frequently nations have perverted the ideal of a special mission into the dangerous idea of a chosen people with a mandate to impose ideas, institutions, and values on others. Such a fierce belief propelled the French Revolution into the Napoleonic empire and was the marrow of imperialism. Lenin revived it to justify class war. The sense of national mandate underlay U.S. wars in the Philippines and Vietnam and campaigns in Nicaragua, Panama, El Salvador, and other Central American countries. An assumed mission to impose values was widespread in World Wars I and II, and it drove the twentieth-century holocausts. More recently it appeared in Bosnia. It is the zealous kind of patriotism that fortifies nationalistic walls and pushes them outward. Moreover, especially in wartime, superpatriots turn pride of country into exclusive, ingrown loyalty and loyalty into obedience. Even in peacetime patriots often equate national worth with military power, and some market national loyalty for economic and political advantage.

Jane Addams surely was not that kind of patriot. She questioned her country's policy in order to improve it. She elevated those national values that were applied equally to all. She saw America as responsible to other nations. Addams promoted peaceful institutions and processes because she understood the limits of the nation-state system. She hated war because she loved humankind. She was the kind of patriot she was because of the kind of pacifist she was.

In her address to the City Club, Addams used the word *pacifist* several times. What sort of pacifist did she have in mind? And what difference did her kind of pacifist make?

Addams referred to those pacifists who had worked to create international habits, attitudes, and institutions of peace. She herself represented a hundred years of such pacifism. From 1815 onward groups of citizens in the United States and Europe, and eventually in Russia and

Japan, organized themselves to influence the policies of their countries. They began by preaching the Christian gospel. Increasingly they spoke the newer languages of political economy, sociology, history, and anthropology. Their essential question was not whether to accept military service but how to contain and eventually replace warfare.

In the nineteenth century the containment of warfare was not regarded as feasible, or even desirable, to the extent it is today. In that century the friends of peace had to sell even the ideal of peace. They reached out to legislatures, cabinets, and the literate public. They held international congresses and enlisted political and intellectual leaders. They advocated international cooperation and even a United States of Europe. They promoted the peaceful settlement of disputes, treaties to restrict warfare, international law, and eventually international organization. By 1914 there were small peace societies among the business, professional, and laboring classes from the Rockies to the Urals, as well as several international peace associations.

Among nineteenth-century peace advocates there were some absolute pacifists, but by the end of the century the absolutists were found mainly in England and North America. Russia's Leo Tolstoy was an absolute pacifist, but he disdained the programs of organized peace advocates, as he also disdained patriotism.

A critically important point is that the pacifism of those nineteenth-century peace advocates was necessarily patriotic. The idea that citizen organization and initiative could make a difference in international relations was a major innovation in thinking about peace. The patriotic kind of pacifism was a form of citizen action possible only in the modern nation-state. The early friends of peace were trying to change political cultures from within. Their strategies, rhetoric, and agendas were shaped by the political cultures of their respective nations. Their pacifist vision was international, but their perspectives and their audiences were national. Peace advocates could claim a higher, enlightened patriotism only insofar as they were patriots.

As a result, at the beginning of the twentieth century European peace advocates invented the words *pacifism* and *pacifist*. They popularized those terms because militarists had become highly organized and extremist and because virulent militarists accused peace advocates of being cowards and traitors. The advocates of peace were trying to contrast their own kind of international, peaceful patriotism with the nationalistic, militaristic kind. They assumed that sovereign nations were the basic political and cultural units, but they believed that international institutions and understanding could redeem nationalism by endowing it with cosmopolitan, nonexclusive loyalties. They were the kind of pacifists they were because of the kind of patriots they were. They were patriots without walls.

Such broad-minded pacifism grew in the United States as well, where it was known also as internationalism. It attracted lawyers, reformers, businesspeople, and political leaders. In the decade before World War I some forty-five societies were organized, some of them well-funded by business leaders such as steelmaker-turned-philanthropist Andrew Carnegie. The major Protestant churches created a peace society within the new Federal Council of Churches of Christ in America. Internationalists forged networks with European counterparts and made key contacts in the State Department. In 1907 they assembled the National Arbitration and Peace Congress to influence the U.S. position at the Second Hague Conference. That congress attracted 1,200 delegates, including cabinet officers, Supreme Court justices, and leaders from labor and business. When Europe plunged into war seven years later, the American internationalists promoted an international peacekeeping organization, with explicit backing from former president William Howard Taft and from President Woodrow Wilson.

What happened to this movement during World War I? Under the pressures of war a new kind of pacifism emerged. Addams identified with the newer pacifism, and that is why in May 1917 she spoke of the older kind in the past tense. Yet the older stream of pacifism did not simply fade away. It has endured to this day, still associated with patriotism.

Most of the established internationalists supported the U.S. war effort. They influenced American war aims and, in turn, the peace settlement. Despite the fact that the United States rejected that settlement, the League of Nations, and the World Court, internationalism continued to be a legitimate expression of patriotism. It still is. What difference has it made?

Organized advocates of peace-through-internationalism kept the league and the court before the country until World War II, when they directed the massive campaign that created a national consensus for the United Nations (UN). Even in the interwar period they cooperated with the problem-solving international agencies that later led to the UN Relief and Rehabilitation Administration, an international monetary system, the Food and Agriculture Organization, and the World Health Organization. The ever-expanding international system became an extension of American institutions and loyalties.

Moreover, peace advocates contributed to the development of nongovernmental organizations, or NGOs. These organizations range from economic and professional associations to the World Council of Churches; from peace groups like the International Fellowship of Reconciliation and the Women's International League for Peace and Freedom to human rights agencies like Amnesty International; and from environmental groups like Green Peace or the World Fund for Wildlife to service agencies like CARE, the American Friends Service Committee (AFSC), or the Mennonite Central Committee. The number of NGOs multiplied from a few hundred in 1919 to more than 12,000 today. They link people across boundaries. They generate new intergovernmental programs and agencies. Virtually every international institution and peacekeeping procedure existing today originated in the proposals and campaigns of nongovernmental, citizen peace advocates. They connect persons and nations with the world and expand loyalties.

Such pacifists made another important contribution to American patriotism: they turned the just-war tradition into an antiwar instrument. For most of them, war could be justifiable if it met certain criteria. The point was to tighten the criteria. The Geneva Convention of 1864 tightened the criteria regarding treatment of the wounded, and the St. Petersburg Declaration of 1868 did the same regarding weapons; the Hague Conferences of 1899 and 1907 similarly tightened the criteria for warmaking through promotion of arbitration. The criteria were tightened further in the league covenant following World War I and in the 1928 Kellogg-Briand Pact, which outlawed aggressive war. Obviously the pact did not prevent war, as was hoped, but along with the league covenant and later the UN charter, the pact did help to limit the kinds of war the international community regarded as legitimate. Later more stringent standards were applied as political realists such as Reinhold Niebuhr and Hans Morgenthau condemned the nuclear arms race and the Vietnam War on the grounds that they violated the criteria for a just war.

Atrocious war crimes in the conduct of the Vietnam War received wide condemnation—condemnation derived from the internationalist kind of pacifism. After World War II, when it cosponsored the Nuremberg trials, the United States had applied the principle of war crimes and created a legally binding precedent. The country became vulnerable to the charge of war crimes in Vietnam because it had incorporated the internationalist principle into its own national institutions and policy. To be sure, internationalism in U.S. history has been self-serving and militaristic insofar as Americans have seen the world as a field for their exclusive or preeminent interests or have imposed their values and institutions on other peoples. The pacifist dimension of internationalism has been the idea of acting responsibly with others.

One scheme delineates three competing forms of internationalism.[7] The first is that of the vast national security bureaucracy of the cold war, a bureaucracy bent on seeing U.S. leadership continue along established lines. Its force is weakening. The second is corporate internationalism, for national boundaries are often irrelevant to a global, market-oriented economy. The third is the internationalism of the growing phalanx of NGOs concerned with global issues and causes such as the environment. Persons using this threefold scheme have concluded that economic and cause-oriented internationalism is defining the future, and with it American identity.[8]

What of the pacifism of Jane Addams in her 1917 speech, the pacifism that emphasized a national mission? It too has been bound up with patriotism. "Are pacifists cowards?" Addams asked. Do pacifists put "'safety first,' [do they] place human life, physical life, above the great ideals of national righteousness?" Certainly not, she answered, for against the tide of the majority, the pacifist "asserts his conviction and is ready to vindicate its spiritual value over against the world." Addams had much to learn about the wartime majority.

A new kind pacifism began to form during 1914–17, while Americans were watching Europeans descend into the abyss. Some peace advocates drifted toward intervention, but others led public, political campaigns against military preparedness and war. When the nation went to war anyway, the latter group's ranks thinned again. The older peace societies endorsed the fight or looked past it to a postwar world. Mainline churches sanctified the crusade: preachers presented arms. The ranks of pacifists were reduced to those few who rejected war altogether and refused to support it. "Yellowbacks," they were called: "pacifists."

The word *pacifist* was transformed into a term of contempt, especially in England and the United States. It was thrown at those who rejected World War I altogether and refused to support it. Pacifists of this kind included not only sectarian nonresistants but also men and women who resisted war from other religious traditions, from humanism, or from socialism. The religious among them often responded to the social gospel, with its emphasis on Jesus acting in history, on the church as servant, and on the centrality of peace and justice. Quakers who entered the peace movement during World War I tended to reflect this religious tradition.

Whatever their backgrounds, these pacifists cared most about people and about social values. They organized new societies, and each new name identified a value: the Fellowship of *Reconciliation,* the American Friends *Service* Committee, the Women's International League for *Peace* and *Freedom.* Jane Addams reflected this value orientation when she called for "newer ideals of peace" and emphasized that all peoples and their problems are interrelated. The new values were transnational: they embraced humankind. Pacifists such as Addams thought about the needs of a human community that pervaded and transcended the atomistic world of sovereign states. They cared even across the lines of wartime alliances, and their caring set them apart from most wartime patriots.

Pacifists in World War I, and later ones in World War II or the Vietnam War, were like the bottled-up people in the 1983 East German child's drawing. If they were not isolated in conscientious objector (CO) camps or in prison, they were ostracized—separated from their countrymen by a patriotism that acted like barbed wire. Consider the poster image of eyes looking through a keyhole. That could have been a picture of staunch pacifists in the Great War and of others in World War II and the Vietnam War. From places of sanctuary or incarceration pacifists looked out on the national crusade while their compatriots looked in on them with disdain, or hatred, or mere indifference. Pacifist journals were held up in the mails and pacifists' speech was abridged; the particular war was unquestionable, the flag became a test of conformity, and governmental war power tended to be arbitrary. The experience was briefest, but also most intense, in World War I. And the challenge of wartime patriotism created a new kind of pacifist.

No significant change takes place suddenly. It took decades to play out the insights, potential, and dilemmas of the pacifists who emerged during the Great War. Nevertheless, a generation of leaders emerged: John Nevin Sayre, Emily Green Balch, Kirby Page, A. J. Muste, Mildred Scot Olmsted, Norman and Evan Thomas, Ray Newton, Frederick Libby, Clarence Pickett, Raymond Wilson, Dorothy Detzer, Devere Allen, and many more. What was special about them, and what difference did they make to the rest of the country?

Their kind of pacifism was special because it was a response to wartime patriotism. They challenged that kind of patriotism. Warfare cannot be judged by its ideals, they insisted; warfare must be judged by what it is. War is not only a battle or a series of battles; it is not only fighting, killing, or destruction. War is a social process. It transfers citizen loyalties from the national community to the nation-state. For the duration, government takes on an aura of absolute value, and it tends to assume absolute authority. That is what Randolph Bourne meant when he wrote, "War is the Health of the State."[9] That is why Evan Thomas chose conscientious objection and Leavenworth prison. Of such pacifism he said, "It is the way of the only true freedom, and therefore the way to love, for freedom and love can never exist apart from each other in the heart of man." Conscientious objection, Thomas believed, "is the way of example as opposed to compulsion. It is the way of belief as opposed to disbelief. It is the way of toleration as opposed to intolerance. Finally, it is the way that frankly accepts the fact of individual responsibility."[10]

War is a social system, the new pacifists insisted, and warfare is a social process. It systematically organizes and applies violence, doing so through destructive, arbitrary force. War is organized violence, violence is inherently unjust, and so war is injustice. In religious terms, "war is sin." If war is injustice, if war is sin, then the cause of peace is also the struggle for justice. If violence is inherently unjust, then the struggle for justice must be waged without violence.

The pacifists who reached this conclusion were oriented toward reform. Faced with war and social injustice, their impulse was to engage society. They made a difference by the ways in which they engaged society, through humanitarian, political, and direct nonviolent action.

Some of those pacifists found a way in love, through reconciliation and service. During and after the war Jane Addams herself promoted food relief to the victims of war on both sides. The AFSC and the Mennonite Central Committee developed around the idea of service as promoting peace. After both world wars pacifists organized international programs of reconciliation. During and after World War II the AFSC and the peace churches mounted famine relief and refugee work. In 1947 the Nobel Peace Prize was awarded to American and British Friends (Quakers) for what the Nobel committee called "the silent help from the nameless to the nameless."

The Nobel prize has been awarded often to humanitarian groups, and today we take for granted what was not at all obvious to people seventy years ago, namely, that individuals and governments have a responsibility to people abroad who are starving and ill and dispossessed. Most Americans feel that programs of humanitarian aid are a national virtue. Certainly humanitarianism cannot be attributed exclusively to pacifists, but this kind of pacifism has imbued Americans' patriotism.

Many pacifists found significant ways to engage society in political activism and tried to influence foreign policy. They made a difference. In the 1930s, when collective security seemed futile, they campaigned to keep the United States neutral. When the nation returned to war, they tried to mitigate the worst excesses, like the horrendous civilian bombing and the unjust internment of Japanese Americans. They cooperated in the campaign for the United Nations, where they pressed especially for recognition of universal human rights. In the 1950s they challenged nuclear weapons and cold war ideology. In the 1960s they were at the core of the antiwar movement. During the 1980s they spearheaded the Nuclear Freeze campaign and the Central American solidarity movement.

In each of these cases a small core of pacifists assembled a broad-based coalition of civic groups, and the coalition in turn mobilized large numbers of citizens to generate significant political pressure. In each of these cases these engaged pacifists addressed national policy, challenged conventional wisdom about war, and confronted bureaucratic power. They mobilized people for action in the arena most closed to public participation, the arena known as "national security." Their actions required people to define their patriotism and to make choices about national purpose in a world context.

Finally, pacifist engagement also took the form of war resistance and nonviolent direct action. War resistance was organized in the 1920s through the War Resisters League and truly became a social force forty years later in the Vietnam War. Nonviolent direct action owed much to the philosophy and strategy of Indian pacifist Mohandas K. Gandhi, whose efforts received serious Western attention throughout the interwar period. After World War II pacifists espousing nonviolent direct action applied their methods to the problem of white racism in America. During the 1956 Montgomery bus boycott Martin Luther King Jr. worked with advisers from the Congress on Racial Equality and the Fellowship of Reconciliation. Both groups were experienced in nonviolent action. At about the same time other pacifists applied the tactics of nonviolent action in the campaign against nuclear weapons. And of course such action became an integral part of the opposition to the Vietnam War.

Nonviolent action was effective when it dramatized the disparity between American institutions or policy on one hand and national ideals and values on the other: racism versus civil rights and fairness, a suicidal arms race versus peace and security, and an atrocious and futile war versus dignity and compassion.

Although nonviolent action sometimes reinforced traditional political action," it sometimes confused issues. Such scrambling of issues happened dramatically during the antiwar movement of the 1960s. The experience of Tom Hayden illustrates such confusion and helps to clarify the dynamic relationship between pacifism and patriotism. Hayden was not a pacifist by principle, but in his life patriotism intersected with the pacifism of engagement—as humanitarianism, politics, and direct nonviolent action.

Born of Irish-American Catholics in Royal Oak, Michigan, Hayden eventually attended the University of Michigan, where he became editor of the student newspaper. Contact with the student-rights and sit-in movements made him an activist and a leader of the Students for a Democratic Society, or SDS. He largely drafted the SDS's 1962 manifesto, the well-known "Port Huron Statement," and for three years he responded to his own call for participatory democracy by working at community organizations in Newark, New Jersey. In 1965, when President Lyndon Johnson began the bombing war, Hayden was only twenty-six; nevertheless, that winter he accepted an invitation to North Vietnam, where he arranged for the release of three prisoners of war. By 1968 he saw the war as undermining the ideals and institutions for which he had become an activist. Persuaded by David Dellinger and others of the power of mass, nonviolent demonstrations, he helped to organize antiwar protest at the Chicago Democratic national convention. Caught up in the turmoil, Hayden felt trapped between protest symbols that came across as being anti-American and police who came across as being patriotic but brutal zealots. Hayden's vision of America and his understanding of himself was shattered. He withdrew to the West Coast and into himself.

Gradually Hayden re-created purpose in his life by teaching children about the Vietnamese. In 1972 he returned to the antiwar movement with actress Jane Fonda. Together they raised funds for Vietnamese relief and worked for George McGovern's antiwar presidential campaign. Hayden was again in the political system. Antiwar activism "does not mean condemning your country," he insisted, "but means that it must be rescued and changed."[11]

In Hayden's life, as in the Vietnam ordeal for America, the pacifism of engagement intersected with patriotism. In the crisis of action Hayden lost his balance and his perspective. What began as a test of purpose turned into a test of will—within the movement and within the nation. Fortunately Hayden, like most engaged pacifists, recovered a sense of purpose. And America?

War is a test of will. Peace is a matter of purpose. The real foreign policy issues were and are questions of purpose. The real achievement of the antiwar movement of the Vietnam era—much like the quieter personal resistance to the two world wars and the more strictly political challenge to nuclear weapons and Central American policy—was to raise the question of purpose. The real question of national identity was and is a matter of purpose. What was the U.S. purpose in Southeast Asia? What is the U.S. role in the Middle East? What is the role of the United States in refashioning the obsolete nation-state system, restructuring the global economy, encouraging accountable self-government, protecting and respecting human rights, expanding equity, or reviving our environment? To describe national purpose is to define national identity. To clarify national purpose is to refine patriotism.

During most of American history pacifists of all kinds have been challenged to clarify what they meant by peace and by their roles in pursuing it. They have been challenged by the changing character of the nation's institutions, its values, and its relationship to the rest of the world. In short, they have been challenged by all kinds of patriotism. Pacifists in turn dared their society to redefine its purpose in the light of a changing world. Pacifism has been part of the process by which the American people, along with others on this endangered planet, have been challenged to form alternatives to war as an instrument of national policy. It has been part of the process by which Americans have been challenged to institutionalize peace as an instrument of justice. "Vertrauen wagen, damit wir leben können"—again, with the dove on the high-tension wire, "dare to trust, that we may live."

In fifth-century B.C. Athens Isocrates blamed the decline of public morality and democracy on Athens's imperialist wars. He warned that "the soul of a state is nothing less than its polity."[12] No matter how global may be American influence and power, the nation's soul will shrink to the narrowness of its national interest or the exclusiveness of its values. By the same measure, insofar as Americans acknowledge their responsibility to the society of nations, embrace humanity, and envision the whole planet as an extended homeland, the national soul will enlarge. Americans will mature in that kind of patriotism insofar as they nurture that kind of pacifism.

NOTES

1. Peter Brock, *Freedom from Violence: Sectarian Nonresistance from the Middle Ages to the Great War* (Toronto: University of Toronto Press, 1991), ix.

2. This was a 1916 political cartoon by Morris, "As Others See Us," published in the *Tampa Tribune*.

3. Morton Grodzins, *The Loyal and the Disloyal* (Chicago: University of Chicago Press, 1956), 5.

4. Quoted in ibid., 30.

5. William James, "The Moral Equivalent of War," *McClure's Magazine* 35 (Aug. 1910): 463–68; reprinted in idem, *Memories and Studies* (New York: Longmans, Green, 1912), 167–96.

6. Jane Addams, "Patriotism and Pacifists in War Time," *The City Club Bulletin* (Chicago) 10, no. 9 (June 16, 1917): 6–7, 22; reprinted in idem, *Peace and Bread in Time of War* (New York: Garland, 1972).

7. A recent Stanley Foundation seminar offered this scheme.

8. *Global Changes and Domestic Transformations: New Possibilities for American Foreign Policy*, Vantage Conference 1992 (Muscatine, Iowa: The Stanley Foundation, 1992).

9. "The State" (1919) in Randolph Bourne, *War and the Intellectuals: Essays by Randolph Bourne 1915–1919*, ed. Carl Resek, 64–104 (New York: Harper Torchbooks, 1964).

10. Private letter to Norman Thomas, Apr. 12, 1917, in Charles Chatfield, ed., *The Radical "No": The Correspondence and Writing of Evan Thomas on War* (New York: Garland, 1974), 112.

11. Charles DeBenedetti with Charles Chatfield, *An American Ordeal* (Syracuse, N.Y.: Syracuse University Press, 1990), 338 n. 83.

12. "Areopagiticus," in *Isocrates*, 2 vols., trans. George Norlin (Cambridge, Mass.: Harvard University Press, Loeb Classical Library, 1929), 2:113.

PART I

❧

PENTECOSTALISM, WHITE AND BLACK

❧

2

⁓

PACIFISM IN PENTECOSTALISM

The Case of the Assemblies of God

⁓

Murray W. Dempster

The year 1914 witnessed both the beginning of the Great War and the formation of the Assemblies of God. News of the war hit the headlines of the *New York Times;* the formation of the pentecostal denomination in Arkansas elicited two small notices in the *Hot Springs* (Arkansas) *Sentinel*. At the time these two events scarcely touched, or so it seemed. Yet in the short span of three years the war's global impact would reach even the fledgling denomination.

By April 28, 1917, only about three weeks after the United States had declared war on Germany, officials of the denomination's governing body, its General Council, formulated a resolution on military service. Moving on, they negotiated with the church's Executive and General Presbytery to approve it and prepared to send it to President Woodrow Wilson. A cover letter accompanying the resolution requested the right of conscientious objection for Assemblies of God members, and the resolution itself read as follows:

> While recognizing Human Government as of Divine ordination and affirming our unswerving loyalty to the Government of the United States, nevertheless we are constrained to define our position with reference to the taking of human life.
> WHEREAS, in the Constitutional Resolution adopted at the Hot Springs General Council, April 1–10, 1914, we plainly declare the Holy Inspired Scriptures to be the all-sufficient rule of faith and practice, and

WHEREAS the Scriptures deal plainly with the obligations and relations of humanity, setting forth the principles of "Peace on earth,
good will toward men" (Luke 2:14); and

WHEREAS we as the followers of the Lord Jesus Christ, the Prince
of Peace, believe in implicit obedience to the Divine commands and
precepts which instruct us to "Follow peace with all men," (Heb.
12:14); "Thou shalt not kill," (Exod. 20:12); "Resist not evil," (Matt.
5:29); "Love your enemies," (Matt. 5:44); etc., and

WHEREAS those and other Scriptures have always been accepted
and interpreted by our churches as prohibiting Christians from shedding blood or taking human life;

THEREFORE we, as a body of Christians, while purposing to fulfill
all the obligations of loyal citizenship, are nevertheless constrained
to declare we cannot conscientiously participate in war and armed
resistance which involves the actual destruction of human life since
this is contrary to our view of the clear teachings of the inspired Word
of God, which is the sole basis of our faith.

April 28th, 1917[1]

In August 1967, five decades after formulating the denomination's
policy on military service, the General Council of the Assemblies of God
gathered in Long Beach, California, and changed its official statement
from pacifism to a position that enshrined "the principle of individual
freedom of conscience as it relates to military service." Adopted when
many Americans were agonizing in conscience over continued U.S. involvement in the Vietnam War, the statement read:

As a movement we affirm our loyalty to the government of the
United States in war or peace.

We shall continue to insist, as we have historically, on the right of
each member to choose for himself whether to declare his position
as a combatant, a non-combatant, or a conscientious objector.[2]

The 1967 statement simply codified a change in the church's position on
military service that had occurred much earlier. Scholars have made
various attempts to understand the nature and the demise of pacifism
in the Assemblies of God, as well as in the larger pentecostal movement.[3]
By far the most comprehensive and insightful study is Jay Beaman's book
*Pentecostal Pacifism: The Origins, Development and Rejection of Pacific
Belief among the Pentecostals.*[4] Beaman's work, although largely focusing on pentecostalism in the United States, sought to establish the pen-

tecostal movement worldwide as being almost entirely officially pacifistic during World War I, until certain events and developments of the 1940s and 1950s triggered a basic shift in pentecostal belief about Christians bearing arms in military service. Beaman took care to describe the diversity of positions on military service that existed among pentecostals even during World War I. Even though the pentecostal movement was not a monolithic group of individual pacifists, Beaman demonstrated that at the official level the pentecostal church was a pacifist church.

The predominant rejection of pacific belief among the pentecostals, according to Beaman, can be traced to the assimilation that pentecostals experienced into the cultural and religious mainstream during World War II and beyond. The "moral" interpretation of World War II, the institutionalization of the pentecostal chaplaincy, the leadership role of the Assemblies of God and its membership in the National Association of Evangelicals, and the social and economic mobility experienced by pentecostals since World War II are the factors Beaman identified to account for the movement's cultural accommodation and the corresponding demise of pacifism among pentecostals.[5]

Given the sectarian profile that characterized much of early pentecostalism and its eventual transition into a denomination, Beaman's sociological explanation for the loss of pacifistic belief among pentecostals makes good sense. As I have stated elsewhere, however, "something is not quite kosher in this portrayal of a majority pacifist movement shifting to a non-pacifist movement within such a short period of time, especially in light of the intensity with which the pacifists held their convictions on this matter."[6] What Beaman's thesis presupposes is that during World War I and through the interwar years pacifism among early pentecostals reflected the movement's antiworldly sectarianism and eschatological mind-set. With that assumption intact, the cultural assimilation theory gives an intelligible explanation for the loss of pentecostal pacifism. Certainly the link that Beaman assumed to exist between pacifism, the sectarian character of early pentecostalism, and the group's eschatological mind-set does rest on demonstrable facts. The question is whether, alongside the anticultural expression of pacifism, other justifications for pacifism can also be found.

From my own research into North American pentecostal pacifism, particularly within the Assemblies of God, I have found that the arguments used by those pentecostals who were absolute pacifists in advocating Christian pacifism reflected a variety of theological and ethical convictions. Arthur S. Booth-Clibborn, his son Samuel H. Booth-Clib-

born, Frank Bartleman, and Stanley Frodsham were four of the major
absolute pacifists who were influential in cultivating pacifist sentiment
and shaping pacifist belief among early North American pentecostals.
More specifically, during World War I their writings were the ones that
were most often advertised for purchase, reprinted, or cited by the leadership of the Assemblies of God in promoting pacifism in the periodicals of the newly formed denomination.[7] Despite different justifications
for pacifism that can be found in their writings, all agreed that a pacifist
ethic was compatible with the option of noncombatant service in a time
of war. Three discrete arguments for pacifism recur regularly in the
popular writings of these pentecostal absolute pacifists. Although the
three arguments did promote an anticultural "come out from the world"
justification for pacifism, they also connected pacifism to the church's
redemptive witness to the world.[8] Without question the pacifism of
Bartleman and Frodsham represented a more narrow sectarian strain
of world-denying pacifism, whereas the two Booth-Clibborns related
pacifism more positively to the global character and witness of the
church. Nonetheless, maintaining that typification categorically seems
to be arbitrary given that all four pacifists formulated arguments that
at times embodied an anticultural attitude and at other times reflected
a pro-Christian rationale for pacifism. Although classifying the variety
of theological and ethical convictions in a way that makes sense remains
to be done, one point has become clear. Pacifism was not an expression
of a common cohesive social philosophy among the absolute pacifists.

Another salient factor becomes evident when these arguments are set
against the denomination's own practices, at least at the leadership level. The Assemblies of God was a pacifist denomination at the official
level during World War I, but at the practical level pacifism was a controversial position among denominational officials and pastors, at times
even generating a divisive spirit. Diversity of opinion on military service was often marked by heated controversy. The official statement on
pacifism and the three major arguments used to support pacifism in the
popular literature seem to be at odds with the intense sparring that was
revealed at times in the denominational politics surrounding the war
issue.

To make sense of these disparate details in the story of pentecostal
pacifism within the Assemblies of God and to indicate how these details
may shed fresh light on the demise of pacifism in the denomination are
the purposes of my essay. First I examine three of the principal pacifist
arguments put forward to convince North American pentecostals, par-

ticularly those affiliated with the Assemblies of God, during the period of World War I and shortly thereafter. The method will be to analyze these arguments so as to reveal dual effects of pacifism within the pentecostal worldview. In one effect pacifism expressed believers' moral requirement to separate themselves from the dominant values and practices of human culture. In its other effect pacifism expressed the moral value that Christians believe God places on all members of the human family. After examining the content of the three arguments in order to get inside the conceptual world of the pentecostal pacifists, I demonstrate that as the war progressed, some influential Assemblies of God leaders developed a growing aversion toward pacifism. Based on my analysis of the arguments and on identification of factors influencing the denominational politics of the time, I propose a revision of the cultural assimilation thesis as an interpretive framework to explain the demise of pacifism within the Assemblies of God.

RESTORING THE APOSTOLIC FAITH: PACIFISM AS THE MORAL SIGN OF A RESTORED NEW TESTAMENT APOSTOLIC CHURCH

The leaders of the pentecostal movement chronicled its "restorationist" character from its inception.[9] In 1912 Charles Parham recollected his own restorationist vision: "My first position, given July 4th, 1900, was a God-given commission to deliver to this age the truths of a restored PENTECOST, during which time I was called the Projector of the Apostolic Faith Movement."[10] Pentecostals proclaimed the modern-day, worldwide outpouring of the Holy Spirit, commonly associated with Azusa Street, Los Angeles, to be the restoration of the baptism of the Spirit and the supernatural work of the Spirit from the New Testament times to the twentieth-century church. Azusa Street was the Day of Pentecost revisited, a latter rain of the Spirit that portended the imminent return of Jesus Christ. A code phrase within early pentecostal discourse that symbolized this restorationist interpretation of the twentieth-century outpouring of the Spirit was "Bible days are here again." "This reversion to the New Testament," B. F. Lawrence told his readers, "was directly responsible for the Movement." Only to highlight his claim did Lawrence recognize that the church had a history: "The Pentecostal Movement," he wrote, "has no such history; it leaps the intervening years, crying '*Back to Pentecost.*'"[11]

In contrast to Lawrence, with his denigration of church history, some early pentecostal leaders employed an apologetic construction of church history to support their restorationist claim. Frank Bartleman and some others delineated the historical scenario of restoration as follows: The early church was a vital organism that proclaimed the apostolic faith found within the New Testament through the first three centuries of church history. The *Pax Romana* that eventually joined church and state in the common cause of promoting Christian civilization culminated in the Dark Ages, during which the light of the gospel finally flickered out. The once-vibrant organism had become "a backslidden" organization, using holy water to baptize the world and its ways.

Nevertheless, the argument ran, God by grace intervened in the church's history to restore New Testament Christianity. Starting with the Reformation, God used Martin Luther to restore to the church the reality of justification by faith. Later, in the Great Awakenings, God used John Wesley to restore the reality of sanctification through consecrated holy living. In the twentieth century God acted sovereignly again, this time to restore the reality of Spirit baptism and the supernatural gifts to the church that come through the outpouring of the Holy Spirit. This latter-day outpouring of the Spirit, which pentecostals called the "Latter Rain," was sent by God to empower Christians to gather the harvest of lost men and women into God's kingdom before the impending return of Jesus Christ.[12]

Variations on the restorationist theme were present among pentecostal leaders, but those leaders all shared the view that the pentecostal movement was God's means of restoring the full gospel of the New Testament proclaimed by Jesus and the apostles. Moral commitment to pacifism among early pentecostals has to be appreciated in the light of this restorationist understanding of church history. From the pentecostal perspective militarism entered the church's life when the church backslid and forged a political alliance with the Roman state. In this context pacifism represented the restoration of the Christian ethic from the apostolic church of the New Testament to the twentieth-century church.

As a consequence of this logic, one of the apologetic features of the pentecostal argument was to demonstrate that pacifism was the normative position on military service within the early church. "For the first three centuries," according to Samuel Booth-Clibborn, "Christians abstained totally from carnal warfare."[13] Both Booth-Clibborns provided evidence for such an assertion; for example, they listed pacifist quotations from the church fathers and related anecdotes about Roman soldiers becoming converted and immediately casting their weapons to the ground.[14] According to the younger Booth-Clibborn, early church history "simply swarms" with such accounts of soldiers' conversions to pacifism.[15] Meanwhile, Bartleman claimed that until the fifth century Roman soldiers were denied Holy Communion because they engaged in the immoral practice of killing other human beings.[16]

Arthur Booth-Clibborn clearly drew out the moral implications of this apologetic for the normativeness of pacifism in the early church in the light of the restorationist interpretation of church history. He made the point in his culminating argument in *Blood against Blood.* "Wherever there is a revival of the spirit of Apostolic Christianity," he wrote, "there also appears a revival of the conviction and the testimony that war is anti-Christian."[17] From this pentecostal restorationist perspective, pacifism was the concrete moral practice that signaled the recovery of the original, eschatological apostolic faith of the New Testament. The key phrases pentecostals used most typically to portray the eschatological character of Christian life that pacifism encapsulated were "the heavenly citizenship of the Christian" and "the pilgrim role of the church." Shortly after the war began, Frank Bartleman orchestrated these themes together in his forthright challenge to the pentecostal readership of *Word and Work:*

> War is damnation in the end to all concerned. . . . The present nations at war declare they will fight to a finish. . . . The hopelessness of all such efforts for peace should cause every true Christian to separate himself from it, confessing themselves [sic] but "strangers and pilgrims" in this world. . . . We are not of this world, but "our citizenship is in heaven" from whence we await our Savior. We must be separate from "nationalism." . . . The early church occupied a position of separation from nationalism completely separated unto God, and so must the church of the end.[18]

Basing his reasoning on the believer's heavenly citizenship and pilgrim role, Stanley Frodsham in the October 1915 issue of *Word and Witness* criticized the viewpoint of fellow pentecostals who argued in *The Evangel* that "the children of God should preserve an attitude of strict neutrality to the warring nations in Europe." In Frodsham's view to remain neutral on the war issue was to support the patriotism that fired up the war spirit. Such national pride was an "abomination in the sight of God." Moreover, according to Frodsham, "one of the old things that pass away when one becomes a new creature in Christ" was such "cultural love for the nation where one happened to be born." To be translated into the kingdom of God's dear son meant that "loyalty to the new

King should swallow up all other loyalties." Frodsham argued that this new center of loyalty destroyed the possibility that a Christian could remain neutral on the war. A pentecostal who sang "this world, this world is not my home" should not remain neutral toward "the nations who have drawn the sword to kill those of the same blood in other nations . . . with their policy of 'War on earth and illwill toward men.'" Because the bellicose rulers of this world denied the truth that God "hath made of one blood the nations of men," Frodsham claimed that they had set themselves "against the Lord and against His anointed." The options were clear: "Is any child of God going to side with these belligerent kings? Will he not rather side with the Prince of Peace under whose banner of love he has chosen to serve?"[19]

Some aspects of Frodsham's argument are enigmatic, and the meaning is difficult to track. One clear track, however, is his conception that an eschatology that "made this world not his home" required a pacifism that resisted compliance with the world's pugnacious ways and witnessed to the universal values of the gospel. This grounding of Christian pacifism in restorationist understanding connected closely with the notion that the church had a prophetic mission to unmask the sinful pretensions of the world. During the war that second line of argument recurred with rhythmic frequency.

UNMASKING THE REALITY OF SOCIAL EVIL: PACIFISM AS THE MORAL CRITIQUE OF THE EXISTING SINFUL SOCIAL ORDER

The prophetic indictment of the war by pentecostal pacifists was based also on a fundamental conviction about fallen human nature. War both expresses and is rooted in human sinfulness. As the Apostle James declared in his epistle, war arises from "the lusts of man." This is why war bears all the features of human sin, namely, cheating, greed, hatred, hypocrisy, lying, murder, pride, spying, vengeance, and so forth. Marked by such vices, war explicitly exploits the victim while it subtly dehumanizes the victor. Thus, for Bartleman, war was "insanity, madness." It was "a great insane asylum turned out of doors."[20]

According to Bartleman and other absolute pacifists, war was more than individual human sinfulness on the loose. It was institutionalized evil that reflected the sinful power structure of the world system. "Men's laws of destruction," "organized iniquity," and "systematized sinning" are some of the phrases Arthur Booth-Clibborn used against war in *Blood against Blood*.[21] "The Scripture shows us," he wrote, "that organized sin is much worse in the sight of God than are the sins of individuals." The church, to its shame, has been complicit at times in legitimizing "the organized slaying of millions in the wars" through an "unholy alliance" with emperors and governments.[22]

Pacifist pentecostals targeted two groups within the power structure—the ruling politicians and the rich class—because political policies and practices of those groups revealed the structural evil that war represents and perpetuates. The ruling politicians, Bartleman believed, used the war machine to consolidate their power. Weaker nations were blamed for the failed domestic policies and misguided international relations of stronger nations, and thus the weaker nations were cast into the role of the enemy. Military conscription of civilians provided a mechanism to acquire the soldiers to fight the enemy and as a consequence to ameliorate otherwise unsolvable social problems.[23] Sounding like Old Testament prophets, the pacifist preachers cataloged the warring nations, unmasking the sins each tried to cover and pronouncing the war to be God's judgment on the nations for their "brazen hypocrisy."[24] For example, Samuel Booth-Clibborn listed the social sins that generated "the present cataclysm":

> *England* is being punished for her increasing and overbearing pride, coupled with wretched hypocrisy in trying to cover such sins as her cowardly Boer War, her Chinese opium scandal, her drunkenness and oppression of the poor. . . .
>
> *Germany* for her military pride and greed of conquest, her boastful and blasphemous philosophies which have developed unbelief in numberless young minds, and for her subtle and clever higher criticism which has been Satan's best weapon for undermining man's faith in God's Holy Word as being true and inspired.
>
> *France* for her blatant infidelity and unspeakably vile morals . . . trying hard to beat Sodom's record for disgusting immorality, [while] making frantic but useless efforts to cover it all up with an outward show of art, architecture and science.
>
> *Belgium* for her recent Congo atrocities, her widespread immorality and drunkenness. . . .
>
> *Russia* for her continual and cruel treatment of God's chosen people, the Jews, not to speak of her over-bearing tyranny on her own subjects.
>
> *Italy* for her general wickedness and anarchy, which sins have been encouraged rather than reproved by the Roman Catholic Church, the "harlot" of Revelation (see Rev. 17:5, 9).[25]

The pentecostal pacifists saw the United States as also being brought under divine judgment for blatant idolatry. The war was God's judgment on America for its "degrading and long-continued worship of the golden calf—the almighty (?) dollar."[26] The war camouflaged these national sins and provided a mechanism for the rule of the stronger nations under the guise of patriotism to compete for "the spoils" of the weaker ones.[27] Drawing a clear distinction between civilian populations and government officials, Bartleman unhesitatingly blamed government bureaucrats for the carnage of war: "Crimination and recrimination among politicians . . . proves to us beyond the shadow of doubt that human governments are simply rotten. Men in public office and ruling positions rule their fellow-men, produce wars or avoid them, according to their own fancies and welfare. . . . The souls of men are used up as so much fodder for their own wills and wishes."[28]

Even though politicians used the military system for the accumulation of power, economic expansion, and amelioration of social problems at home, the pacifists considered the beneficiaries of this material production to be the rich classes of the world's nations. They thought this was especially true in the United States. An American "'money bag' despotism"—as Bartleman labeled it[29]—of the ruler and the capitalist exploited the poor and working classes in at least two ways. Economically the war increased the disparity between rich and poor: the rich got richer and the poor got poorer until finally "the rich man's dog gets more meat than the poor man's family."[30] The capitalist viewed the war as a commercial enterprise that produced profits. Reprehensibly the profits came from exploiting the misfortune of others. In the war economy the prices for munitions, as well as for wheat and other staples of life, were driven up for profit. And who received the profits? Bartleman listed them as "Wall Street interests, Pork Barrel administration, Brewer's Corporation, Syndicate and Monopoly, Steel Trust and Armor Plate, Powder Trust, etc. without end."[31] Meanwhile, Bartleman noted, "the poor must live on half rations. The sick must die. We cannot buy new clothes. We cannot buy good food. We cannot travel. Rent prices are criminally high." In Bartleman's view the most galling part of this hypocrisy was that the politicians who had enough power to "commandeer a nation" into war did nothing about this "handful of exploiters."[32] "Human leeches" is how he characterized such monopolists.[33]

Observing the shrewd way that the wealthy used the government's promotion of patriotism to their own benefit, Bartleman chided the rich for their ingenuity in finding schemes to rip off the common worker in a war economy: "Patriotism in most cases has proven to spell 'Graft.' 'Dollar' patriotism. War bonds are reduced in price until the poor man is either forced or frightened into unloading. Then they suddenly soar above par. Stung again! They are now in the hands of the patriotic Broker."[34] Individual greed, the capitalist free-market system, and the politicians who made public policy coalesced to institutionalize the unequal distribution of wealth. In Bartleman's judgment the distance between the classes in wartime constituted such an egregious criminal act that it "cries to heaven." "Think of Charlie Chaplan, the popular movie actor, getting around a half million dollars and over, for one year's salary while millions are starving."[35]

Economic exploitation of the poor by the rich is only one area of war's evil social functions. The other area that the pacifists dwelled on was the cost in human life. From the war's outset the pacifists emphasized that the American wealthy class was profiting financially from the bloody transaction of human killing. For example, Samuel Booth-Clibborn recalled how the rich profited without regard to human suffering when the Allies looked to U.S. firms for millions of tons of munitions. "Did these millionaires 'stand by the president' by keeping strictly neutral??? No!!! Not while there was a chance of piling up dollars, even though every one of them was dripping with the blood and tears of tortured Europe."[36] A new pool of the poor and working class helped to revitalize this "blood money" exchange of human lives for profit after America entered the war. The ultimate irony that Bartleman saw in this exploitation was that "the innocent are sent to do the killing, and be killed," while "those responsible for the wars are generally beyond its reach."[37]

Arthur Booth-Clibborn recalled a personal incident that made the systemic evil involved in this exchange of life for money crystal clear to him. He had visited a dock at Cork, in Ireland, where a ship was en route to war. He saw firsthand the "organized inequity" that, in his words, used "human flesh as 'food for cannon'":

> As I looked at a mass of . . . factory lads from Lancashire packed on the forward deck of a great transport ship . . . and talked to them from one ship to the other, there was a horrid squeezing at my heart. The scene reminded one of slavery, or the Irish cattle market preceding the shambles. Poor lads! How hollow their laughter sounded. How shy they looked when I passed them across some religious literature. A shilling a head was their price. The Queen's shilling, taken perhaps outside some cor-

ner saloon. And some widow's prodigal boys were probably among them.
My heart felt like bursting.[38]

The Booth-Clibborns and Frank Bartleman were absolute pacifists who
shared the belief that war was institutionalized violence under the cover of law. For them, a Christian should resist complicity in the social evil
called war through the practice of pacifism. Living by the principles of
Christian pacifism was a way to critique the power structure of the world
order and to do so with definite moral action.

For such pacifists, an essential part of the church's moral witness was
to remind the world and its military, economic, and political systems of
God's judgment on human sin, both individual and corporate. Moreover, resisting cultural assimilation into the world's power structure was
the only way for the church to maintain its loyalty to Jesus Christ and
keep its true identity as an eschatological community. Early pentecostal pacifism built on these theological and ethical convictions. Bartleman succinctly expressed such ethics without pulling his punch: "The
war church is a harlot church," he wrote. It persecuted its pacifists to sell
its own members for blood money, in exchange for the favor of the
powerful and the rich.[39] He saw a commitment to pacifism as the moral way to express the truth that "the 'body of Christ' is not the Body of
'a harlot.'"[40] Pacifism was a way to remind the world, in practical behavior, that the church and its moral conscience were not for sale to the
highest bidder.

The church was called to do more than stand against the world, however; it also was called to witness proactively for the fundamental value
of human life.

AFFIRMING THE VALUE OF HUMAN LIFE: PACIFISM AS THE CERTIFICATION OF THE UNIVERSAL VALUE OF HUMANITY

The decision of whether to participate in war's killing or in making peace
clearly revealed the Christian's ultimate loyalties, values, and disposi-
tions. To kill another human being in war was to demonstrate through
one's conduct that one's ultimate loyalty was to what Arthur Booth-
Clibborn called "the Earth Empire." The earth empire "selfishly cuts up
humanity as a whole in the supposed interest of a part . . . [and] places
kings and countries between the soul and Christ." It disseminated propaganda for "the organized discouraging of any good and kind information about 'the hereditary enemy' or rival nationality." And it will-

fully cultivated a "blind and narrow spirit," which was "the seed of war."[41] In contrast, Christians are people who give their ultimate loyalty to Jesus Christ after experiencing a genuine conversion to God. In Booth-Clibborn's words, this life-changing transformation, in which all Christians share, lifts their minds "above the fogs of prejudice or party, of politics or nationality." It makes them into "overcomers, whose spiritual stature makes their heads come over little partitions which separate nations and organizations—enabling them to examine universal truths in a spirit of universal love, and recognize fellow men everywhere and brethren in those born again."[42]

Intentionally or not, the brand of pacifism that the Assemblies of God leaders promoted among early pentecostals through Arthur Booth-Clibborn's book *Blood against Blood* is, in the author's word, "pro-Christian." Ultimately Booth-Clibborn's pacifism was rooted not in a spirit of antimilitarism but rather in the attempt to actualize the way of Christian peacemaking in the world. The practice of Christian pacifism required the transforming power of the gospel, however. In Booth-Clibborn's view, any effort to build international harmony without a true spiritual life led only to the delusion of a false peace; the real war could be won only by killing "the war spirit" within, through spiritual transformation. "In the trans-Calvary empire alone," he wrote, "can peace be found either for a world or for an individual soul. But those who have been born again alone dwell there. The words 'enemy' and 'foreigner' are not in their language." The ultimate distinction between "the Earth Empire" and the "trans-Calvary Empire" was "an essential difference in *spirit and disposition* and *in the means employed to remedy the evils in the world.*" For the unregenerate "it is carnal power and worldly war, expressed in hatred and ending in death; to the Christian, it is spiritual power and gospel war, expressed in love and ending in life."[43]

For these men Christian pacifism not only reflected a pursuit of peace based on a spiritual foundation; in a very explicit way it also certified the gospel that the church proclaimed to a war-ridden world. For instance, Bartleman stated flatly that the Christian who went to war against fellow human beings thereby betrayed "the principles of the Christ who died for all men."[44] "God's grace and Gospel are international," he declared; "Christ died for all men."[45] In the same vein Samuel Booth-Clibborn expressed disbelief at the dehumanizing effects of war. War causes people to become calloused toward the human lives Jesus came to save: reading about "thousands upon thousands of precious souls *'for whom Christ died'* being blasted into eternity or sunk in the ocean, causes the average person no more feeling than as if they were so many swat-ted flies or drowned rats."[46] In the view of these pentecostal pacifists, those spent lives had value—a value placed on them by Jesus Christ in his redemptive death.

Moreover, it is not only Christ's redemptive death that certifies the value that God places on all people. Redemption only discloses that which God has deemed of value in creation. All people were part of a common humanity already in Adam, a humanity loved by God. So kill-ing humans in war denies a central truth of natural law: by definition, it denies that all people are a part of a common humanity. Arthur Booth-Clibborn expressed the point eloquently: "Those persons who died out yonder belonged, after all, to no empire, to no church, to no organiza-tion or sect. They belonged to God, to humanity, to each of us, as we belong to them." According to Booth-Clibborn, the truly converted per-son recognized that in belonging to Christ, he or she also belonged "to humanity and not to any nation." This, wrote he, "will settle the ques-tion of war for him forever."[47]

According to this logic, when a Christian believer kills his fellow Christian in war, the act creates a double moral evil. In the words of the elder Booth-Clibborn: "In war the worldling denies one kind of tie in killing his fellow-creature; the Christian denies two kinds—he kills his *fellow-creature* and his *fellow-Christian*."[48] Bartleman agreed. The very idea of "converting men by the power of the Gospel, and later killing these same converts, across some imaginary boundary line," he wrote, "is unthinkable."[49]

These men thus saw Christians killing Christians as a violation both of natural law and of Christ's law; moreover, it violated the church's identity as the community of individuals who made visible the new humanity that exists in Christ. Samuel Booth-Clibborn emphasized this principle from Paul's teaching, quoting or citing 1 Corinthians 12:13, 27 ("For by one Spirit are we all baptized into one Body whether we be Jews or Gentiles, whether we be bond or free"), Colossians 3:11 ("Where there is neither Greek nor Jew, circumcision nor uncircumcision, Barbarian, Scythian, bond nor free; but Christ is all and in all"), and Romans 12:5 ("So we being many, are one Body in Christ, and every one members of another"). From these biblical affirmations Booth-Clibborn adduced that the body of Christ is composed of people of different national iden-tities who have been united into "one mystical Body of which Christ is the Head." He claimed that "as a member of that Body," a Christian "must love its members irrespective of their nationality." In the younger Booth-Clibborn's mind, Paul's portrayal of the church was inconsistent with Christians' fighting, hating, and killing fellow Christians from other countries. Therefore, in saying yes to Christ, the Christian as a member of Christ's body must say no to the wars of the world.[50]

Thus the pacifist pentecostal writers put forward three major arguments against killing in war: the value of a common humanity created by God, the value of a humanity headed toward redemption in Christ, and the value of a new humanity already existing as the body of Christ. But Arthur Booth-Clibborn thought that however argued, the ethical question boiled down to the same basic moral value. "And so, as in all such questions of right and wrong," he reflected, "everything comes finally to a point, and that point is *life*—human life."[51] In this theological context pacifism was moral because it valued all people created by God and for whom Christ died and because it gave visible expression to this prolife witness in its own transnational community of regenerated believers.

In the light of the three salient arguments used by early pentecostals to justify their pacifism, and of the pacifist Assemblies of God statement of 1917, it seems justifiable to infer that the Assemblies of God was "officially" a pacifist church during World War I. Furthermore, we may infer that the Assemblies of God was "officially" a pacifist church because a majority of its members held a pacifist belief in concert with the denominational statement and in keeping with the arguments that the leaders marshaled to support pentecostal pacifism. The official denominational statement and the way in which the denominational literature promoted the writings of the absolute pacifists support these inferences. Consequently, it seems perspicacious and convincing to use the cultural assimilation thesis to explain pacifism's later demise, which became codified in a denominational statement on military service in 1967. The cultural explanation is all the more plausible in the light of the upwardly mobile membership of the Assemblies of God during the 1940s and 1950s.

Nonetheless, the pacifist confession contained in the statement of 1917 and the content analysis of the pentecostals' arguments for pacifism tell only the conceptual part of the story of Assemblies of God pacifism. When the official statement and the pacifist rationale are interpreted within the denominational and political contexts in which they were written and distributed, another part of the story becomes significant for understanding the demise of the Assemblies of God pacifism. The definite contextual features of the story suggest that the official pacifist statement and the pacifist arguments may not have represented a position held by a majority of members in the denomination after all—and therefore that the cultural assimilation thesis needs to be modified to explain the loss of pentecostal pacifism, particularly in the case of the Assemblies of God.

PENTECOSTAL PACIFISM, DENOMINATIONAL DEALINGS, AND POLITICAL PRESSURE: REVISING THE THESIS OF CULTURAL ASSIMILATION

After the Executive Presbytery of the Assemblies of God sent the pacifism statement of 1917 to President Wilson, officially declaring its denomination to be a pacifist church, the *Weekly Evangel* published the statement with an explanation to readers. The explanation justified the action of the denomination's leaders on three grounds: (1) that pacifism represented the movement's "Quaker principles"; (2) that pacifism represented "every branch of the movement, whether in the United States, Canada, Great Britain or Germany"; and (3) that some part of the pentecostal movement needed to take responsibility to speak for the movement as a whole in the light of the U.S. conscription law.[52]

The first justification alluding to the movement's Quaker principles is enigmatic given pentecostalism's theological roots,[53] but the second—that pacifism pervaded all branches of the pentecostal movement—can easily be documented. For example, in his study of pacifism Jay Beaman noted that for the twenty-one pentecostal groups that had formed by 1917, he had found evidence that thirteen of them adhered to pacifism.[54] Nevertheless, to some degree the issue of the scope of pacifism pervading all sections of the movement is logically distinct from the issue of the number of pacifists within each branch or section of the movement. The issue of representation is sticky. In fact, from the time of the original discussions about it, pacifism appears to have been controversial among North American pentecostals. That was true especially within the ranks of the Assemblies of God. From 1914 and onward, that is, as early as three years prior to the statement of 1917, the *Christian Evangel* and its successor, the *Weekly Evangel,* carried exchanges—sometimes rather pointed ones—on the pacifism versus military service issue. Although from 1915 onward the editorial policy of these magazines moved cautiously but deliberately toward pacifism, a backlash of reaction clearly indicated that not all Assemblies of God preachers agreed with their church's official magazine.[55]

The 1917 statement brought additional reactions from the clergy. For example, the Texas District Council, one of the denomination's strongest regional powers at the time, resolved in its 1917 session to cancel the credentials of any preacher who spoke against the government. Of course such a resolution applied directly to pacifists. Sensing the pressure of the Texas delegation about the inappropriateness of antigovernment statements some pacifists were making, the General Council in 1917 concurred. "Such radicals," it said, "do not represent this General Council."[56]

The antipathy of fellow members toward the pacifists within the Assemblies of God was not restricted to Texas. As the war progressed, some of the denomination's leaders tried to restrict explicit pacifist expression among the church's preachers. This occurred especially after the government established conscription in May 1917 and even more following the Espionage Act of 1917 and the Sedition Act of 1918. For example, when some pentecostal preachers were among a half-dozen clergy who were jailed by U.S. marshals for violating wartime laws, E. N. Bell, editor of the *Weekly Evangel* and himself not an absolute pacifist, used the occasion to address the Assemblies of God clergy. In the magazine's January 5, 1918, issue he sternly warned the clergy to register for the draft in order to make their exemption legal and not push their pacifist convictions into the political arena. Bell told the clergy that if they were arrested for making what the government regarded as treasonous remarks, he doubted that the pentecostal movement would stand with them. In fact, Bell wrote not only as editor of the denomination's paper; he also had been the first to serve as chairman of the General Council, in 1914. He concluded in a foreboding tone: "So let all our preachers be duly warned not to do anything rash, like these other preachers, that will land them in a Federal Penitentiary, or up before a shooting squad for Treason to the Country."[57]

Only seven months after Bell had issued his warning, he urged his paper's readers to destroy one of Frank Bartleman's tracts on pacifism.[58] Part of his motive may have been a quarrel within the pentecostal movement, for as the war progressed Bartleman and his fellow pacifist Samuel H. Booth-Clibborn had come to associate more closely with a faction known as the Oneness Pentecostals. As historian Edith Blumhofer has pointed out, however, as the Oneness branch splintered off from the Assemblies of God, it sustained the radical restorationist vision of the early movement without compromise, even under the pressures of the war.[59] In calling on readers to destroy Bartleman's tract, Bell was no doubt concerned that the content of the pamphlet might invoke the government's reprisal under the Espionage Act. Whatever his intent, the effect of Bell's action was to marginalize Bartleman's influence within the Assemblies of God. Ironically, only three years earlier, in 1915, the *Weekly Evangel* had reprinted Bartleman's tract in its columns. Now the editor of the same *Evangel* called the Assemblies of God faithful to destroy the pamphlet.[60] An influential voice whom the denominational leaders had earlier used to provide the rationale for pacifism within the Assemblies of God was now being muted.

With the proverbial mighty pen, Bell kept up his campaign. In October 1918, two months after calling for Bartleman's tract to be destroyed, he went on record flatly opposing the pacifists' contention that killing in war is murder. "When a soldier obeys his country in executing just punishment on the criminal Hun," he wrote, that soldier is not a murderer as long as his motive is not personal hatred of the enemy.[61] The fault line along pacifism was widening. Denominational leaders such as Bell had become increasingly disaffected with the pacifist position after the United States entered the war. Some pacifists, such as Frank Bartleman and Samuel H. Booth-Clibborn, had apparently become disenchanted with the Assemblies of God. They preferred to associate with more radical restorationist pentecostal groups.

Along with the growing strain in relations between some denominational leaders and some leading pacifist spokespersons, the government's concerted effort to clamp down on pacifist activity and the patriotic spirit that swept through the country after America entered the war caused many pentecostal Christians to break ranks with those who were conscientiously opposed to the war. When the war was over, Frank Bartleman, who had a global assessment of the pentecostal church and its practice of pacifism, stated bluntly that during the war "the Pentecostal failed to stand by the Lord."[62] It was clear to Bartleman that World War I had robbed "the church of her sacred calling and 'pilgrim' role" and plunged it headlong "into the vortex of world politics and patriotism, with all its fallen prejudices and preferences, avarices, cruelties, hates and murders."[63] In a two-part article published in the *Pentecostal Evangel* in 1930, Donald Gee concurred with Bartleman's assessment. Like Bartleman, he concluded that the church as a whole had imbibed the patriotic spirit during World War I and had betrayed its pacifist principles.[64] Thus the second claim—that pacifism pervaded all branches of the pentecostal movement—turned out to be hyperbole, despite the denomination's use of this argument to justify its pacifist statement of 1917.

The third and final justification used by the Assemblies of God executives when they registered the denomination as a pacifist church claimed that someone had to speak for all pentecostals in response to the conscription law. This argument really constitutes a disguised confession of the political coercion the church's leaders were experiencing. Under both the press of deadlines imposed by the U.S. government and the conditions established by Congress for religious denominations to qualify their members for conscientious objector status, the Assemblies of God leadership registered the denomination as a pacifist church.[65] In other words, the action was politically necessary to give draft protection to those pentecostals who were indeed pacifists. Only if the church as a whole registered as a pacifist denomination could its pacifist members—whatever their number—receive official status as conscientious objectors. Accordingly, the statement itself and the rationales developed to justify it simply do not provide reliable measures of how deep or broad pacifist belief was in the Assemblies of God movement as a whole. The official position adopted by the church was not necessarily based on a majority consensus of the church's membership; rather, it was an action—by the leaders' own confession—that the denomination's leaders took to protect those members who wanted to claim conscientious objector status. Moreover, for the denomination's clergy the official position provided a way to secure ministerial exemptions. That was true both for preachers who were principled pacifists and for those who were not but who nonetheless believed that the clergy as a class should not be involved in combatant service and the taking of human life.

Considered in its context, the denomination's pacifist statement of 1917 does not point to the uncritical conclusion that the Assemblies of God was a pacifist movement during World War I. Officially the denomination did register itself as such with the government. At a practical level, however, the Assemblies of God was made up of regional district councils, some of whose leaders expressed explicit sympathy for the American war effort, and of individual members, many of whom chose as a matter of personal conscience to participate in military service. However, pentecostal believers who were conscientious objectors would have that option only if the Assemblies of God leaders took the official action that they did.

The political context also casts fresh light on the significance of the three arguments used here to interpret Assemblies of God pacifism. The theological and ethical arguments for pacifism demonstrated that pentecostal thought encompassed a variety of justifications for pacifism as a normative moral position. Pacifism was tied to the idea of restoring a vibrant apostolic faith, to resisting assimilation into an exploitive, war-ridden world, and to affirming the value of human life. Accordingly, for some pentecostals pacifism became the moral sign of a restored New Testament faith, the moral critique of the existing sinful social order, and the moral certification of the universal value of humanity—a humanity created by God, redeemed by Jesus Christ, and finding visible expression in the church. All these arguments intoned the dissonance that early pentecostals as a whole felt toward the world of human culture. According to the pentecostal absolute pacifists, a pacifistic way of life is an expression of a sojourner's mentality that makes it clear that this world is not the pentecostal pilgrim's home.

Nonetheless, the arguments to support the normativeness of pacifism indicate just as clearly that pentecostalism's absolute pacifists viewed a pacifistic way of life as a positive expression of the truth of the gospel. Pacifism was understood as a way of life that both resists accommodation to the world and expresses the truth of God's love for all human beings. It validates the church's proclamation that God is the creator of human life, that Jesus died to save all people, and that the church is a multinational community.

Given the sturdy theological and ethical content of these arguments— whatever the ambivalence between anticultural and pro-Christian sentiments—and the intensity with which the pacifists presented them, it seems almost incredible that the denomination could lose its pacifism as rapidly as it did. It seems doubly incredible if pacifism and its rationale were held by a majority of pentecostals within the Assemblies of God.

In fact, my investigation reveals yet another consideration: the absolute pacifists' arguments had a definite advocacy character. Their goal was to persuade, not to describe an established denominational position. The arguments were written by pentecostals to other pentecostals. To be sure, the popular-level literature functioned to express and consolidate some already existing sentiment, but its main function, or at least the hope, was quite clearly to bring more pentecostals into the pacifist fold.

· · ·

When the theological and ethical content and the persuasive functions of these arguments are coupled with other factors of the time, it seems that the cultural assimilation theory needs to be nuanced in an important way. Only then can the theory account for the demise of pentecostal pacifism, at least in the case of the Assemblies of God. Given the advocacy character of the pacifist literature, the theological and ethical content of the pacifistic arguments, the political nature of the 1917 statement, the disaffection between the denominational leaders and some of the spokespersons for pacifism as the war progressed, and the eyewitness appraisal of pacifists such as Bartleman and Gee—given all these, the change the Assemblies of God made between 1917 and 1967 with regard to military service needs a religious as well as a cultural explanation. In religious terms, the denomination lost a prophetic pacifist minority. These minority pacifists, while holding some overlapping ideas and common arguments, used a variety of theological frameworks and ethical principles to justify Christian pacifism.[66] Before they had an opportunity to cultivate a pacifist *tradition,* however, history had overtaken them and the nation's patriotic war spirit had invaded the house, never to leave. Without a theologically informed ethical tradition to sustain the pacifists' numbers and to perpetuate their beliefs to new generations, the demise of pentecostal pacifism within the Assemblies of God was only a matter of time. That demise would become all the more apparent in World War II, the Korean War, and the Vietnam War, but the unraveling of a pacifist contingent within the Assemblies of God church was already in motion by the end of World War I.[67] The loss of the prophetic strain of pacifists within the movement grew out of theological and ethical conditions that allowed for the denomination's subsequent cultural accommodation.

Ironically, the statement on military service adopted in 1967 put into denominational policy what had been *practiced* within the Assemblies of God even in 1917: "We shall continue to insist, as we have historically, on the right of each member to choose for himself whether to declare his position as a combatant, a non-combatant, or a conscientious objector."[68] When the pluralism of pentecostal conscience was moved from the level of practice to official policy, however, the 1967 statement forfeited the opportunity to claim conscientious objector status for the denomination's youth. The Selective Service Act of 1967, like U.S. conscription laws ever since 1917, granted conscientious objector status only to those whose conscience was grounded in a pacifism nurtured by religious conviction and teaching.[69] Apparently the need to be sensitively inclusive of those in the Assemblies of God who were conscientious objectors by keeping the pacifist statement at the official level of the denomination's constitution and bylaws no longer existed as it had in World War I. The fact is that, since 1917, both the conscription laws and the court decisions interpreting them had made conscientious objection more and more a matter of individual conscience and far less a matter of membership in a church officially recognized as pacifist. Therefore, between 1917 and 1967 the denomination's need to maintain an official policy of pacifism so as legally to protect its pacifist minority declined dramatically.

Nonetheless, the change in the official statement adopted during the agony of the Vietnam War did indeed disclose that pacifism was past history within a culturally accommodated Assemblies of God. The accommodation left believers alone with an individual right of conscience but with no church teaching, one way or the other, to inform the exercise of that right in a morally responsible manner.

NOTES

1. "Resolution Concerning the Attitude of the General Council of the Assemblies of God toward Military Service Which Involves the Actual Participation in the Destruction of Human Life," printed in *Weekly Evangel,* Aug. 4, 1917, p. 6. Each biennium from 1927 to 1965 a slightly modified version appeared in published, official minutes of the denomination's General Council; see *Minutes of the Thirty-First General Council of the Assemblies of God* (Springfield, Mo.: Gospel, 1965), 134 (such minutes hereinafter cited as "General Council *Minutes,*" with year).

2. General Council *Minutes* (1967), 35. This statement continues verbatim through the most recent meeting of the General Council, Aug. 6–11, 1991, in Portland, Oregon; see General Council *Minutes* (1991), 220.

3. Lack of knowledge about pacifism in classical pentecostalism began with omissions in the first histories by academically trained historians: Carl Brumback, *Suddenly from Heaven* (Springfield, Mo.: Gospel, 1961), and Klaude Kendrick, *The Promise Fulfilled: A History of the Modern Pentecostal Movement* (Springfield, Mo.: Gospel, 1961). Their omissions are puzzling since by 1954 Irvine John Harrison's Th.D. thesis, "A History of the Assemblies of God" (Berkeley Baptist Divinity School, Berkeley, Calif.), had treated military service as an early "theological storm." Nils Bloch-Hoell, *The Pentecostal Movement: Its Origins, Development and Distinctive Character* (Oslo: Universitetsforlaget; London: Allen and Unwin; New York: Humanities, 1964) was also silent on pacifism. John Thomas Nichol's *Pentecostalism* (New York: Harper and Row, 1966) did mention pacifism in the International Pentecostal Assemblies but treated it as merely isolated and aberrational. The first histories to recognize early pentecostalism's pacifism were William W. Menzies, *Anointed to Serve* (Springfield, Mo.: Gospel, 1971); Walter J. Hollenweger, *The Pentecostals: The Charismatic Movement in the Churches* (Minneapolis: Augsburg, 1972); and Vinson Synan, *The Holiness-Pentecostal Movement in the U.S.* (Grand Rapids,

Mich.: Eerdmans, 1975). Robert Mapes Anderson, in *The Vision of the Disinherited: The Making of American Pentecostalism* (New York: Oxford University Press, 1979), broke fresh ground by developing pacifism's significance and offering an interpretation that it grew out of pentecostals' socioeconomic disfranchisement. See also Roger Robins, "Our Forgotten Heritage: A Look at Early Pentecostal Pacifism," *Assemblies of God Heritage* 6 (Winter 1986–87): 3–5; idem, "A Chronology of Peace: Attitudes toward War and Peace in the Assemblies of God: 1914–1918," *PNEUMA: The Journal of the Society for Pentecostal Studies* 6 (Spring 1984): 3–25; James R. Goff Jr., *Fields White unto Harvest: Charles F. Parham and the Missionary Origins of Pentecostalism* (Fayetteville: University of Arkansas Press, 1988); Edith Blumhofer, *The Assemblies of God: A Chapter in the Story of American Pentecostalism, Volume 1—To 1941* (Springfield, Mo.: Gospel, 1989); Mickey Crews, *The Church of God: A Social History* (Knoxville: University of Tennessee Press, 1990); and above all Jay Beaman, *Pentecostal Pacifism: The Origins, Development and Rejection of Pacific Belief among the Pentecostals* (Hillsboro, Kans.: Center for Mennonite Brethren Studies, 1989). Beaman argued that pentecostals lost their pacifism through assimilation into the American mainstream.

4. See end of n. 3. The book is the slightly revised publication of Beaman's 1982 M.Div. thesis by the same title, completed in April 1982 at North American Baptist Seminary, Sioux Falls, S.D.

5. Beaman, *Pentecostal Pacifism,*107–21.

6. Murray W. Dempster, review of Beaman, *Pentecostal Pacifism, PNEUMA: The Journal of the Society for Pentecostal Studies* 11 (Fall 1989): 59–64.

7. These absolute pacifists were influential in promoting and shaping pacifist sentiment within the Assemblies of God. Notable writings were Arthur Booth-Clibborn, *Blood against Blood,* 2d ed. (Springfield, Mo.: Gospel, 1914); Frank Bartleman's pieces in the group's official *Weekly Evangel* (June, July, Aug. 1915); Samuel H. Booth-Clibborn's writings in the *Weekly Evangel,* especially "The Christian and War," serialized in issues of Apr. 28 and May 5 and 19, 1917, with some of the same content reappearing in his booklet *Should a Christian Fight? An Appeal to Christian Young Men of All Nations* (Swengal, Pa.: Bible Truth Depot, n.d. [ca. 1917–18]). See note 23 for more bibliography. Stanley H. Frodsham was influential for Assemblies of God pacifism in a *Word and Witness* article critical of neutrality early in World War I and in his role as the denomination's executive secretary. Frodsham wrote and sent the letter of April 28, 1917, to President Wilson, accompanying the resolution on military service.

8. See my "Reassessing the Moral Rhetoric of Early American Pentecostal Pacifism," *Crux* 26 (Mar. 1990): 23–36, whose thesis is that pacifism gave pentecostals the rudimentary principles of a social ethic and disclosed a pentecostal social conscience. I argued further that with the loss of pacifism, pentecostals also lost a wholistic conception of the church's mission in the world. Such arguments appear also in a paper I read in 1991 in Switzerland, "'Crossing Bor-

ders': Arguments Used by Early American Pentecostals in Support of the Global Character of Pacifism," later published in *EPTA Bulletin: The Journal of the
European Pentecostal Theological Association* 10, no. 2 (1991): 63–80. My analysis offers revision of Jay Beaman's cultural assimilation thesis for explaining the
demise of pentecostal pacifism. Critics have noted that at least four of the five
pacifists I treated—Bartleman, Frodsham, and the Booth-Clibborns—were
influential primarily in the Assemblies of God and may not have been important in other pentecostals' pacifism. The present essay demonstrates my appreciation for that criticism. I wish also to thank Professors Augustus Cerillo and
Lewis F. Wilson for helpful criticisms based on their expertise in pentecostal
history.

9. In *The Apostolic Faith* Charles F. Parham wove restorationism through
many of his articles—see especially "The Apostolic Faith Movement," *The Apostolic Faith,* Dec.-Jan. 1912–13, pp. 1–2—and he linked his restorationism with
pacifism. The present essay does not include Parham because, as a function of
his doctrinal excesses, his racist attitudes, and questions about his sexual conduct, he was anathema to the Assemblies of God from its inception; see Goff,
Fields White unto Harvest, esp. 128–46. For other restorationist interpretations,
see Frank Bartleman's "God's Onward March through the Centuries," *The Latter
Rain Evangel,* July 1910, pp. 2–8, and his later *How Pentecost Came to Los Angeles—How It Was in the Beginning* (1925), reprinted as *Asuza Street* (Plainfield,
N.J.: Logos International, 1980); D. Wesley Myland, *The Latter Rain Covenant
and Pentecostal Power* (Chicago: Evangel, 1910); and B. F. Lawrence, *The Apostolic Faith Restored* (St. Louis: Gospel, 1916), both reprinted in *Three Early Pentecostal Tracts,* vol. 14 of *"The Higher Christian Life": Sources for the Study of the
Holiness, Pentecostal, and Keswick Movements,* ed. Donald W. Dayton, 48 vols.
(New York: Garland, 1985); and Elizabeth Sisson, "Acts-Two-Four—Past and
Present," *Weekly Evangel,* Dec. 1, 1917, pp. 2–3. For analysis of restorationism in
early pentecostalism, see Grant Wacker, "Are the Golden Oldies Still Worth
Playing? Reflections on History Writing among Early Pentecostals," *PNEUMA:
The Journal of the Society for Pentecostal Studies* 8 (Fall 1986): 81–100.

10. Charles Parham, "Leadership," *The Apostolic Faith,* June 1912, p. 7.

11. Lawrence, *Apostolic Faith Restored,* 12. Pentecostalism sometimes appears
to be quite ahistorical; for an analysis, see Grant Wacker, "A Profile of American Pentecostalism," in Harold D. Hunter, ed., *Pastoral Problems in the Pentecostal-Charismatic Movement,* 1–88 (Cleveland, Tenn.: Society for Pentecostal
Studies, 1983), esp. 24–36.

12. For an analysis of Frank Bartleman's view of this "process of restoration,"
see the introduction in Cecil M. Robeck Jr., *Witness to Pentecost: The Life of
Frank Bartleman,* vol. 5 of *"The Higher Christian Life,"* esp. xviii–xxi.

13. Samuel H. Booth-Clibborn, *Should a Christian Fight? An Appeal to Christian Young Men of All Nations* (Swengel, Pa.: Bible Truth Depot, n.d.), 32.

14. Arthur Sydney Booth-Clibborn, *Blood against Blood* (New York: Charles

C. Cook, n.d. [reprint of preface in the 2d ed. is dated 1914]), 106–10; S. Booth-Clibborn, *Should a Christian Fight?* 32–35.

15. S. Booth-Clibborn, *Should a Christian Fight?* 33.

16. Frank Bartleman, "Christian Preparedness," *Word and Work,* ca. 1916, p. 114.

17. A. Booth-Clibborn, *Blood against Blood,* 146.

18. Frank Bartleman, "War and the Christian," *Word and Work,* ca. 1915, p. 83.

19. Stanley H. Frodsham, "Our Heavenly Citizenship," *Word and Witness,* Oct. 1915, p. 3.

20. Bartleman, *War and the Christian* (undated tract), 4.

21. A. Booth-Clibborn, *Blood against Blood,* 39, 82, 73.

22. Ibid., 87–88.

23. These indictments were repeated by Bartleman in a variety of articles: "Present Day Conditions," *Weekly Evangel,* June 5, 1915, p. 3; "The European War," *Weekly Evangel,* July 10, 1915, p. 3; "What Will The Harvest Be?" *Weekly Evangel,* Aug. 7, 1915, p. 1; "The War—Our Danger," *Word and Work,* Nov. 1915, pp. 300–301; "Christian Preparedness," *Word and Work,* ca. 1916, pp. 114–15; "Not of This World," *Word and Work,* ca. 1916, pp. 296–97; "The World War," *Word and Work,* July 1916, pp. 296–97; "The World Situation," *Word and Work,* ca. 1916, pp. 344–45; "In the Last Days," *Word and Work,* Sept. 1916, pp. 393–94; "The Money God," *Word and Work,* ca. 1916–17, pp. 274–75; "A Time of Trouble," *Word and Work* 39 (Apr. 1917), 185–86.

24. S. Booth-Clibborn, *Should a Christian Fight?* 19. Frank Bartleman also used this rhetorical technique; see especially "Present Day Conditions," 3; "What Will the Harvest Be?" 1; and "The War—Our Danger," 300.

25. S. Booth-Clibborn, *Should a Christian Fight?* 19–20.

26. Ibid., 20.

27. Bartleman, "War and the Christian," 82; S. Booth-Clibborn, "What Will the Harvest Be?" 1.

28. Bartleman, "War and the Christian," 83.

29. Bartleman, "The War—Our Danger," 301.

30. Bartleman, "In the Last Days," 393.

31. Bartleman, "War and the Christian," 83.

32. Bartleman, *War and the Christian,* 4.

33. Bartleman, "In the Last Days," 393.

34. Bartleman, *War and the Christian,* 4.

35. Bartleman, "Christian Preparedness," 114.

36. S. Booth-Clibborn, *Should a Christian Fight?* 42.

37. Bartleman, *War and the Christian,* 4; cf. idem, "The War—Our Danger," 301.

38. A. Booth-Clibborn, *Blood against Blood,* 83.

39. Bartleman, *War and the Christian,* 4.

40. Bartleman, "War and the Christian," 83.

41. A. Booth-Clibborn, *Blood against Blood,* 26.

42. Ibid., 31.

43. Ibid., 125, 99, 95, 14 (his emphasis).

44. Bartleman, *War and the Christian,* 3.

45. Frank Bartleman, *Christian Citizenship* (tract, ca. 1922), 2.

46. S. Booth-Clibborn, *Should a Christian Fight?* 18.

47. A. Booth-Clibborn, *Blood against Blood,* 30.

48. Ibid., 32.

49. Bartleman, *Christian Citizenship,* 1.

50. S. Booth-Clibborn, *Should a Christian Fight?* 14–15.

51. A. Booth-Clibborn, *Blood against Blood,* 16.

52. "The Pentecostal Movement and the Conscription Law, *Weekly Evangel,* Aug. 4, 1917, p. 6.

53. Quaker principles may have been brought into the everyday discourse of pentecostals through influential leaders. Frank Bartleman's mother had nurtured him in the Quaker faith. Arthur Sydney Booth-Clibborn in the third edition of *Blood against Blood* traced his own pacifist heritage back to John Clibborn's conversion to the Quaker faith in 1658 (appendix C, 166–76). Arthur passed on his Quaker-based pacifism to his son Samuel. Nonetheless, given the theological roots of the pentecostal movement, the allusion to the movement's "Quaker principles" remains puzzling. For a comprehensive analysis of the theological roots of the broader movement, see Donald W. Dayton, *The Theological Roots of Pentecostalism* (Grand Rapids, Mich.: Zondervan, 1987); for a more specific analysis of the origins of pentecostalism that bears on the formation of the Assemblies of God, see Blumhofer, *The Assemblies of God,* 17–64.

54. Beaman, *Pentecostal Pacifism,* 30.

55. This pacifist-militarist exchange is analyzed by Roger Robins, "A Chronology of Peace: Attitudes toward War and Peace in the Assemblies of God: 1914–1918," *PNEUMA: The Journal of the Society for Pentecostal Studies* 6 (Spring 1984): 3–25.

56. General Council *Minutes* (1917), 17–18, reported that the Assemblies of God reached a consensus on loyalty to government and honoring the flag and agreed that radicals on such matters did not represent the general council's views.

57. E. N. Bell, "Preachers Warned," *Weekly Evangel,* Jan. 5, 1918, p. 4. Interestingly, the resolution on pacifism was formulated during a brief period when E. N. Bell was not serving as an officer within the Assemblies of God. Bell seemed to conform to the pacifism of the movement on his return to the ranks of denominational leadership, yet as time passed his own unease with pacifism rose more and more to the surface.

58. E. N. Bell, "Destroy That Tract," *Weekly Evangel,* Aug. 24, 1918, p. 3.

59. Blumhofer, *Assemblies of God,* 1:434 n. 16.

60. The tract was Bartleman's *Present Day Conditions;* the *Weekly Evangel* had printed it in its June 5, 1915, issue.

61. E. N. Bell, "Question and Answers," *Weekly Evangel,* Oct. 19, 1918, p. 5.

62. Bartleman, *War and the Christian,* 4.

63. Bartleman, *Christian Citizenship,* 2.

64. Donald Gee, "War, the Bible and the Christian," *Pentecostal Evangel,* Nov. 8, 1930, p. 6.

65. "The Pentecostal Movement and the Conscription Law," 6.

66. Even a cursory examination of representative pacifist literature suggests that early pentecostals did not set forth a unified set of theological convictions and ethical principles to justify Christian pacifism. A typology of the North American pentecostal pacifism examined in this essay might be characterized as follows: "sectarian" pacifism (Frodsham); "dispensationalist" pacifism (S. Booth-Clibborn); "prophetic" pacifism (Bartleman); and "ethical-humanitarian" pacifism (A. Booth-Clibborn). Including other pacifists in addition to the four examined in this essay might expand the data base within each of these types or expand the variety of types.

67. Writing in 1954, when the church was still officially pacifist, Irvine John Harrison observed that Assemblies of God people had radically changed their practice by World War II. He noted that the executive's 1917 statement was still held officially and that "at least theoretically the Assemblies of God are still a church which holds in common with Quakers, Mennonites and others their refusal to bear arms even to resist aggression." But he also noted that in World War II only an infinitesimal fraction of members had chosen conscientious objection, and he expressed personal support of the U.S. war effort in grandiose rhetoric; see Harrison, "A History of the Assemblies of God," 156–57. No doubt a great majority of Assemblies of God members shared Harrison's patriotism, yet vestiges of the earlier pacifism remained. Jay Beaman has noted that of approximately 12,000 World War II objectors in Civilian Public Service, pentecostals numbered about 131, of whom about 20 can be identified as Assemblies of God members. For the period from World War II through 1967, the time of the change in the official statement, Beaman chronicled various developments (including some behind-the-scenes maneuvering) that culminated in that change; see Beaman, *Pentecostal Pacifism,* 103, 107–18.

68. General Council *Minutes* (1967), 35.

69. Selective Service Act of 1967 (PL 90–40), 81 Stat. 100.

3

❧

RACE AND CONSCIENTIOUS OBJECTION IN WORLD WAR I

The Story of the Church of God in Christ

❧

Theodore Kornweibel Jr.

During World War I, alarms about "enemy aliens," "Wobbly" anticapitalist labor agitators, fifth columnists, and a legion of "slackers" gripped the emotions and prejudices of an anxious U.S. public. With such fears rampant, the arrests of obscure black southern preachers on charges of obstructing the war effort elicited no national headlines. Although grand juries ultimately vindicated accused leaders of the Church of God in Christ (COGIC), widespread efforts of government officers and vigilante mobs to compel patriotism and military service reveal troubling pressures on wartime free speech and religious expression. Yet the story also demonstrates that the legal system could rise to the occasion and resist the inflamed passions of the day.

By World War I the Church of God in Christ was scarcely two decades old and had not established any tradition of pacifism. Its founder, Charles Harrison Mason, had been born in 1866, shortly after his parents exchanged slavery for wage labor on farms and plantations in Tennessee and Arkansas. As a child Mason attended school only to the fourth grade, yet he did not lack for scriptural training. His Missionary Baptist parents taught him, and even as a child he displayed unusual spiritual depth. In 1893, at age twenty-six or twenty-seven, he assumed leadership of a revival in Preston, Arkansas, where many found repentance. Later that year, believing that formal education would make him a better preacher, he enrolled in Arkansas Baptist College, but he left after only three weeks. "The Lord showed me that there was no salvation in schools and colleges," he declared. Instead, salvation would come through the preaching of a twofold blessing: conversion—that is, a saving knowledge of Jesus Christ through a personal relationship with him—and sanctification—that is, the believer's purification from all sin. Meeting with like-minded preachers, Mason planted the seeds of a new pentecostal church. The seeds bore fruit in 1897 in an old gin house in Lexington, Mississippi, where Mason founded the first Church of God in Christ.[1]

During the early years of the twentieth century, dormant spiritual embers burst into flame in widespread corners of the world, nowhere more dramatically than in an "Azusa Street" revival in Los Angeles led by William J. Seymour, a black evangelist. In the words of David M. Tucker, writer of a book on black church leaders, Seymour began "preaching the new doctrine of a third blessing—baptism by the Holy Ghost and fire—which empowered saints to cast out devils, heal the sick, and speak in other tongues." Soon hundreds of persons, white and black, made pilgrimages to Seymour's renovated livery stable seeking the anointing of the Spirit.[2] This third blessing provided Mason with the missing experiential and theological pieces of the holiness puzzle. Now based at Memphis, Mason went to Los Angeles, received the gift of tongues, and returned to spread the fire of revival. Five weeks of all-night meetings aroused dramatic interest in the new pentecostal worship and belief.[3]

In 1907 the first General Assembly of the Church of God in Christ named Mason the church's Chief Apostle. Rapid growth took place among urban mill hands and rural sharecroppers in Tennessee, Arkansas, and Mississippi.[4] By the 1910s, a time when black Texans were stepping up a migration to the West Coast, the church spread to southern California, where Elder E. R. Driver assumed leadership. Eastward, churches were planted in Norfolk, Pittsburgh, Philadelphia, Detroit, Harlem, and Brooklyn, while expansion up the Mississippi Valley led to outposts in St. Louis, Kansas City, and Chicago. By 1917 the Church of God in Christ had congregations in the major urban centers to which blacks were streaming in the "Great Migration"—although the majority of its members were still concentrated in Arkansas, Florida, Louisiana, Mississippi, Oklahoma, Tennessee, and Texas.[5] The church would have remained invisible to most whites, who little noticed the growth of urban storefront or rural southern sanctified congregations, had it not been for World War I. But the war brought unanticipated challenges and attention from public authorities and superpatriotic vigilantes. It was the church's time of persecution and testing.

In the supercharged atmosphere of the war, both public officials and superpatriotic organizations manipulated and exacerbated prejudices against conscientious objectors and all other suspected enemy sympathizers. In that atmosphere all but the most single-minded devotees of unpopular causes found it prudent to fall silent, comply, or both. Religious objectors to participation in war suffered considerable persecution, for neither the public nor the government was tolerant of those who believed that God forbade them to render military service unto Caesar. Nonreligious objectors, including some blacks, faced even greater hostility. Given such a popular mood, the top leadership of the Church of God in Christ was fortunate to escape conviction and draconian punishment.[6]

Members and leaders of COGIC first came to the attention of the federal government because their church forbade the shedding of blood, a belief that was bound to create conflict with the draft. Enforcement of selective service regulations was the responsibility of the Department of Justice. United States attorneys prepared legal cases while the rapidly expanding Bureau of Investigation gathered evidence and apprehended nonregistrants or refusers. The government's efforts often trampled constitutional liberties, the most spectacular example being the infamous 1918 "slacker raids." Caught in a crossfire of public intolerance and zealous enforcement of conscription, COGIC members and other religious objectors could nevertheless not betray their understanding of Scripture. Consequently they and federal authorities were on a collision course. That church leadership ultimately escaped prosecution is a tribute to the good sense of two grand juries in eastern Texas that rejected the arguments of federal agents and prosecutors.

Millions had died on the battlefields of Europe prior to April 1917, when America officially entered the war. If the United States was to have a decisive combat role, it had to conscript soldiers quickly. In writing its draft law Congress provided that exemptions be granted only to conscientious objectors who were members of religious bodies opposed to participation in war. Following this, President Wilson declared that members of "a well recognized religious sect or organization" that had a creed prohibiting war service were eligible, but they still had to perform noncombatant military service. (That is, the president made no provision for complete exemption or for alternative service under civilian direction.) To win such limited noncombatant status, applicants had to convince local draft boards of the sincerity of their beliefs. In practice the Quakers, Mennonites, Church of the Brethren, and a few smaller long-time pacifist groups such as the Brethren in Christ were the only denominations whose men had their pacifism recognized without undue difficulty. Moreover, the government demanded that even they don military uniforms and work under military command and discipline.[7] Of those who refused to cooperate, hundreds were court-martialed and sentenced to long, abusive terms at maximum-security prisons such as Alcatraz and Leavenworth. Seventeen received death sentences—although later, in saner times, the sentences were commuted. Public opinion associated conscientious objection with pro-Germanism or Wobbly-style economic radicalism. An assistant secretary of war spoke of marked "dislike and distrust of this small minority of Americans professing conscientious objections to warfare."[8]

The administration of the draft was further compromised by inconsistency and bias on the part of local draft boards. Staffed typically by middle- and upper-class white patriots, southern boards were ill-equipped to assess sympathetically the claims of members of the Church of God in Christ for exemption on the basis of conscience. Blacks in general were much more likely to be declared fit and available for induction than were whites, and they were less likely to receive exemptions for hardship, family support, or agricultural necessity. Not surprisingly, the proportion of black to white draft "delinquents" was more than two to one.[9] As for the general public, it often made no distinction between disloyalty and conscientious objection: a refusal to bear arms was tantamount to treason. Given such policies and attitudes, Bishop Mason and the Church of God in Christ were all but guaranteed trouble in 1917 and 1918. The southern white populace lived in fear that German agents were stirring blacks to disloyalty or even revolt. Agents of the Bureau of Investigation probed hundreds of such rumors. Consequently, despite COGIC assurances of patriotism and love for country, the public misunderstood the church's stand against participation in war. To many southern whites, imprisoned by ancient anxieties, black dissent could be interpreted only as the product of outside agitation and the desire for vengeance.

Church of God in Christ doctrine included an unambiguous prohibition against combatant military service. The virtue of brotherly love and the sinfulness of hating others were principles that Jesus Christ had stressed; therefore, so should humankind. "We believe the shedding of human blood or taking of human life to be contrary to the teaching of our Lord and Saviour, and as a body, we are adverse to war in all its various forms." This view did not lead to sympathies for Germany, however. Addressing a large baptismal gathering at North Memphis on June 23, 1918, Bishop Mason preached a sermon entitled "The Kaiser in the Light of the Scriptures," referring to the German ruler as the "Beast" or Antichrist depicted in Revelation 13, a man of warfare, pillage, and suffering. Christ, by contrast, represented peace. Mason even found scriptural approval, in Matthew 5:42, for the purchase of Liberty Bonds, and eventually he claimed to have raised more than $3,000 for the government. His sermon ended in prayer not only that all peoples would beat swords into plowshares and study war no more in anticipation of the second coming of the Prince of Peace but also that the "German hordes" would be driven back behind their borders.[10] Despite such patriotic assurances, however, Mason encouraged male parishioners to seek conscientious objector status. In the eyes of many southern whites, that in itself was treasonable.

Bishop Mason first drew federal scrutiny in September 1917 when an alarmed chancery clerk at Lexington warned authorities that Mason "openly advised against registration and made treasonable and seditious remarks against the United States government."[11] The church had many members around Lexington, situated in Holmes County in Mississippi's Delta region. In that area blacks constituted nearly 80 percent of the population, and local whites worried not only about racial domination but also about meeting draft quotas.

Bureau of Investigation agent M. M. Schaumburger, whose territory included rural Mississippi and Louisiana, tried to verify the allegations. Interviewing indignant whites who had attended Mason's assemblies, he learned that the "negro revivalist preacher" conducted nightly meetings the first two weeks in August, always to overflow crowds of two or three thousand. A magnetic speaker, Mason was said to exert as much influence over his race as did Billy Sunday among whites—and to have amassed considerable personal wealth, including a $60,000 mansion in Memphis. Informants alleged that he taught opposition to bloodshed and war and that he said his church's members need not register for the draft. Worse, Schaumburger learned that Mason allegedly labeled the present conflict a rich man's war and a poor man's fight, a war in which blacks had no grudge against the Germans, a good people who treated blacks better than did other whites. At a baptism Mason was said to have praised Germany so profusely that one of his fellow preachers threatened to quit the church. Schaumburger believed all this was enough to convict Mason for treason, obstructing the draft, and giving aid and comfort to the enemy—especially since two church members had not reported for induction.[12]

Confident of prosecution, Schaumburger took sworn statements from members of both races. Unfortunately for him, the affidavits of four members of the (black) Mississippi Cavalry who had attended Mason's meetings were couched in such racially guarded language that they proved to be useless. Schaumburger noted ruefully that "while all the men know by reputation that Mason is a menace to the country, they are unable to furnish direct testimony."[13] Hence on its first attempt the government, possessing only hearsay evidence, was unable to prosecute Mason. Of course this failure did nothing to allay the racial as well as the patriotic anxieties of local whites and federal authorities.

The next person to come under government suspicion was Rev. E. R. Driver, overseer of COGIC churches in California and one of the denominations's founding elders. (Driver was later prominent in Marcus Garvey's Universal Negro Improvement Association.) Summoned to the Bureau office in Los Angeles in February 1918, he was accused of being "pro-German and bitter toward the Government." Although Driver insisted on his loyalty while defending the church's opposition to taking life, agent George T. Holman remained skeptical of Driver's patriotism. "This colored minister is supposed to have considerable influence among a number of people of his race and his attitude is very aggressive with reference to this country's entrance into the war," Holman declared, believing "that it would be possible for him to be of considerable menace to the country." The agent vowed to keep Driver under observation and curtail his activities should they become "pronounced."[14] Such confrontation was rather typical. Bureau conscription files are replete with records of inquisitional interviews in which agents argued with suspects, assailed them with patriotic bombast, and threatened them to gain compliance with the draft.

Many southern whites suspected that German gold was financing the subversion of blacks' loyalties; such subversion seemed to be confirmed on April 1, 1918. A headline in the *Vicksburg Post* proclaimed, "Draft Evasion in Holmes County Due to Pro-German Teachings among Blacks." The state adjutant general's office, the paper reported, had found it "virtually impossible" to get blacks to comply in Lexington because of Mason's allegedly pro-German sermons and his advice to "resist" conscription. Investigators learned that three weeks earlier one Dimitrius Giannokulion had conducted a meeting at Mason's church, during which time he had also received a message in code. To worried whites there was no coincidence between this information and the allegation that Mason was "suddenly wealthy," enjoying a new brick-and-stone residence in Memphis. What made the situation seem all the more sinister was the fact that in the preceding two months only a small proportion of several hundred black registrants called up for service had reported for induction. (In desperation the state's adjutant general published the names of seventy alleged draft dodgers there, offering a $50 reward for each one delivered to the nearest military post.) The story linking Mason, Giannokulion, and draft resistance was picked up by the national wire services, which spread the alarming tale of German intrigue across the country. It took the black *New York Age* to debunk the idea of enemy subversion through Mason's church. That paper in turn called for an investigation of southern draft boards, alleging that they inducted all black registrants regardless of fitness while exempting many eligible whites.[15]

These "revelations" prompted the Bureau of Investigation to open a new case on Bishop Mason. An agent named Harry D. Gulley received instruction to make a detailed report. At the same time, thanks to the patriotic zeal of a local representative of the U.S. Food Administration, the military intelligence section of the War Department was alerted to this perceived threat to preparedness. Henceforth the Bureau and army officers would share information on Mason and the Church of God in Christ.[16]

Gulley found matters to be somewhat different from the description given by the excited press. Officials in Lexington told him that the number of black draft respondents was indeed alarmingly low but that part of the blame lay with the local board's inefficiency and poor record keeping. Nothing was learned about Giannokulion, although Gulley heard new rumors of five suspicious characters—three Germans, an Englishman, and a Frenchman—all of whom were believed to have some connection with Mason. Draft delinquents held in the local jail were interviewed, but only one had been to Mason's church, and he denied hearing any antidraft propaganda. Hearsay reports charging Mason with supporting Germany and with holding secret antidraft meetings at 3 o'clock in the morning also surfaced. Gulley could substantiate nothing, however, and he concluded that most blacks "had evidently been admonished not to talk 'war talk.'"[17]

One church member who did agree to speak was James Lee, one of five ordained COGIC preachers in Holmes County, but Lee insisted that neither he nor Mason preached antidraft or antiwar messages. Gulley's only success was in obtaining several documents, including a doctrinal statement drawn up the previous August by Mason and elders W. B. Holt (white) and E. R. Driver of Los Angeles. This piece affirmed loyalty to magistrates, civil laws, the Constitution, the president, and the flag, all as God-given institutions. Nonetheless, it also stated that shedding blood or taking life was contrary to the teachings of Jesus, although it allowed church members to perform any other service that did not conflict with the no-bloodshed principle. Of subsequent great interest to the Bureau was a blank petition, signed by Mason and addressed to draft boards, to be used by registrants seeking exemption based on church doctrine. A final document was an earlier doctrinal statement, written by Holt as long before as 1895, forbidding members to shed blood or bear arms.[18]

Despite finding no direct evidence, Gulley was convinced that church leaders had caused blacks to disobey the draft law and that doctrinal statements against war were adopted merely to increase membership. Overcome by fears and disregarding Holt's 1895 statement, Gulley concluded that COGIC's recent association with white churches in the West could well have resulted from German activities to hinder the draft. Nevertheless, he recognized the need for more concrete evidence, so he urged the U.S. attorney in Jackson and Bureau offices in Memphis and Los Angeles to investigate Mason, Holt, and Driver further.[19]

Ironically, Gulley's investigation gave Mason temporary protection from outraged Lexingtonians by assuring the townsfolk that the "menace" was being taken seriously. Events elsewhere showed that when worried patriots felt that no governmental action was forthcoming, vigilante action was likely. One victim of such action was Rev. Jesse Payne, a COGIC pastor in Blytheville, Arkansas. In an incident on April 18, 1918, Payne was fortunate to escape with his life. Under the headline "Negro Preacher Tarred," the *Memphis Commercial Appeal* reported that this

pastor of the colored holly [sic] roller church in the southeast suburbs of this city, was given a coat of tar and feathers last night as a result of alleged seditious remarks for some months concerning the president, the war, and a white man's war.

Earlier in the evening the preacher is alleged to have said something about the kaiser being as good a man as the president, and that the kaiser did not require his people to buy bonds and some one landed a solar plexus on him sending him into the ditch, from which he got up running. . . .

[After the tarring and feathering, Payne] repeated the soldier's oath, and promised to talk Liberty Bonds and Red Cross to the end of his life and the end of the war.

It is said his flock has shown no interest in the war work, while the negroes of other churches have been most liberal, $2000 having been subscribed by the Methodist and Baptist churches Sunday night. This church is circulating literature which he says was sent to him by a brother preacher in Memphis, showing from Bible quotations that it is not right for Christians to fight. The literature is scattered broadcast over the country.

The newspaper ended its report by editorializing that the punishment inflicted "will result in great good to demonstrate to not only blacks but some whites that it is time to get into the war work and quit talking such rot as is attributed to Payne."[20]

Bureau investigations proceeded in the South and on the West Coast. Mason agreed to an interview with Memphis agent in charge W. E. McElveen, stressing that he had advised men of draft age who became church members after passage of the draft act to register but to claim conscientious objector exemptions, for he believed that church members should respect and obey current laws. Furthermore, Mason had sent a telegram to President Wilson after the draft act was passed, explaining the church's doctrines and offering to meet with him. Regulations concerning conscientious objection were sent to Mason, and he claimed to have followed them. In addition, Mason avowed his support for Liberty Bond, war stamp, and Red Cross drives. McElveen was particularly concerned about possible German influence in the church, but Mason denied both outside funding and pro-German preaching in COGIC pulpits. Finding little to confirm suspicions of subversion, McElveen concluded that the bishop was less extreme than religious objectors such as the Seventh-day Adventists.[21]

McElveen's lack of alarm notwithstanding, surveillance of Mason continued. When the preacher conducted a camp meeting in late May at E. R. Driver's Los Angeles church, the local American Protective League (APL) supplied the Bureau with an excited report of dramatic increases in COGIC membership due, it was believed, to members getting noncombatant status. The web of suspicion went farther, with the APL reporting that several Germans were members of Driver's church and that other wealthy Teutons gave generous donations. "Fine autos quite frequently stop at the above church and their occupants are of a strong German type," the APL charges ran. Neighbors did not appreciate the late night revivals and reported angrily that their protests had brought threats in return.[22]

In the opinion of Bureau chief A. Bruce Bielaski, enough evidence from Mississippi, Tennessee, and California had been amassed by late spring 1918 to support prosecution of Mason. Believing "that there is some special basis for complaint of pro-German activities in these sections of the country," he directed that "a strong case should be prepared in order to make a striking example of some of the alleged agitators."[23]

At this point events overtook the Justice Department, forcing it to protect the life of the man it held in suspicion. Bishop Mason returned to Lexington in early June 1918, perhaps not realizing the antipathy of local whites who blamed him for the alarming decline in draft compliance. Many black registrants were unwilling to appear for induction. When apprehended, they exhibited COGIC petitions expressing religious objections to war. Moreover, white residents reported Mason telling would-be converts that "if you want to stay out of this war you must get right with God, and join my church. There is no occasion for the negroes to go to war; the Germans are the best friends the negroes have. Germany is going to whip the United States for the mistreatment accorded the negroes, if for no other reason. This is a rich man's war anyway." A lynching appeared likely, and so the local sheriff quickly arrested Mason for obstructing the draft. This development, plus news of an imminent investigation by the Bureau, momentarily quieted the mob spirit. When agent Eugene Palmer arrived in Lexington, however, he found local whites unpacified by the arrest. Fearing the worst, Palmer borrowed the sheriff's car, got Mason out of jail, and drove him to Durant, where he caught an Illinois Central train and took Mason to safety in Jackson. Arraigned on draft obstruction charges, Mason pleaded not guilty, waived a preliminary hearing, and had to post a $2,000 bond guaranteeing that he would appear in federal court in November. Meanwhile, back in Lexington, a "large number" of men said to have been influenced by Mason were summarily rounded up and sent to Camp Pike, Arkansas, for induction.[24]

In numerous cases during the war, alarmed southern whites found it difficult to believe that blacks could hold antiwar beliefs or be disenchanted with the war without being manipulated by enemy agents. The *Jackson Daily News* hailed Mason's arrest as "an important step in countering German propaganda," saying that the preacher was responsible not only for the large group of Holmes County blacks who allegedly evaded the draft but also for "making false statements for the purpose of promoting the cause of Germany, and detrimental to the military welfare of the United States." When agent Palmer examined Mason's suitcase for incriminating evidence, however, he found nothing to establish an enemy connection, other than several pieces of an "anointed cloth" and a bottle of German cologne with which to perform the consecration.[25]

Meanwhile, military intelligence was mustering its own evidence against Mason. Any activity threatening to impair enlistments was of concern to its chief, Col. Marlborough Churchill. Churchill instructed officers in Los Angeles and St. Louis to investigate Elders E. R. Driver, W. B. Holt, and Randolph R. Booker to determine whether there was German influence behind the church's nonparticipation policy. He addressed a similar letter to Bureau chief Bielaski recommending further investigation of COGIC propaganda and its leadership and urging that "the inquiry concerning William B. Holt should be especially rigid." Churchill explained that Holt "is a white man, very insulting and overbearing in manner, and [that he had] travelled all the way from Los Angles to Jackson to arrange bail for Mason, putting up $2000 in cash."[26]

Soon thereafter the Bureau of Investigation opened a case on Henry Kirvin, pastor of the Paris, Texas, congregation of COGIC. Not only did the Bureau believe that his actions had undermined military preparedness; it also expected to implicate Bishop Mason. Agent DeWitt S. Winn, a former Burns detective, unearthed information that, if provable, would have damned the entire leadership. Kirvin was alleged to have referred to the Red Cross as the "blood of the Beast" described in the book of Revelation and to have warned his flock not to contribute to that charity or wear its button. More important, Winn continued, Kirvin's congregation raised $125 so that Kirvin could accompany Mason to Washington to gain draft deferments from Woodrow Wilson. Not surprisingly, the two had not visited the president but had instead met with a draft official who supposedly arranged immunity from the draft and from Red Cross, Liberty Bond, and war thrift stamp contributions for every member. Henceforth each one—adult and child—was assessed twenty-five cents monthly, allegedly on the authority of the president, to ensure their exemption. So ran the charges.[27]

Learning that Kirvin, Mason, and Holt were in Austin raising legal defense funds, Winn phoned agent Claude McCaleb to urge investigation, although not a hasty arrest. McCaleb covered Mason's meeting but could report nothing incriminating.[28] Undeterred, Winn, McCaleb, and U.S. attorney Clarence Merritt continued to prepare a case for prosecution. Records of the Paris church were examined. Holt, whom Mc-

Caleb believed to be a German, was already jailed in Paris on charges of possessing a gun, which suggests that state and federal authorities were cooperating on the case. But Mason and Kirvin were as yet uncharged. When grilled by McCaleb, Henry Kirvin detailed how on orders from Mason all members of the church had been registered the previous January and assessed twenty-five cents monthly for legal representation of men who might be drafted. He denied discouraging Red Cross participation and said, "I am now teaching that nations ought to chastise one another."[29]

Although that part of the church creed detailing opposition to military service was first printed in 1917, after the draft law was passed, Mason maintained it had long been church doctrine; there simply had been no need to publish it earlier. As to unpatriotic motives, Mason claimed that he was "just trying to teach the scriptures." Answering questions about Holt, he declared that the white man had joined the church in May 1917 and had become its superintendent of Spanish missions. Concerning Holt's arrest for weapons possession, Mason explained that Holt carried a badge and gun as a deputy sheriff in California.[30]

On July 16, 1918, Charles H. Mason and Henry Kirvin were arrested. They and William B. Holt were charged with pretending to be federal officers and conspiring to commit offenses against the government. The former infraction carried a maximum three-year sentence and $1,000 fine, the latter permitting two years incarceration and a $10,000 penalty. Mason was said to have told church members that he was an emissary of President Wilson with authority to collect the twenty-five cents monthly to ensure their exemption from military service. The *Paris Morning News* cynically simplified the issue, declaring that Mason was "charged with working holy roller negroes." Holt remained in jail in lieu of a $5,000 bond that he could not raise, while the others were released on their own recognizance. Given the climate where suspicious white outsiders were assumed to be enemy agents, the white man was deemed the more dangerous. A trial date was set for late October, which suited the federal prosecutors, who needed time to work up a credible conspiracy case.[31]

In Los Angeles Bureau agent Killick gathered additional data on the three defendants by interviewing COGIC leader E. R. Driver—who, incidentally, denied he was a Negro, claiming his father was an East Indian who married a black woman after the son's birth. Driver described Mason as devoted heart and soul to his religious work but also as sometimes misunderstood because of his lack of education. He had never heard Mason criticize the government or encourage evasion of military duty; on the contrary, Mason had said that COGIC members who were drafted should seek positions "that did not necessitate their engaging in the actual taking of human life." Killick tried to trap Driver in a logical inconsistency by arguing that noncombatant soldiers were culpable, since they helped the combatants who did take life. Driver agreed, but he believed that noncombatants were absolved before God of any wrongdoing. Convinced of neither Driver's nor the church's sincerity, Killick concluded that

> his attitude was very commanding and dictatorial, and his general personality very repugnant. I could easily imagine that this man, if crossed and aggravated, might become wildly fanatical on any issue which might confront him. In my opinion, I do not believe that the principle of opposition to warfare was ever established as a fundamental of this church prior to the entrance of the United States into the war. . . . I believe that the members of this church were anxiously desirous of evading military service in every respect.[32]

But could such conspiratorial intent be proven in a court of law? The sum of the Bureau's evidence to this point was not likely to convince an impartial jury.

Meanwhile, the fear of German subversion still preoccupied army officials. The Bureau of Investigation sent copies of Winn's reports to the Military Intelligence Division, which in turn requested still more surveillance to determine whether enemy aliens were promoting obstruction of the draft laws. Military Intelligence Division operatives tapped E. R. Driver's telephone in a vain attempt to prove a German connection.[33] Col. Churchill's office waited impatiently for the trial of Mason, Kirvin, and Holt, stressing to John Lord O'Brian, the special assistant to the attorney general overseeing Espionage Act cases, that prosecution was "fairly important for our counter-propaganda work, as there are outcroppings of this negro religious agitation in other parts of the country with which we have to deal." This was a reference to the Pentecostal Assemblies of the World, Churches of the Living God, Church of God and Saints in Christ, and black Church of Christ congregations, all of which opposed participation in the war.[34]

If the Department of Justice was to succeed in prosecuting Mason and his associates, hearsay evidence would not be enough. Credible testimony by church members who were not themselves under indictment was essential. The most promising witness appeared to be a Rev. W. C.

Thompson, who had left the church in disagreement over the issue of military service. Interviewed by Bureau agents in Chicago, Thompson charged that COGIC members were discouraged from buying Liberty Bonds because Mason wanted them to give money to him for his new house. He charged further that Henry Kirvin's antiwar stand was simply for personal gain. To the Bureau's chagrin, however, Thompson defended Mason and Kirvin as basically patriotic citizens, even if mistaken. This was hardly the conclusive testimony that the Justice Department needed to convict the church leaders.[35]

The government suffered another setback when the sudden death of DeWitt Winn in the influenza epidemic left the Bureau without its most informed, diligent, and professional operative on the case.[36] His replacement, agent Lewie H. Henry, continued with U.S. attorney Merritt to prepare the case for presentation to the federal grand jury. Using the Paris church registry, Henry took detailed statements from thirteen members, including two lay preachers. They related how, after his trip to Washington to see the president, Kirvin instructed the congregation to pay twenty-five cents to register so that the president would know who were the saints of the church. All those paying and so registered would not have to go to war, but those who did not would be cut off from the church and afforded no protection from military service. Women were urged to register too, so as to avoid forced labor in Red Cross work. Members were also told to purchase, for fifteen cents, a document entitled "Doctrinal Statement and Rules for Government of the Church of God in Christ." This document stated that "we believe the shedding of human blood or the taking of human life to be contrary to the teachings of our Lord and Savior, and as a body we are adverse to war in all its various forms." If men were inducted, Kirvin was alleged to have said, they could use the pamphlet to plead for mercy and not be put in the front-line trenches. Members were admonished that in all circumstances they must "live the life" if they expected their church to stand behind them. The investigators also examined church finances, but nothing damaging came to light except the fact that Holt had failed to pay the printer for the doctrinal statements. None of this "evidence" was likely to guarantee a conviction. What most shocked Henry was testimony that Holt hugged and kissed Mason. Culturally ignorant, the Bureau agent interpreted this as a shocking display of interracial intimacy rather than as what it was: the "holy kiss," a scriptural form of Christian greeting.[37]

On October 29, 1918, even as newspaper headlines were proclaiming the imminent collapse of Germany and its allies, a federal grand jury convened in the Texas town of Paris to weigh the evidence against Mason, Holt, and Kirvin. A large number of church members attended the hearing, whose presiding judge was DuVal West of San Antonio—a jurist who was no stranger to cases of suspected black disloyalty. Not surprisingly, the grand jury declined to indict on the charge of conspiring to hinder the draft, for it found that the three preachers' operations "were not conducted in a way that was covered by any federal statute." It found no more merit in allegations of impersonating government officials. Disappointed but not defeated, the assistant U.S. attorney suggested that the three be charged in Lamar County Court for swindling in connection with the monthly assessments. Agent Henry persuaded county attorney Grady Sturgeon to prosecute, promising full access to evidence gathered by the Bureau; on November 1 the defendants were back in custody.[38]

Local prosecution was still potentially dangerous, for racial passions might easily be manipulated. The press focused particularly on Holt because sworn affidavits reported him eating and lodging with blacks and hugging and kissing black fellow preachers. Kirvin and Mason made bond, but again Holt was not so fortunate. The *Paris Morning News* reported that "the white man who was arrested with the negro holy roller preachers on the charge of swindling is still in jail. None of the brethren have so far made bond for him, although the darkies have been released."[39]

The final attempt to prosecute the leaders of the Church of God in Christ must be pieced together from only a few extant clues. After November 5 the *Paris Morning News* did not mention the trio. The minutes indexes for both the county and the district courts of Lamar County fail to note the disposition of the swindling case, and at that time the county grand jury did not keep minutes. It seems quite apparent that the local grand jury failed to support the county attorney's attempt to prosecute using the evidence supplied by the Bureau of Investigation. Only William B. Holt was convicted: on December 6 he pleaded guilty to vagrancy and was fined one dollar. This was the last recorded act of harassment against the white official of COGIC.[40]

Bishop Mason saw his legal travails in Mississippi and Texas as nothing less than persecution, and evidence supports his interpretation. In all likelihood the church's antiwar doctrines antedated the imposition of the draft in 1917. Clearly neither Mason nor other officials were pro-German. Mason's sermon "The Kaiser in the Light of the Scriptures" expressed a clear antipathy to German policy and a willingness to support Liberty Bond campaigns. There was simply no conspiracy to obstruct either the draft or any other government operation. Nevertheless, public officials and ordinary citizens were not inclined to differentiate between religious objection to all wars and opposition to the immediate conflict. Part of the reason was that other blacks did express unmistakable political dissent. Socialists such as A. Philip Randolph and Chandler Owen, editors of the *Messenger*, viewed the war as the exploitive product of international capitalism. Hundreds of expatriate black southerners, trapped in northern urban ghettos where the Promised Land seemed as remote as ever, saw no reason to fight in the "white man's war."[41] By contrast, Church of God in Christ doctrine was apolitical. The church should have excited no more disfavor than did the Quakers.

Regarding the later charge that Mason impersonated a government official, the evidence is no stronger. The extant documents suggest that the twenty-five-cent assessments were to pay for the legal costs of Mason and other arrested leaders and of those seeking draft exemptions.[42] This was probably the easiest way to raise a defense fund, and the money collected seems to have gone for its intended purposes. The bishop may have naively assumed from his talks with draft officials in Washington that the government "recognized" his church's antiwar doctrines as sufficient to ensure exemption from conscription, at least for those men who were members before passage of the selective service law. Inexperienced in dealing with the wider world, Mason relied less on the nuances of law than on the strength of the sovereign God—whom he knew far better.

But the mood of 1917 and 1918 was intolerant of any nonconformity. Even established peace churches such as the Mennonites and Quakers had difficulties. Newer denominations, without long-established traditions, or sects about which the government had no reliable information were treated even less sympathetically. Given this climate, and the racially biased operation of many southern draft boards, it was almost inevitable that black religious objectors would be perceived as tools of the enemy and their leaders would be seen as traitors. Neither was to be tolerated. In this respect white southern responses to the Church of God in Christ simply echoed the vocal majority of the country, which had no patience for anyone, whether religious sectarian, political dissident, or slacker, who refused to demonstrate rabid patriotism. Wartime passions led to wartime excesses, and the Bureau of Investigation, whose agents were white, male, middle class, and patriotic, was not immune. Most agents worked in areas to which they were native, so those serving in the South were likely to hold traditional views on race relations and suspicions of black nonconformity.

Years later Bishop Mason narrated his tribulations during World War I. His chronology was not exact, but the interpretation was clear:

> In 1918 I was called to appear before the judge of the Kangaroo Court in Paris, Tex. The presiding officers [*sic*] looked at me and laid down his books, and said, "You all may try him; I will not have anything to do with him."
>
> In 1918, at Lexington, Miss., I took a scriptural stand against the ungodly deeds of the various races, about how many souls were being hurled into eternity without chance of seeking God for their soul's salvation, knowing that without the hand of the Almighty there could be no remedy for the same.
>
> The Holy Ghost through me was teaching men to look to God, for he is their only help. I told them not to trust in the power of the United States, England, France or Germany, but trust in God. The enemy (the devil) tried to hinder me from preaching the unadulterated word of God. He plotted against me and had the white people to arrest me and put me in jail for several days. I thank my God for the persecution. "For all that live godly must suffer persecution." 2. Tim. 3:12. . . .
>
> Later in the same year I was called to Jackson, Miss., to answer to the charge that the devil had made against me. The presiding officers talked with me, after which they told me that I was backed up by the Scripture, and would not be hurt by them. . . . If God be for you, who can be against you![43]

Reasons for the federal government's failure in its efforts to prosecute Mason in Jackson must be inferred from sketchy evidence. It may be that proceedings were simply dropped after the armistice on November 11, 1918. The Justice Department continued to pursue other wartime cases for many months after the end of hostilities, however, so it is more likely that a grand jury found insufficient grounds on which to indict. Such actions were usually not recorded, and thus the absence of information in the minutes and dockets of the district court can be understood as mute evidence in support of that conclusion.[44]

Many federal officials during World War I believed the country to be imperiled by enemies within the gates. From the attorney general to private citizens, that suspicion included the notion that the gullible black population's loyalties were being manipulated by a sinister adversary. Considering the experiences of other groups and individuals who opposed the war on political or religious grounds, Bishop Mason and his associates were fortunate to find vindication through the legal system.

The Justice Department, charged with enforcement of selective service regulations, had a legitimate interest in the church and its leadership. The tragedy in this case is not the fact of federal scrutiny but the degree to which an overenergized Bureau of Investigation, encouraged by military intelligence, succumbed to popular fears and prejudices that compromised its objectivity. Some agents, such as DeWitt Winn, conducted themselves professionally, but in this and other cases many of Winn's peers personified the anxieties and prejudices of the fearful white populace. The relentless pursuit of COGIC leaders and their arrests on farfetched conspiracy and impersonation charges lend credence to Bishop Mason's claim to persecution by federal authorities, his ultimate exoneration notwithstanding.

What happened to the Church of God in Christ's pacifist tradition after World War I? Anecdotal evidence suggests that during World War II the men whose membership antedated that conflict did not fight, but how many were successful in gaining recognition as conscientious objectors is unknown. Only twelve members worked in Civilian Public Service camps, so very likely the total was small. The church's membership grew rapidly during the 1950s and 1960s, and its pacifist heritage faded from view. A new generation of members performed combat duty in Vietnam.[45] Today, church doctrine still states that "the shedding of human blood or the taking of human life is contrary to the teachings of our Lord and Saviour, Jesus Christ, and as a body, we are adverse to war in all its forms." Should members be drafted, the official doctrine says they are to submit to induction as conscientious objectors, undergo only basic training, and refuse any "advanced weapons training given to combatant soldiers," serving instead in noncombatant capacities.[46] But few seem to know of, much less follow, that noncombatant doctrine.

Pacifism was nurtured by the early restorationist Church of God in Christ. Sadly, however, as happened in other sects that grew in membership and sought to enter the denominational mainstream, conscientious opposition to war became a forgotten tradition.

APPENDIX

Using U.S. Government Records to Research Pacifism and Conscientious Objection during World War I

Federal records in the National Archives and its regional branches contain a gold mine of information on antiwar organizations, peace churches, and individual conscientious objectors and pacifists during World War I. The Bureau of Investigation (renamed the Federal Bureau of Investigation [FBI] in 1935) was zealous in tracking down suspected "slackers" and "deserters," while its parent, the Justice Department, was equally intent on prosecuting spies, "enemy aliens," draft evaders of whatever belief, and other opponents of the war. The army's Military Intelligence Division conducted widespread surveillance on civilians and cooperated with the Bureau in investigating those who opposed the war or military service. In addition the Post Office Department monitored periodicals and pamphlets suspected of disloyalty or hindering the war effort and exercised censorship with a heavy hand. The wartime years and "Red Scare" immediately following not only produced the most intolerant era in U.S. history but also gave birth to the nation's modern political intelligence practices.

Abundant sources on pacifism and conscientious objection are available at the National Archives in Washington, D.C. The best starting place is the "Old German" case files of the Bureau of Investigation: 594 reels in collection M-1085, constituting part of record group 65, documents pertaining to the FBI. The archives offer a printed guide, *Investigative Case Files of the Bureau of Investigation: 1908–1922*. An additional 111 reels of microfilm reproduce a million or more index cards listing the names and case file numbers of every individual, organization, and publication suspected of violating a federal statute or of being pro-German, subversive, antiwar, or unpatriotic. With luck the researcher who wishes to study Bureau investigations of a particular religious denomination may find citations to that church in the index reels. In my research, however, I had to depend on names of individuals, since in most cases individuals, not the organization itself, were the foci of the investigations. Ultimately I located 2,000 separate case files on African-American draft violators, many of whom had only unwittingly transgressed a regulation or requirement. Of the willful noncooperators, most were not religious objectors.

Many of the Bureau's case files, however, are rich not only in biographical detail but also in description (or caricature) of specific theological positions held by persons who refused to render military service unto Caesar. For instance, there was Harvey J. Anderson, a black soapbox preacher who experienced sanctification in an unnamed Cincinnati holiness church in 1915. Convinced that he had received a prophetic call from God to deliver judgment on a wayward nation, he condemned as murderers not only President Woodrow Wilson but also even the U.S. soldiers in the trenches. The thirty-six-year-old Mississippi native supported himself intermittently as a barber, hod carrier, and common laborer, but he was so poor that just before his arrest he had pawned his clothes. Anderson languished in jail for sixteen weeks until his case came before the federal grand jury—a month after the Armistice, in late 1918. By that date the attorney general had issued orders that this type of case no longer be prosecuted, and Anderson was released, one of many victims of local and federal zeal against harmless religious dissenters.[47]

Another example is Dan McNairy, a black in Marshall, Texas. He was a member of the Jehovah's Witnesses, the religious group that suffered the greatest persecution during World War I.[48] McNairy served six months in jail for disparaging the president, criticizing the conduct of the war, questioning the value of Liberty Bonds, and asserting that the book of Revelation proved that Kaiser Wilhelm II was destined to rule the world. Noting that the man was well-educated and had considerable influence over other blacks, the Bureau's investigating agent concluded that his "crime" was "of such a vile nature" and his advocacy so "bold" that formal prosecution was warranted.[49] McNairy's case illustrates the value of another source: federal court records. These are especially helpful because some Bureau of Investigation case files do not indicate how cases were resolved.

Researchers will also want to use War Department records. During World War I the Military Intelligence Division engaged in widespread spying on civilians, including investigations of alleged draft evaders or those encouraging resistance to conscription. Again, one must begin with the names of individual suspects or denominations and sects. Military Intelligence Division materials in record group 165 at the main branch of the National Archives in Washington are well indexed, and archivists in the Military Reference Branch will respond to letters of inquiry.

Many opponents of military service, including many who either failed to appear for induction or went to the military camps and then refused orders, faced military trials. The army still retains the indexes for World War I–era trials. To use the indexes, it is best to request the docket number for the individual case from the deputy clerk of the court, Department of the Army, United States Army Judiciary, NASSIF Building, Falls Church, Virginia. With that number, the military reference division at the archives branch in Suitland, Maryland, can locate trial documents in record group 153 (Judge Advocate General, Army). Shuttle vans run daily between Suitland, a Washington suburb, and the main archives in Washington.[50]

A final important source of federal records pertaining to pacifism and conscientious objection is Post Office Department materials in the National Archives in Washington, since under the Espionage Act of the World War I era the Post Office had responsibility for monitoring the press. Investigative records of newspapers, pamphlets, and other periodicals published by pacifist groups and churches are likely to appear in the Espionage Act enforcement case files in record group 28. Researchers will do well to know the names of denominational newspapers and pamphlets. Archivists in the Civil Reference Branch will respond to inquiries. Case files on these same publications will also likely be found in the Bureau of Investigation microfilms; researchers should check its index for both the periodicals and their editors.

Researchers using federal records to chart the trials and tribulations of those who suffered for the sake of conscience during World War I will ultimately discover the emergence of America's modern political intelligence network. For instance, representatives of the Justice Department (particular its Bureau of Investigation), the Military Intelligence Division, and the Post Office Department met weekly and sometimes daily to discuss cases with their counterparts in the Office of Naval Intelligence and the State Department. Information on suspects was shared, investigations were coordinated, and prosecutions were planned. The government stifled much dissent without resorting to prosecution, just by using intimidating investigations, "black bag" jobs (break-ins), and threats of legal action.

Historians are reconstructing pieces of this story, but there is much fertile ground yet to be tilled. Persons who wish to see a fuller description of the sources may consult my article "Bishop C. H. Mason and the Church of God in Christ during World War I," *Southern Studies* 26 (Winter 1987): 261–81; parts of this appendix are reprinted from that essay, with permission of the editor.

NOTES

An earlier version of this essay appeared as "Bishop C. H. Mason and the Church of God in Christ during World War I: The Perils of Conscientious Objection" in *Southern Studies* 26 (Winter 1987): 261–81. I offer the current version by permission of the Southern Studies Institute.

1. German R. Ross, *History and Formative Years of the Church of God in Christ* (Memphis: Church of God in Christ, 1969), 14–16; Lucille J. Cornelius, *The Pioneer: History of the Church of God in Christ* (N.p.; n.p., 1975), 9–12.

2. Cornelius, *The Pioneer*, 3–5, 11–13; Ross, *History and Formative Years*, 17–18; David M. Tucker, *Black Pastors and Leaders: Memphis, 1819–1972* (Memphis: Memphis State University Press, 1975), 88–90.

3. Tucker, *Black Pastors and Leaders*, 91. Not only was the church the first black pentecostal denomination, but it remains the largest; see Lawrence Neale Jones, "The Black Pentecostals," in Michael P. Hamilton, ed., *The Charismatic Movement*, 145–58 (Grand Rapids, Mich.: Eerdman's, 1975), 150.

4. Vinson Synan, *The Holiness-Pentecostal Movement in the United States* (Grand Rapids, Mich.: Eerdmans, 1971), 177.

5. Tucker, *Black Pastors and Leaders*, 95–96. By 1926 there were seven hundred congregations and thirty thousand members, two-thirds residing in the South, with more congregations in urban areas than in country districts; see Charles E. Hall, *Negroes in the United States, 1920–1932* (Washington: U.S. Government Printing Office, 1935), 532, 538–50.

6. A good survey of this intolerance is H. C. Peterson and Gilbert C. Fite, *Opponents of War, 1917–1918* (Seattle: University of Washington Press, 1968). Other useful sources are Zechariah Chafee Jr., *Free Speech in the United States* (Cambridge, Mass.: Harvard University Press, 1941); Donald Johnson, *The*

Challenge to American Freedom: World War I and the Rise of the American Civil Liberties Union (Lexington: University of Kentucky Press, 1963); Harry N. Scheiber, *The Wilson Administration and Civil Liberties, 1917–1921* (Ithaca, N.Y.: Cornell University Press, 1960); William Preston, *Aliens and Dissenters: Federal Suppression of Radicals, 1903–1933* (Cambridge, Mass.: Harvard University Press, 1963); Julian F. Jaffe, *Crusade against Radicalism: New York during the Red Scare, 1914–1924* (Port Washington, N.Y.: Kennikat, 1972); Paul L. Murphy, *The Meaning of Freedom of Speech: First Amendment Freedoms from Wilson to FDR* (Westport, Conn.: Greenwood, 1972); and idem, *World War I and the Origin of Civil Liberties in the United States* (New York: Norton, 1979). For details on treatment of black conscientious objectors, see Theodore Kornweibel Jr., "Apathy and Dissent: Black America's Negative Responses to World War I," *South Atlantic Quarterly* 80 (Summer 1981): 331.

7. Peterson and Fite, *Opponents of War*, 121–25.

8. U.S. War Department, *Statement Concerning the Treatment of Conscientious Objectors in the Army* (Washington: U.S. Government Printing Office, 1919), 7–9, 14–19.

9. Arthur E. Barbeau and Florette Henri, *The Unknown Soldiers: Black American Troops in World War I* (Philadelphia: Temple University Press, 1974), 35–37; U.S. Provost Marshal General's Office, *Second Report of the Provost Marshal General to the Secretary of War on the Operation of the Selective Service System to December 30, 1918* (Washington: U.S. Government Printing Office, 1919), 459, 461.

10. Cornelius, *The Pioneer*, 68; Ross, *History and Formative Years*, 25–28.

11. Agent M. M. Schaumburger to Bureau of Investigation, Sept. 24, 1917, Old German case file 144128, Record Group 65, Investigation Case Files of the Bureau of Investigation, National Archives (hereinafter RG65, BI, NA).

12. Agent M. M. Schaumburger to Bureau, Sept. 26, 1917, OG64788, RG65, BI, NA.

13. Schaumburger to Bureau, Sept. 26, 1917, OG172841, and Sept. 27, 1917, OG64788, RG65, BI, NA.

14. Agent G. T. Holman to Bureau, Feb. 27, 1918, OG64788, RG65, BI, NA. Driver's involvement in the UNIA is noted in agent A. A. Hopkins to Bureau, Apr. 2, 1921, case file BS198940–113, RG65, BI, NA, and in Emory J. Tolbert, *The UNIA and Black Los Angeles* (Los Angeles: Center for Afro-American Studies, University of California, 1980).

15. *Vicksburg Post*, Apr. 1, 1918; *New York Globe*, Apr. 1, 2, 1918; *New York Sun*, Apr. 2, 1918; *New York Age*, Apr. 6, 1918.

16. H. Leider, field representative, U.S. Food Administration, to Col. Ralph H. Van Deman, Apr. 2, 1918, case file PF1811–2; Van Deman to Maj. Walter H. Loving, Apr. 12, 1918, case file PF1811–3, Record Group 165, War Department, Military Intelligence Division, National Archives (hereinafter RG165, MID, NA).

17. Agent Harry D. Gulley to Bureau, Apr. 2, 1918, OG64788, RG65, BI, NA.

18. Ibid. The church's antiwar doctrine is printed in Cornelius, *The Pioneer,* 68.

19. Gulley to Bureau, Apr. 2, 1918.

20. *Memphis Commercial Appeal,* Apr. 18, 1918, p. 11.

21. Agent W. E. McElveen to Bureau, May 2, 1918, OG64788, RG65, BI, NA.

22. Agent V. W. Killick to Bureau, June 3, 17, 1918, OG64788, RG65, BI, NA. The presence of whites in the church was not unusual, for there were many mixed pentecostal congregations in the early twentieth century, following the interracial Azusa Street revival; see Jones, "The Black Pentecostals," 148.

23. Chief A. Bruce Bielaski to agent J. P. Finlay, May 17, 1918; Bielaski to Division Superintendent Forrest C. Pendleton, May 17, 1918, OG144128, RG65, BI, NA.

24. Agent E. Palmer to Bureau, June 20, 1918, OG227347, RG65, BI, NA (quotation); *Chicago Defender,* June 29, 1918. No record has been found to identify the men sent into the military or to determine whether they persisted in claiming to be conscientious objectors. Such summary "justice" obviously narrowed their options.

25. Palmer to Bureau, June 20, 1918, OG227347, RG65, BI, NA; *Jackson Daily News,* June 19, 1918.

26. Col. Marlborough Churchill to F. Sullens, editor of the *Jackson Daily News,* June 25, 1918; Sullens to Churchill, June 29, 1918; Churchill to Bielaski, July 13, 1918 (quotation); Churchill to Intelligence Officer [IO], Los Angeles, June 19, 1918; Churchill to IO, St. Louis, July 13, 1918, 99-7; RG165, MID, NA.

27. Agent DeWitt S. Winn to Bureau, July 16, 1918, OG64788, RG65, BI, NA.

28. Agent Claude McCaleb to Bureau, July 15, 1918; OG245662, RG65, BI, NA.

29. Winn to Bureau, July 16, 18, 19, 1918, OG64788; McCaleb to Bureau, July 15, 1918, OG245662, RG65, BI, NA (quotation).

30. McCaleb to Bureau, July 15, 16, 1918, OG245662, RG65, BI, NA.

31. *Paris Morning News,* July 17, 1918; Winn to Bureau, July 19, 20, 1918, OG64788; McCaleb to Bureau, July 16, 18, 1918, OG245662, RG65, BI, NA. The trio was charged with violating sections 32 and 37 of the U.S. Penal Code.

32. Killick to Bureau, July 19, 23, 25, 1918, OG64788, RG65, BI, NA.

33. Killick to Bureau, Aug. 6, 1918, OG64788, RG65, BI, NA.

34. Alfred Bettman to Lt. Van Dusen, Aug. 8, 1918, OG64788, RG65, BI, NA; Carlton J. H. Hayes, MIS, to Special Assistant to the Attorney General John Lord O'Brian, Sept. 4, 1918 (quotation); U.S. attorney Clarence Merritt to Attorney General Thomas W. Gregory, Sept. 21, 1918; case file 195341, Record Group 60, Department of Justice, National Archives; Churchill to Bielaski, July 26, 1918, 99-7, RG165, MID, NA; Walter J. Hollenweger, "A Black Pentecostal Concept," *Concept* 30 (June 1970): 61–63; Kornweibel, "Apathy and Dissent," 330–31. Information on the other dissenting churches is in case files 99-7 and 99-68, RG165, MID, NA, and case file OG27320, RG65, BI, NA.

35. Division superintendent Charles E. Breniman to division superintendent Hinton G. Clabaugh, Aug. 31, 1918; agent F. G. Habda to Bureau, Sept. 10, 1918;

agent W. Neunhoffer to Winn, Sept. 16, 1918; Neunhoffer to Merritt, Sept. 16, 1918; OG64788, RG65, BI, NA.

36. Winn's death was mourned by his bureau colleagues, who testified to his dedication and professionalism (tragically his daughter also succumbed to influenza on the same day); personnel file of DeWitt S. Winn, obtained from the Federal Bureau of Investigation through the Freedom of Information Act.

37. Agent Lewie H. Henry to Bureau, Oct. 27, 1918, OG64788, RG65, BI, NA; Capt. Moss, IO, Los Angeles, to Department Intelligence Officer, San Francisco, Oct. 18, 1918, 99-7, RG165, MID, NA.

38. Henry to Bureau, Nov. 2, 1918, OG64788, RG65, BI, NA; *Paris Morning News,* Oct. 30, Nov. 2, 1918 (quotation).

39. *Paris Morning News,* Nov. 2, 3, 5 (quotation), 1918.

40. Letter to author, July 23, 1982, A. M. Aiken Regional Archives, Texas State Library, Paris, Texas; Criminal Minutes, Lamar County Court, book 12, p. 290.

41. Theodore Kornweibel Jr., *No Crystal Stair: Black Life and the Messenger, 1917–1928* (Westport, Conn.: Greenwood, 1975), ch. 1; Kornweibel, "Apathy and Dissent."

42. Jones's and Cornelius's "authorized" histories of the denomination and Mason's own accounts do not provide any details on the assessment.

43. Mason quoted in Ross, *History and Formative Years,* 23–24.

44. Letter to author, Aug. 3, 1982, National Archives Branch, East Point, Georgia.

45. This anecdotal information was supplied by Dr. David Daniels, of Mc-Cormick Theological Seminary, Chicago, in a telephone conversation with the author, Oct. 15, 1992. The figure for COGIC men in CPS camps is from Melvin Gingerich, *Service for Peace* (Akron, Pa.: Mennonite Central Committee, 1949).

46. This information was supplied by the office of Bishop George D. McKinney, St. Stephens Church of God in Christ, San Diego, in a letter to the author dated Aug. 31, 1992.

47. Agent Claude P. Light to Bureau, Aug. 17 (2 documents) and 23 and Dec. 10, 1918; agent Ora M. Slater to Bureau, Aug. 12, Sept. 30, 1918; case file OG270244, RG65, BI, NA.

48. See Peterson and Fite, *Opponents of War,* 119–20.

49. Agent DeWitt S. Winn to Bureau, Aug. 2, 4, 1918, OG258197, RG65, BI; *United States* vs. *McNairy,* Record Group 21, U.S. District Courts, Eastern District of Texas, Jefferson Division, National Archives, Ft. Worth.

50. One list is "Religious C.O.'s Imprisoned at the U.S. Disciplinary Barracks, Ft. Leavenworth, Kansas," published by J. D. Mininger, Kansas City, Mar. 10, 1919. Mininger was a Mennonite minister and city missionary in Kansas City who also served his church during the war and afterward by visiting young men in military camps and in the Ft. Leavenworth prison; a copy of this list was kindly supplied to me by Professor Michael Casey of Pepperdine University, who also instructed me in the procedures for locating court-martial records.

4

སྠ

PACIFISM AMONG THE EARLY PENTECOSTALS

Conflicts Within and Without

A Response to Murray W. Dempster and Theodore Kornweibel Jr.

སྠ

Jay Beaman

Murray Dempster's "Pacifism in Pentecostalism: The Case of the Assemblies of God" is a welcome contribution to a discussion of pacifism in religious traditions other than peace churches. Dempster's intention is to retell the story of how the Assemblies of God became an officially pacifist denomination at the time of World War I, only to change its stance later to one that effectively dropped pacifism. In that retelling Dempster has highlighted a conflict between those within the early Assemblies of God who were ardent pacifists and those who objected to that pacifism. The story was not as simple as a straightforward page-length pacifist statement by the Assemblies of God in 1917 seemed to affirm. In 1917 the Assemblies of God was officially a pacifist denomination, but in practice the subject of pacifism was quite divisive in the church, just when the denomination stated its pacifism most clearly. In relating this early conflict over pacifism, Dempster makes an important contribution.

More than half of Dempster's discussion elucidates the positive theological reasons for pacifism among early pentecostals. Dempster examined the writings of five persons who influenced the Assemblies of God on the subject. According to him, that examination was necessary to correct an apparent distortion in an earlier study that I made.[1] He thought that my earlier work pinned the adoption and rejection of pacifism almost exclusively on pentecostals' later movement into the cultural mainstream after an earlier anticultural stance. Dempster freely admits that there is ample evidence for this sectarian strain in pentecostals' early pacifism, but he wishes also to develop another theme inherent in that pacifism, a theme to be found "alongside" the "anticultural expression." Thus on the one hand Dempster distances himself from the sociocultural interpretation of the change in the Assemblies of God from its earlier pacifism, while on the other hand he admits that the positive theological affirmations inherent in the pacifism of early pentecostals "did promote an anticultural 'come out from the world' justification for pacifism." His more central point, however, is that the early pentecostals also "connected pacifism to the church's redemptive witness to the world." This idea of redemptive witness is what Dempster presents in the heart of his discussion.

First, according to Dempster, the early pentecostals positively affirmed pacifism as an integral part of "restoring the apostolic faith"; to them, pacifism was a "moral sign of a restored New Testament Apostolic church." Dempster argues that this restorationist theme included a positive "apologetic construction" of church history affirming that history. That positive affirmation selectively affirmed the first three centuries of the early church and the first two decades of the twentieth century. This "restorationist" perspective led to a positive separation that affirmed citizenship in an "eschatological" community. Such separation was not "passive withdrawal," however; rather, it was "a way to resist compliance with the world's bellicose ways and a way to witness to the universal values of the gospel."

Second, Dempster finds in the early pentecostal pacifists a "moral critique of the existing sinful social order." That social order exhibited a structured evil beyond the individual. For much of social evil, unjust wealth and power were the ends and war was the means. Through war unjust leaders and the wealthy class expropriated profits and labor from the poor, and they cynically maintained their misrule by promoting patriotism. For Dempster this critique resounds like the Old Testament prophets.

Pacifism was a sign of a new "countercommunity" centering in Jesus Christ. Although the group was admittedly sectarian, "resisting cultural assimilation into the world's power structure was the only way for the church to maintain its loyalty to Jesus Christ and keep its true identity as an eschatological community." Dempster finds a dual role for this countercommunity: it did "more than stand against the world . . . ; it also was called to witness proactively for the fundamental value of human life."

This was the third theological base for pacifism. These pentecostal leaders saw "pacifism as the certification of the universal value of humanity." According to this argument, one cannot be committed to Jesus Christ, who died for all humanity, and hold to partisan divisions that would justify taking part in killing some part of humanity. Christ values all human life.

Certainly these ardent pacifists did ground their commitment to peace in the theology of the good news of Jesus Christ. It was not simply a class-based ideological stance. Nor was the later rejection of pacifism simply a matter of pentecostals' relative affluence. Causal models suggesting that class membership determines belief fail to leave open the possibility that some people may simply have been persuaded by preachers' claims that Jesus Christ performed a redemptive work that makes possible a new community. Dempster admits that this theological bedrock also went hand in hand with an "anticultural 'come out from the world' justification" for those vocal early pentecostals who espoused pacifism, but he wishes to "nuance" the anticultural view with the theological justification. To be sure, his thematic organization of this material gives it an added cogency that my earlier narrative presentation lacked.

Dempster's discussion has another effect, however. Reading his material supporting early pentecostalism's second theological justification for pacifism (pacifism as a "moral critique of the sinful social order"), one hears other voices more recent than those of the Old Testament prophets. Although the Booth-Clibborns, Bartleman, Parham, and others did indeed frame their arguments theologically, they also used language from their day's critique of capitalism, language common among socialists and other critics.

Whatever the origin of the early pentecostals' arguments for pacifism, Dempster demonstrates that although the Assemblies of God was officially pacifist, practically speaking the pacifism had little effect. He offers two reasons. First, "not all preachers agreed" with the pacifism that developed in the publications of the Assemblies of God from 1915 to 1917. This was apparent both from the heated debates in the *Weekly Evangel* and from the minutes of the church's general council meetings. Second, during World War I, when the Assemblies of God's most explicit pacifist statement was framed, apparently neither members nor leaders paid

much attention to what it said. Dempster found evidence for this in
Frank Bartleman's and Donald Gee's critique that, along with the church
at large, the pentecostals had become patriotic.

After reviewing the three theological bases for pacifism in the early
Assemblies of God and the tenuous character of that pacifism even at
the beginning, Dempster states his thesis. He says that only a "prophetic minority" in the Assemblies of God really held to pacifism in the first
place. Because this prophetic minority never won the majority to a
shared tradition, a de facto patriotism and a nominal pacifism characterized the Assemblies of God from the beginning. According to Dempster, the pacifism expressed in print was in fact an embarrassing over-
statement to ensure that the minority—"whatever their number—
[could] receive official status as conscientious objectors." Thus the
change away from pacifism five decades later was only cosmetic. Although it included pacifists, as a whole the Assemblies of God had never really embraced pacifism.

If Dempster's thesis is true, there are some serious questions. First of
all, why did a movement with only a small minority of pacifists decide
to be so inclusive or protective of the rights of all, at the cost of making
the whole movement appear unpatriotic at a time when patriotism was
at fever pitch? Why was the Assemblies of God so quick to champion
the rights of its pacifists? Did it really see so much value in them as a
prophetic minority? As we consider Dempster's argument, we have to
ask who, if anyone, among the Assemblies of God leaders made up that
prophetic minority. Although Dempster analyzes five exemplars of
pacifist sentiment, only Stanley Frodsham was a member of the Assemblies of God in the United States. The founder of pentecostalism, Charles
Parham, had been discredited as a leader in 1907;[2] he founded his own
group, the Apostolic Faith, which remained small and distant from the
Assemblies of God. Frank Bartleman was an independent evangelist who
mistrusted all organizations, including the Assemblies of God, and may
have been loosely associated for some time with the Oneness branch of
pentecostalism.[3] The Booth-Clibborns were English Pentecostals initially, even if Dempster places Samuel H. Booth-Clibborn among the Oneness Pentecostals in the United States during World War I. So who constituted the prophetic minority that the Assemblies of God was so keen
to protect with its pacifist statement to the government? Not the group
whose theology Dempster discusses.

Moreover, if pacifism was associated with the fringe of pentecostalism but not important to most of the leadership, why did the Assem-

blies of God not distance itself from those pacifist sentiments? On another issue, the trinitarian controversy that culminated especially from 1913 to 1916, the Assemblies of God both dissociated itself from the official statements of the unitarians and effectively disfellowshipped one-fourth of its ministers in the process.[4] If the main leadership in the Assemblies of God did not believe in pacifism, the time to distance itself would have been during World War I, when pacifism was such an embarrassment. Large portions of the U.S. population had already moved with apparent ease from neutrality to militarism as the nation became involved in the war. The Assemblies of God could have done the same, but its leaders refrained.

I argue instead that the strong biblical basis initially employed by the Assemblies of God to justify its pacifism may have proved to be a serious impediment to its later abandonment. As my book suggests, in the mid-1960s it was necessary for the Assemblies of God to reinterpret biblical texts regarding the taking of human life before the church could change its statement on pacifism, which it then did in 1968.[5] Also, the change may have been difficult until the earlier generation of leaders had passed from the scene. Both arguments suggest that there was deeper affirmation of pacifism than Dempster allows.

Dempster further suggests that the Assemblies of God statement may have been designed to win exemptions for ministers who were pacifists or to satisfy those who believed ministers should be exempted from war. But that suggestion ignores the fact that ministers—and even most ministerial students—were exempted from active service in World War I.

Far more troubling to me is Dempster's attempt to reconstruct my work as exclusively sociological—as if a sociological analysis denigrates the theological in the early pentecostals' experience. Admittedly I found the differing early and later sociocultural contexts surrounding pentecostalism to be important factors in its loss of pacifism. I did not assume, however, as Dempster suggests, that a majority of early pentecostals were absolute pacifists at the time of World War I. Dempster makes a real contribution in his discussion of the division within the Assemblies of God over pacifism, but I did not overlook such division. I tried to make clear (1) that there were early moderators and even serious detractors to pacifism within early pentecostalism[6] and (2) that there was little evidence for widespread conscientious objection to all forms of military service by early pentecostals.[7]

Furthermore, one must distinguish between my explanation for early pentecostals' pacifism and my rather different analysis of the reasons later ones abandoned it. When I explained why pentecostals held to pacifism, I argued that their theology was at the center.[8] Although I placed their theology in a sociocultural context, I did not intend either factor to deny the other. What I did *not* find was how the movement changed its theology and how a change in theology led to dropping pacifism.

Dempster's analysis leaves one wondering how an articulate and theologically informed pacifist minority could be routinely published in pentecostalism's early denominational literature while most leaders and constituents disagreed with the pacifists outright. The dichotomy between belief versus practice and between early versus later statements invites sociological analyses. In trying to distance himself from the sociological interpretation, Dempster does little to tell us why the theological justifications for pacifism apparently lacked potency. He suggests that the arguments used by early pentecostal pacifists were diverse. Did pacifists conflict with each other because of differing theological justifications for pacifism? Dempster suggests that the pacifist minority did not have time to form a pacifist *tradition* from its own theology and ethics. Was there a different theology held by the pacifists and the nonpacifists? What were these theological differences? Did such theological differences generalize to other issues besides pacifism?

Dempster's analysis has made me wonder for the first time whether the division in the Assemblies of God over the Trinity was not the focal point for a whole constellation of differences. If so, was pacifism tied to such theological differences? This possibility is appealing when one reflects on how E. N. Bell, the editor of the *Weekly Evangel,* at one time seemed to support the ardent pacifists and at other times attempted to restrain them. During the same time Bell tried to hold together two alternative views on the Trinity: he was trinitarian and then rebaptized unitarian, and usually he argued for freedom of conscience and unity between the divided groups.[9] It appears that instead of being opposed to pacifism, leaders such as Bell were of two minds and therefore hard-pressed as to how to respond to pacifism.

After Bell read Booth-Clibborn's book on pacifism, he encouraged his readers to read the book and adopt its pacific view. Nonetheless, when the government arrested pacifists, when people went to prison, and when magazines of various groups were confiscated, Bell tried to soften such pacifist convictions. Possibly, many leaders in the Assemblies of God had been convinced of pacifism during U.S. neutrality but had not counted on the high cost of pacifism once the United States entered the war.[10] Analysis of pacifism within the larger context of earlier theological divisions is inviting and enlightening. So also is the changing context of national events.

Finally, the degree to which early Assemblies of God men were pacifist during World War I is still an open question. The U.S. government was not concerned with accurate records on denominational affiliation of combatants, noncombatants, and conscientious objectors. Furthermore, the government did not recognize full conscientious objection; it granted only noncombatant status within the military. Nearly 21,000 men chose such noncombatant status, and only 3,989 persisted in the more absolute stand.[11] The latter were inducted and subjected to severe persecution by the military. We do not know how many of the nearly 21,000 men who chose noncombatant status, many of them either as an expression of pacifism or intending conscientious objection, were members of pentecostal groups, including the Assemblies of God.

According to one source, of the 3,989 who persisted in pacifism after forcible induction, "1300 'originally accepted or were assigned to non-combatant service'; 1200 were furloughed to agriculture and 99 to the Friends Reconstruction Unit in France." Meanwhile, "450 were sent to prison by courts-martial."[12] Elsewhere I have documented at least 33 pentecostals among those persisting in pacifism, at least 17 of whom were court-martialed for their stand.[13] It is not clear how many of those 33 were members of the Assemblies of God.[14]

Dempster makes the point that pentecostals did not have time to develop a shared tradition relative to pacifism. I agree. They were probably completely unprepared for the reality of U.S. government coercion of pacifists to become a part of the military. Early pentecostal young men may really have believed that all they had to do was apprise the government of their conscientious objection and they would be deferred from service. With no history of dealing with the government, their disorganization was surely no match for the government's organization.[15] Scholars should study further the extent of pentecostal pacifism and the men who were inducted against their wills.

For such further study, scholars need to examine new sources of documentary evidence. A good recent example of doing that is Theodore Kornweibel's study "Race and Conscientious Objection in World War I: The Story of the Church of God in Christ."

Kornweibel's work provides new evidence of the serious cost of conscience to some early pentecostals in the Church of God in Christ.[16] It also provides fresh evidence of the actual working out of pacifism by some pentecostal leaders and followers. In the persecutions that Korn-weibel documents, it is not entirely clear how much came from racism, how much from wartime paranoia, and how much from the government's real concern about draft evasion. There is some evidence that both the government and various local vigilantes were very concerned.

Kornweibel's corollary story of interracial friendship and fellowship in suffering is one worth reading again. Here one is reminded of the initially interracial character of the early pentecostal movement and the later change to segregation. The story of the origin and rejection of in-terracial fellowship among pentecostals may be shorter than the story about pacifism.[17] Nonetheless, the juxtaposition of these two stories, which together tell of a comparatively more interracial and pacifist wit-ness at the outset followed by a generally segregated and nonpacifist pentecostal movement, invites a broadening of the debate about the meaning and causes of such changes in their larger context.[18]

Kornweibel notes the astonishment of the government agents who heard testimony of a public display of Christian greeting between Church of God in Christ leaders across color lines in the form of the scriptural "holy kiss." This behavior was so unusual that it was deemed to be tacit evidence of alien (German) influence. This interracial car-ing also had practical application, such as providing $2,000 cash for bail when authorities jailed Bishop Charles H. Mason under suspicion of espionage. Kornweibel also provides a glimpse of how the local congre-gations of the Church of God in Christ organized to raise funds for a structure that would represent members as conscientious objectors be-fore their government. The congregations organized, sacrificed, and backed conscientious objection.

By midsummer 1918 the Church of God in Christ had suffered nu-merous arrests to force inductions into the military and several arrests of key leaders. Mason was arrested more than once. When Mason, Henry Kirvin, and William Holt were arrested together in July 1918, Holt's bail was set at an amazing $5,000. He could not come up with the money. This was one month before an Assemblies of God publication warned people to burn Frank Bartleman's tract because of the danger that pen-tecostals would be interpreted as being pro-German.

Far from being pro-German, the pacifism of Charles H. Mason and the early leaders of the Church of God in Christ was theologically based. A basic COGIC statement, as Kornweibel quotes it, declared "the shed-ding of human blood or taking of human life to be contrary to the teach-ings of our Lord and Savior." Kornweibel explained that Mason regarded the kaiser as the "'Beast' or Antichrist depicted in Revelation 13." He noted further that Mason "prayed for Allied victory," and that the COGIC leader "found scriptural approval, in Matthew 5:42, for the purchase of Liberty Bonds." Kornweibel does not believe that Mason's protest was sociopolitical. He does not consider it to be like the work of "many black sharecroppers and migrants seeking the Promised Land in northern cities," that is, the work of blacks who "saw no reason to fight in what they called the 'white man's war.'" Rather he thinks that "Church of God in Christ doctrine, in contrast, was apolitical." Yet he finds that "in the eyes of many southern whites, Mason's instruction to male parishioners to seek conscientious objector status was simply treason."[19]

Kornweibel's contribution is important for the new historical information he places in a theological and social context and for the story it tells about practical organization at the congregational level. He provides a clear picture of how the public at large accepted massive curtailment of constitutional rights, such as freedom of speech. The government and local citizens valued some things more than democratic freedoms. There was a collusion between local intolerance and war support and the federal government's unyielding prosecution of this early pentecostal group.

There is also historical irony in the unintended consequences of these events. In the long run the reputation and legitimation of Bishop Charles H. Mason as a leader was enlarged because he survived a massive government investigation and prosecution with his character intact. Moreover the federal government's own penchant for surveilling and persecuting citizens, and for documenting its heavy-handedness with copious notes, provided Kornweibel with the evidence for his analysis. This type of documentation and analysis parallels the recent rewriting of Eastern European history based on newly opened secret government vaults. Sometimes in history good may indeed come from evil. Let us hope that we continue to find evidence, and learn even more, about early pentecostals and their struggle for peace.

NOTES

1. Jay Beaman, *Pentecostal Pacifism: The Origin, Development, and Rejection of Pacific Belief among the Pentecostals* (Hillsboro, Kans.: Center for Mennonite Brethren Studies, 1989).

2. J. R. Goff Jr. has noted that Parham was arrested but never proven guilty of immorality, but his reputation was ruined; see his "Charles Fox Parham," in Stanley M. Burgess, Gary B. McGee, and Patrick H. Alexander, eds., *Dictionary*

of Pentecostal and Charismatic Movements (hereinafter *DPCM*) (Grand Rapids, Mich.: Zondervan, 1988), 660–61.

3. C. M. Robeck Jr., "Frank Bartleman," in *DPCM*, 50–51.

4. D. A. Reed has noted that in the 1916 Third General Council of the Assemblies of God, "the Trinitarians entered the meeting in control of the key positions and committees. . . . With the adoption of the statement, 156 of the 585 ministers were barred from membership and with them many congregations." See his "Oneness Pentecostalism," in *DPCM*, 644–51.

5. Beaman, *Pentecostal Pacifism*, 110–18. See also "The Sixth Commandment," in *At Ease*, Summer 1966, p. 9, whose author claims to have adapted the material from *The Holiness Handbook* (Springfield, Mo.: Gospel, 1966).

6. Beaman, *Pentecostal Pacifism*, 73–90. My book has a whole chapter on moderators and detractors from pacifism among early pentecostalists, including some in the Assemblies of God. It deals at length with, among others, E. N. Bell. I also noted those such as S. A. Jamieson, a charter member of the Assemblies of God and one of the group that drew up its doctrinal statement in opposition to the Oneness controversy, who was also a leader in opposing pacifism.

7. Ibid., 21. On that page I noted, "While the early Pentecostal Movement did not require pacifism from members, most early Pentecostal groups give evidence of official pacifist belief. There were open differences of opinion, but overwhelming pacifist belief characterized the movement. The literary witness to such beliefs remains as tacit evidence of the support for pacifism by the key leaders in each group represented."

8. Ibid., vii. On that page I noted such factors as eschatology, concern for missions, literal interpretation of Scriptures, identification with the early church, and renewal of the church in modern times (i.e., restorationism), as well as social class. See also Jay Beaman, "Pacifism and the World View of Early Pentecostalism," a paper presented at the Society for Pentecostal Studies, Cleveland, Tenn., 1983; a photocopied conference volume titled "Pastoral Problems in the Pentecostal-Charismatic Movement" includes this paper. There I argued for the "centrality of pacifism to the early Pentecostal world view" and continued: "Chief among the elements of that world view were intense millennial expectations coupled with anti-nationalistic allegiances. Millennial expectations placed their hopes for a just society outside of the present configuration of power in this world. This fueled an anti-nationalistic sentiment as did their missionary zeal and redemptive identification with other peoples around the world, as well as their sensitivity to their own impoverished socioeconomic status. They found war so repulsive because of its obvious incongruence with the missionary impulse. They did not identify strongly with nationalistic goals because they perceived that, given their social position, those goals were never framed with them in mind. These elements of their world view, coupled with a restorationist or primitivist view of the church, provided a matrix of which

pacifism was an integral part." The paper developed these themes, using many
of the same sources now used by Dempster. Although the sociocultural arguments are at the front, the theological content should not be missed.

9. D. A. Reed, "Oneness Pentecostalism," in *DPCM,* 645.

10. E. N. Bell's call to the readers of the *Christian Evangel* to destroy Frank
Bartleman's tract may have reflected less his antipathy to pacifism than a realistic loss of free speech. Bell noted, "While this tract was merely aimed at sin
high or low, and while the things said would be understood in times of peace[,]
that was entirely too radical for war times"; see "Preachers Warned," *Weekly
Evangel,* Jan. 26, 1918, p. 9, and "Destroy This Tract," *Christian Evangel,* Aug. 24,
1918, p. 4. The government was severely limiting free speech, however, and small
magazines that criticized the war effort were quite vulnerable; see Robert W.
Coakley, Paul J. Scheips, and Emma J. Portuondo, *Antiwar and Antimilitary
Activities in the United States, 1846–1954* (Washington, D.C.: Office of the Chief
of Military History, 1970), 73. At this same time Supreme Court justice Oliver
Wendell Holmes justified imprisonment for some who spoke against the war,
saying, "When a nation is at war many things that may be said in time of peace
are such a hindrance to its efforts that their utterance will not be endured so
long as men fight and that no court could regard them as a constitutional right";
see ibid., 75, citing *Shenck v. United States,* 249, U.S. 47 (1919).

11. Staughton Lynd, *Nonviolence in America: A Documentary History* (Indi-
anapolis: Bobbs-Merrill, n.d.), xxiv.

12. Norman M. Thomas, *Is Conscience a Crime?* rev. ed., foreword by Charles
Chatfield (New York: Garland, 1972), 15.

13. Beaman, *Pentecostal Pacifism,* 102–5. The 33 pentecostals identified by the
government were out of a classification of 1,000 of the nearly 4,000 men who
persisted in pacifism. How many more pentecostals were among the nearly
3,000 unclassified men is still unknown. John Irvine Harrison, "A History of
the Assemblies of God" (Th.D. diss., Berkley Divinity School, 1954), 151, notes,
"A few pentecostal men were taken to military installations and stripped of their
clothing [except] their underwear and forced to go this way for days or else don
the uniform which was lying close at hand."

14. Professor Michael Casey of Pepperdine University, Malibu, California,
has provided me with a photocopy of a list of 359 individuals entitled "Religious C.O.'s Imprisoned at the U.S. Disciplinary Barracks, Ft. Leavenworth,
Kansas," published Mar. 10, 1919, by J. D. Mininger, a Mennonite minister of
Kansas City, Kansas, and apparently compiled by Maurice A. Hess. I count
twenty-five pentecostals in this list, but only three are identified as Assemblies
of God, and these are ambiguous—two are labeled "Pentecostal Assembly[ies]
of God."

15. Sarah T. Parham, *The Life of Charles F. Parham* (Joplin, Mo.: Tri State,
1930), told how Charles Parham's office editor and manager for the *Apostolic
Faith* magazine, Roland Romack, on being inducted into military service, asked

for but was denied exemption from combatant service. Many thousands had been denied all kinds of exemptions. There may have been large numbers of pentecostal young men who asked for exemptions based on conscientious objection but were denied. They may have simply not thought that there was even the possibility of serious resistance. As the few who were successful in their resistance showed, it was almost impossible.

16. For a briefer account of the same story with most of the same characters, but from different sources, see L. Lovett, "Black-Holiness Pentecostalism," in *DPCM*, 81.

17. Hints of the interracial character of earlier pentecostalism are found in the extended Azusa Street revival meetings and in the fact that numerous individuals among the first group of Assemblies of God clergy were previously ordained by Bishop Charles Mason of the Church of God in Christ. Of course, there were opportunistic elements in this story as well as in the story of pacifism. It is likely that the interracial witness was no more consistent than that of pacifism. See both Lovett, "Black-Holiness Pentecostalism," 76–84, and Reed, "Oneness Pentecostalism," 644–51. An interesting analogue could also be drawn to pentecostalism's earlier broader range of women's leadership ministries, including preaching, and its later narrowing of those freedoms. See R. M. Riss, "Women, Role of," in *DPCM*, 893–99.

18. L. Lovett, "Black-Holiness Pentecostalism," 81, suggests that "the statement, 'We are opposed to war in all its various forms and believe the shedding of blood and the taking of human life to be contrary to the teachings of our Lord Jesus Christ,' remains to this day the CGIC [Church of God in Christ] stance." Of course, the story is not completely transparent. In Kornweibel's account one central figure, William B. Holt, was a pacifist and yet carried a gun as deputy sheriff.

19. Quotations are from the draft of Kornweibel's essay that I received before composing these remarks.

PART 2

🙢

CHURCHES OF CHRIST, CHURCH OF GOD

🙢

5

CHURCHES OF CHRIST AND WORLD WAR II CIVILIAN

PUBLIC SERVICE

A Pacifist Remnant

؈

Michael W. Casey

A conscientious objector (CO) who placed himself in a "concentration camp" or a "federal prison" was a "freak specimen of humanity," according to Foy E. Wallace Jr., a leading preacher of the Churches of Christ (C of C), in 1942. The next year E. LeRoy Dakin, of the National Service Board for Religious Objectors, pleaded that it was "only fair" that the C of C "help us in a financial way" to support the C of C COs in the Civilian Public Service camps. "The Historic Peace Churches plead for your partnership in this high enterprise," he wrote. The strange, chaotic, radical congregational polity baffled Dakin. He admitted to one C of C leader, "Since your churches do not have a national headquarters, and many leaders and churches may not be sympathetic toward the Conscientious Objector, I am at a loss to know how to deal with this matter."[1]

The C of C are a part of the Campbell-Stone tradition that also includes the Disciples of Christ and the conservative Christian Churches. Although the division with the Disciples of Christ has roots going back into the nineteenth century, the C of C were first recognized as a separate tradition in the U.S. Census of Religious Bodies of 1906. The central theological tenet of the C of C, which goes back to Alexander Campbell, is the restoration of the primitive, or New Testament, church. The tradition argues that there is a "blueprint," or pattern, for the church that can be discerned by commands or the examples of the primitive church. Any "additions" of human opinion or inventions of humans are erroneous. Division from the Disciples of Christ came, according to the official statement printed by the census bureau, because as "the churches increased in membership and wealth . . . there arose, in the opinion of some, a desire for popularity and for such 'human inventions' as had been deplored in the beginning of the movement. Chief among these 'inventions' were, a general organization of the churches into a missionary society with a 'money basis' of membership, and the use of instrumental music in worship."[2]

The missionary society preempted congregational autonomy and replaced the church as the agent of mission work. The C of C thus was—and is—radically congregational, eschewing all denominational structure or bureaucracy. Instrumental music was seen as a "human addition" to the divine pattern of a cappella music. All other religious traditions had deviated from the primitive pattern and were corrupt. The C of C had recaptured the glorious apostolic church, so that all Christians needed to come out of the denominations and join it. This prompted the C of C to remain aloof from all other traditions, except to debate. The thought of cooperating with other traditions never occurred. The C of C fit the classic sectarian model.[3]

Civilian Public Service (CPS), a labor of love for the historic peace churches, included a cacophony of obscure and bizarre sects and radical political pacifists. About two hundred men from the C of C were in CPS and constituted the fourth largest non–peace church tradition in its camps.[4] Like most sects in CPS, the C of C men withdrew into their own tightly knit circles and stayed aloof from most others—one more odd sect, it might seem, passing through CPS. Reviled and consigned to oblivion by most of their brethren and misunderstood by most others, including the historic peace churches, these men beg to be understood.

I will attempt a "thick description" of the COs from the C of C based on oral history interviews supplemented by written historical sources. The purpose is to gain access to their conceptual world, both for those outside the tradition and for those inside it who do not understand them. These men and their experience in CPS are a microscopic but important part of the larger history and tradition of peace within the C of C. Because of the availability of ministerial deferment, most of the CPS men from the C of C were not preachers but had blue-collar vocations and tended not to write about their pacifism. Whereas the more elite preachers of the C of C were more oriented toward print culture, the CPS men's culture was oral. Traces of the print culture remain, but the oral culture is rapidly disappearing as CPSers from the C of C die.[5]

The CPS story really begins with World War I. During that war COs were treated horribly in the United States. They basically had two options: noncombatant service or prison.[6] As World War II approached, the historic peace churches recognized that this situation could be repeated, and they successfully lobbied Congress for some type of alternative service. The result was a compromise, CPS. In CPS the COs were to do "work of national importance under civilian direction." The catch was that the men (draftees were all males) would not receive any pay. Indeed, each one had to pay $35 a month to cover expenses and had to provide his own clothes. If the CPSer or his church could not or did not pay the expenses, the historic peace churches ultimately had to bear the cost—regardless of the man's religious background.[7]

The type of work varied. Most CPSers did conservation work at old Civilian Conservation Corps camps or built roads or dams, trimmed trees, or fought forest fires. Some worked at mental hospitals, in agricultural projects, or for public health programs. A few, volunteering as "guinea pigs," put themselves at risk for medical and scientific experiments.

The U.S. government's Selective Service ran the overall program, controlled the assignments of the individuals in CPS, and operated some camps, while each peace church (Quaker, Mennonite, and Church of the Brethren) had a network of camps it paid for and administered. The CPS rested on a unique church-state relationship. It also created constant tensions for control between Selective Service and the National Service Board for Religious Objectors (NSBRO), the organization the historic peace churches created to deal with the government. Usually, NSBRO lost.

Pacifism was an important part of the Campbell-Stone tradition. Alexander Campbell, Barton Stone, and other Disciples of Christ leaders were pacifists. David Lipscomb, the leader of the emerging C of C from 1866 to 1912, argued that Christians should not fight in wars but live by the principles of the Sermon on the Mount. After Lipscomb died in 1917, and with the pressures of World War I, most C of C congregations abandoned pacifism.[8]

After the C of C evolved into a separate tradition, diversity existed. In the CPS camps three distinct groupings of the C of C were represented: the one-cup churches; the non–Sunday school, or nonclass, churches; and the "mainline" churches (ones that had Sunday schools and used multiple cups in communion). These groupings existed because, soon after the division with the Disciples of Christ had solidified, the question had arisen whether local congregations could organize Sunday school classes to study the Bible. A minority opposed this as a "human invention." Starting in the late 1910s and continuing through the 1920s, numerous churches began abandoning their one-room wood church buildings for somewhat more "upscale" frame or even brick buildings that had extra rooms for Sunday school classes. The nonclass minority saw this as a sign of "worldliness."[9]

While the majority of the mainline C of C churches were abandoning pacifism, the nonclass churches were tenaciously holding on to it. In 1928 R. F. Duckworth, the editor of the leading nonclass journal, petitioned Congress to get the C of C recognized as a peace church. Both churches and individuals were put on record as being opposed to war.[10]

Also in the 1920s many congregations, copying their Baptist and Methodist neighbors, began to use individual communion cups for the Lord's Supper. A small sectarian minority opposed this as yet another "human innovation," however. Most of these churches divided from the nonclass churches and represent the most sectarian form of the C of C. By World War II, pacifism was a minority position even in the nonclass churches, but it was different with the one-cup churches. They are still on record with NSBRO (now NISBCO) as a peace church.[11]

Some pacifism remained in the mainline C of C, sometimes because of isolationist sentiment, but Pearl Harbor sharply reduced it. By about the time of Foy E. Wallace's attack on COs, it took courage to remain pacifist.[12] In general the more sectarian a church was, the greater its support for pacifism during World War II.

Despite a common heritage and similar experiences in CPS, there were significant differences among the CPS men from the C of C. Their attitudes toward war and Christians participating in war, although similar, were not identical, and the men had to learn to deal with their differences as well as with differences with outsiders.[13]

For the C of C men, the rationale for being a CO rested mostly on primitivism. Houston Martin, from a one-cup church, believed that "the New Testament as a whole" did not support killing. "I just couldn't see it myself—killing one another. I just couldn't go for that." Phil Teague, from the nonclass background, recalled:

> I do remember that back in the thirties I just could not stand violence. I could see that there was an incompatibility between the military and Christianity. The teachings of Jesus said love your enemies, don't go

shooting at them. Says if your enemy's hungry feed him, that's the way it would be. But that's not compatible with the way of the world: the eye for an eye and a tooth for a tooth and get his hide first and skin it. And I remember when we were attending church, I was about twenty years old. I spoke one Sunday at a little country church in Arkansas, and one old bird said, "Phil, you're right; a Christian would not make a very good soldier."

Glen Stice, from a mainline congregation, said: "I tried to think biblically, and I know that we have a lot of Scriptures that say you should not kill. . . . It talks a lot about love an awful lot in the Scriptures, about loving your neighbor as yourself and that you're to love your enemies and 'Vengeance is mine, thus sayeth the Lord.' All these had some influence on me."[14]

Some men were influenced by their fathers who had been COs in World War I or by their mothers. Phil Himes recalled: "I expect there were expectations developed at an early age. My father taught me about being a conscientious objector in World War I, although on examination he flunked the physical and wasn't called up." Carl and Everette Kessler's father also had been a CO in World War I, but he was not drafted. Family influence to take the CO position was not unusual. Elton Wyly, from a nonclass church, said: "By the time I could know anything right or wrong, my mother was my teacher. . . . She was always a pacifist. We were just brought up to understand the cruelties of war [and] the carnality of war."[15]

Preachers and local congregations also played a part in shaping CO attitudes. Elton Wyly recalled that "the general leadership at the church where we were going [at Friona, Texas] stood on this premise that carnal warfare is not Christian." Carl Kessler remembered that preachers from Alabama and Georgia came to Rincon, Georgia, endorsing the CO position. J. C. Eager was influenced to be a CO by Alvah Davis, an elder at the Hamby church in Abilene, Texas, who had been a prisoner at Ft. Leavenworth as a CO in World War I. Several CPSers came from small churches in rural counties where local preachers were apparently handing down pacifist views from generations before. For example, several were from Clay County, Alabama, where people of the nonclass churches did not read any periodicals and never received visits from nationally known preachers.[16]

R. F. Duckworth's efforts to influence the government to recognize the C of C as a peace church definitely had an impact on men from the one-cup and the nonclass churches. Duckworth influenced Elom Harbin of Littlefield, Texas, to take the CO stand. Orba Miller of Floydada, Texas, and J. C. Eager went on record with Duckworth to prove their CO status. Duckworth's efforts helped Phil Teague to think more on the issue.[17] Undoubtedly others responded to Duckworth's influence, especially in Texas.

These men were not illiterate: they read pacifist books and C of C periodicals. During the Civil War David Lipscomb had written the classic pacifist work of the tradition, *Civil Government*. In this book he argued that it was wrong for Christians to participate in politics in any form, even to vote. Directly or indirectly, Lipscomb's ideas influenced many of the CPS men. Several, agreeing with the idea that Christians were citizens of a different kingdom, never voted. A few of the COs had read *Civil Government* before going into camp, whereas others read it after entering. Usually men from the most sectarian group, the one-cup churches, and occasionally men from the non–Sunday school churches did not vote. Most of the men whom I interviewed were not as extreme as Lipscomb, however, and they did vote. They saw voting as a privilege that allows Christians to influence government.[18]

During the war there were a number of books published that supported the CO position. One of the most influential was *The Christian Conscientious Objector*, by James D. Bales, a doctoral student at University of California, Berkeley, and a mainline C of C preacher. Bales refused to take the ministerial deferment and was prepared to enter CPS. When a federal judge intervened and gave Bales the deferment anyway, Bales accepted it on the grounds that the government had made the choice for him. Bales's book is a compendium of some leading pacifist scholarship of the time. On practical matters, Bales explained how to fill out forms to obtain CO status and how to answer draft boards' questions. His book concluded that "the CPS camp seems to offer a more effective testimony to the cross. In fact, many non-pacifists are convinced that noncombatant work is inconsistent with the c.o. profession. . . . I believe the most consistent course is to refuse to join the army." James David Hamm of Valdosta, Georgia, read Bales's book and was convinced to enter CPS in 1944.[19]

Most C of C men read the leading periodicals of their particular C of C segment, all of which supported pacifism. Men from the one-cup churches read *Old Paths Advocate*. The non–Sunday school men read *Gospel Tidings* and the *Church Messenger*. Most of the men from the mainline churches read the *Gospel Advocate* or smaller journals that advocated pacifism.[20]

Every CO in war has to confront the government's system for dealing with the CO "problem." The response of the C of C pacifists differed from pacifists of other traditions. Not a single person I interviewed considered not registering for the draft. Winfield Skinner of Valdosta, Georgia, was typical: "I felt like it was my responsibility to obey the law as far as I could. Now if they had not allowed me to be a conscientious objector, I might have gone in a more drastic way." Skinner was clearly following what the leadership of the church advocated.[21]

After registering, men were subject to the call of Selective Service and had to deal with their local draft boards. Although the treatment of COs was better in World War II than in World War I, many objectors in the C of C had difficulties. Phil Himes, one of several Pepperdine College students who sought CO status, had grown up in Odessa, Missouri; Morrilton, Arkansas; and finally Sumas, Washington. His father influenced him to be a CO, and so did J. N. Armstrong, one of the founders of Harding College, in Arkansas.[22] Himes thought when he registered that he would work with the draft board in Sumas. His three older brothers, who also were Pepperdine students, easily obtained CO status through that local board. After Himes registered, however, a draft board in Los Angeles took his case. When he filled out the forms, he claimed CO status and asked to be classified IV-E (CPS), but the board classified him I-A.[23]

Himes inquired of the board concerning the reclassification. They replied that they had granted him the IV-E, but, as he later recounted, "an attorney for the board recommended that, because a large number of Pepperdine students had registered with that board, . . . they change my status to I-A. When I appealed that, they gave me a I-A-O (noncombatant), but I would not accept that either. So I appealed again and was turned down." After receiving an order to report for induction in 1943, Himes informed the government that he would not do so and that he was staying at Pepperdine. "I got a call on August 1 from an FBI agent named Joe Wells," Himes has recalled. "He apologetically said, 'Could you come down to my office tomorrow morning? Frankly I have to arrest you.' And he gave me assurances that I would be released on my own recognizance." Instead Himes was jailed overnight. The next day Wade Ruby, an English professor at Pepperdine, showed up at the hearing to help. Himes remembered: "When the judge said, 'You can be released on a thousand dollars bail,' Ruby stood up and said, 'Why?' The judge said, 'Well, we've had some experience that these guys disappear.' So a couple of my brothers [who were] college students raked up a thousand dollars, and I got out on bail that day."[24]

Meanwhile Himes had started the process of appeal to the president for reclassification. Before his next court appearance Guy Click, a jailhouse lawyer and C of C preacher, accompanied Himes on a visit to the federal prosecuting attorney. Himes remembered, "We asked . . . for permission to plead nolo contendere." This allowed Himes to keep the presidential appeal alive but made him subject to conviction without admitting his guilt. Himes recalled that only after some persuasion did the prosecutor consent. When Himes appeared before Judge Harrison, of the federal district court, the judge also accepted the nolo contendere plea. Himes remembered that the judge "kept postponing the trial date a month at a time until the appeal to the president was heard from." The appeal was refused in December 1943. Then the judge surprised Himes by saying, "I can't order the local draft board to reclassify you, but I am going to send your file back to them, and I suggest that you contact them and see what else they need to help them make a decision about this." Himes gave the draft board another reference that they requested, and after they reviewed his case again, they reclassified him IV-E. Himes has recalled being in Pepperdine's dining hall when "I got a telephone call . . . saying that I had been reclassified. . . . I went out in front of the dining hall and let out a war hoop or some such thing. And it wasn't long—March—I was called up into CPS."[25]

Several men were working in jobs that qualified them for deferment from the draft, but bosses or persons in the community learned about their CO convictions and had their status changed, forcing them into CPS. Winfield Skinner is one example. He obtained a deferment from military service by working for the U.S. Army Corps of Engineers. He was sent to Bainbridge, Georgia, to help build an air base, thinking he "was going to be on permanent status there." His boss, a military captain, wanted all the civilian employees to buy war bonds, however. Skinner recalled: "There were some of us who didn't make much money and were married. My wife was expecting and under a doctor's care. I just couldn't buy, and I told him I couldn't, and it wasn't long after that I got my draft notice. This captain said he didn't know whether he was going to report me to the draft board. He had to make up his mind, but apparently he did after I still refused to buy the war bonds."[26]

Men from the C of C served in all types of CPS camps and activities, but there were two camps where significant numbers of them worked: a Church of the Brethren camp at Magnolia, Arkansas, and the first government-run camp at Mancos, Colorado. At least fifty-three men, more than a fourth of the C of C men who participated in CPS, were stationed in Magnolia for at least part of their service. At least thirty-nine men from the C of C served at Mancos, probably making the C of C the largest religious group at the camp.[27]

Camp 7 in Magnolia, Arkansas, opened before the United States entered the war. Phil Teague from Tolar, Texas, recalled: "I first went to camp in August of '41 and I was there for about 9 months." After Pearl Harbor more members of the C of C entered CPS and went to Magnolia. Murray Wilson, a mainline preacher from nearby Waldo, Arkansas, became aware of these men and their need for support, since none of them was being supported by the churches. Wilson appealed in church journals: "We can eliminate this situation by each congregation sending their contribution, monthly to the superintendent of the camp or to me."[28] Even in those early days, the non–Sunday school churches began trying to support the men at Magnolia. At first they sent food to the camp, but after Pearl Harbor they began to send money. The one-cup churches were a little slower to coordinate their efforts, but through the urging of a California preacher named Ervin Waters, Carl Nichols of Hollywood, California, collected money that was sent to the Church of the Brethren.[29]

When the men first entered CPS, their attitude and outlook was very positive. Batsell Moore wrote: "A more democratic way of life cannot be found than the way of life in these camps, and a better opportunity to develop leaders and teachers for the church cannot be had." Bertram Jack recalled that most who went into CPS thought of Magnolia as "the good old days." Most appreciated the educational activities that the Church of the Brethren sponsored. Coleman Boyd recalled that the camp ran a grocery store on the honor system, leaving a change box unattended and letting each man leave his money and make change. The store ran for months with no thefts. The Magnolia camp worked mostly at conservation: digging ponds, fighting fires, and doing farm work. H. C. Welch has recalled: "We were in the Soil Conservation Service. We were building terraces and doing things out on the land, farms and stuff there. And my job, I was a truck driver on one of these projects." Gus Winter, a preacher who visited his son at Magnolia, wrote, "I found myself in a very cheery, friendly atmosphere and everyone imbued with the spirit of service and lending a helping hand." He spent seven days at the camp and did not hear "one word of profanity" or "one questionable thing."[30]

Not everything was positive at Magnolia, however. The men from the different segments of the C of C had to try to worship together. Initially they all met in a small cabin at the camp. Phil Teague recalled: "We had men who were pro–Sunday school. We had men that were [of] the one-cup persuasion. We had men that were [of] the nonpreacher persuasion. We were all meeting together, and nobody objected to it." Later Hugh Coleman Boyd came to the camp, and Teague said that Boyd and the mainline men "wouldn't meet with us, because we had men that were non–Sunday school." Boyd recalled that he liked to debate the non–Sunday school men as well as men from the other traditions. In the debates, Boyd remembered, "We had quite a bit of discussion. They were real nice fellows, and we never got angry. . . . [But] they never did believe like we did."[31]

There were problems with the local church at Magnolia, especially for the men from the mainline churches. The Magnolia church was very patriotic and prowar, and according to Landon Hatley, it "felt very strongly against conscientious objectors." One CO wrote to Jimmy Lovell, a California church leader, that the Magnolia church would allow the COs to attend worship but did not allow them "to take part in the services." Coleman Boyd recalled: "Some of them there were so critical of religious objectors. They in a shrewd way would try to indoctrinate us that we were wrong. There was a song that said, 'Must I be carried through the skies on flower beds of ease while others fought to win the prize and sail through bloody seas?' Then it said 'No, I must fight if I would win, increase my courage Lord.' It goes on and talks about how we are to fight the Christian battle—the spiritual battle. But they took it as a fleshly, physical battle, and so they kept on suggesting that song and so finally those of us who were religious objectors, we got to the place that every time they would ask for suggestions, we would suggest that song, and they quit singing it altogether. They refused to suggest it anymore."[32]

Other people in the local community were not very favorable to the CPS men either. Marie Welch, wife of a C of C man in the Magnolia camp, later recalled: "The people there were pretty hostile. I think probably the most hostile." Her husband, H. C. Welch, added, "The worst of any place we were." Marie went on to recount that she

worked for a little while there in a cloth factory. The guy that managed and hired us, he was okay, he was a nice fellow. H. C. made a habit of coming down during . . . [the times] when I was off [for] my supper break. There was a guy there that was very prejudiced against COs, and he told everybody in the building that he was going to beat H. C. up, and everybody knew it but me. When H. C. came that night, all these people came out, and they were ready for the confrontation. . . . This guy started his loud mouth and his cursing and ranting. Well, I jumped out of the car and H. C. drove off. That was the end of that, and I think that was the end of his coming in the evenings, too. But I think some of the other guys went in groups. They didn't really get out by themselves, because some people were really hostile.

The camp at Magnolia was closed when a tornado destroyed its buildings. Marie remembered that "the common thinking of the townspeople was that God was really trying to punish the COs, because otherwise it wouldn't have happened, it wouldn't have been right there in such a concealed area. And that really confirmed their ideas that they were right in the first place, now the Lord really was after COs."[33]

Between the mainline men and the more sectarian ones there also were differences in how they thought about having churches run the camps. Phil Teague took the lead in changing several men's opinions; as a result many from the nonclass and one-cup churches requested transfers to a government camp. Teague later recalled: "I never thought a whole lot about it to begin with, but then I thought no, if the government is going to take my time, they're the ones who should support us, and not the Church of the Brethren. Nothing against the Church of the Brethren, but it wasn't their obligation."[34] Teague also wrote a letter to the periodicals of the nonclass and the one-cup churches, declaring:

> It is the business of civil governments to pass and enforce laws. The "Peace Churches" assumed a part of this carnal activity when they asked for the administration of these camps.
>
> A law has been passed and enforced, taking men away from their homes and families, forcing them to work without pay and leave their families to get along any way they can. Such an action, just or unjust, is to be done by a carnal civil power, if done at all.
>
> Our prayer is that the body of Christ, the group who has been called out of the world, will separate themselves and cease to take part in the carnal functions of worldly affairs . . . [and] that all support, sanction and administration by the churches of Christ of such camps, should cease. Support the men in the camps as brethren in need if you will, but to assume support of the camps is to assume an obligation that belongs to civil powers.[35]

In contrast the mainline men felt it was all right for the peace churches to support them. Coleman Boyd recalled: "I felt like they [the historic peace churches] had shouldered that responsibility as a group, and as long as they were satisfied with it and as long as I was working for the government in work of national importance, I felt like I had accomplished my goal. I never really considered a government camp."[36]

The lack of pay was also a factor for some individuals who transferred to government camps. The plan created hardships for many of the men who had families. Many of these men changed to noncombatant status, through which they received regular pay and benefits. Almost universally the lack of pay was despised by the Church of Christ men. Boyd typically "thought it was a form of slavery," declaring that he thought so then and still does now. "I feel like it was a blessing to have folks like the Brethren, Mennonites, and the Quakers that would shoulder that kind of responsibility, but I felt like we had gone the second mile when we worked nine hours a day for the government for not one red cent."[37]

The government camps differed markedly from the church camps. Spirit and morale began to darken, especially over the lack of pay. Government camps offered modest pay for the men, but they were more repressive than the church camps and became a dumping ground for many "misfits." The C of C men from the sectarian segments noticed the difference. Bertram Jack recalled that Mancos, Colorado, the first government camp, was "hard" in comparison to the church camps. Most CPSers there felt they were simply "doing time." The camp had a large number of political objectors, and they changed the tone. Clarence Eager recalled about Mancos: "I'd say that half of them were not there on religious convictions. And they were troublemakers. Of course some of them refused to work. They got so many RTWs [Refusals to Work] they sent them to prison. The camp directors weren't slavedrivers; we didn't work hard. Nobody that I knew of was mistreated. But some of the campers felt mistreated—I never felt that way—it was mainly those who didn't have religious convictions that felt like they were in prison. And some of them did choose to go to prison." Most of the C of C men did not like the political objectors.[38]

Although the number of political objectors was high, other aspects of camp life were similar to those at the church camps. At Mancos the men built a huge irrigation dam and did other types of conservation work. The camp was near the town of Mancos, so some families of campers came to live near the men, which also occurred around church camps. Conscientious objectors were given leave and were able to visit their families. At Mancos, as at many church camps, the local citizens were sometimes hostile to the COs.[39]

The COs once again had to deal with differences among themselves. Most in the non–Sunday school segment considered the one-cup men to be "too radical." Bertram Jack reported in 1946 about a meeting that the one-cup COs sponsored at Mancos, saying: "The meeting . . . finally brought a criticism of us who feel differently. Two hours of last Sunday afternoon was spent in discussing our differences. I am unable to see through some of their arguments." Clarence Eager also remembered such problems. "Sometimes they wouldn't get along," he recalled. "The only trouble we had was when Ervin Waters came up there and H. C. Welch. We talked about it—we were satisfied, we just had one cup. We all worshiped together until Ervin Waters came up there and convinced them even though we had one cup, we believed it was all right to have more than one, so we didn't worship together anymore after that. Otherwise we were friendly toward each other." Eventually several mainline men also transferred into Mancos, but they never created any problems and worshiped with the non–Sunday school men.[40]

What was the longer-term effect? The divided perspectives of the CPS men continued after their CPS experience was over. The one-cup churches maintained their stand as a peace church. Ervin Waters even testified in Congress in 1952 against a universal military training act and argued for alternative service for COs, which was eventually adopted.[41] Despite such efforts, the one-cup churches have been so few and so poor that they have had very little influence. The non–Sunday school churches continued to produce some COs in later wars, but the CO position has been a minority one in this extremely small segment of the Churches of Christ. The mainline churches have all but forgotten their tradition of peace. Few mainline members know the story of the CPS men.

So what happened to the CPS men from the C of C? Although many are leaders in their congregations, all but a few remain quiet about their CO experiences. One response to my question about teaching others about the war issue was typical. "I'm not a radical person on this subject. I've never been one to try to force my beliefs on someone else. In fact, maybe I'm not strong enough sometimes about trying to influence you because I don't feel I have these rights to try to influence you. I've never publicized that I was a conscientious objector—that I take this side."[42] In contrast to the humble churches of the one-cup and nonclass segments, the mainline C of C have ascended in wealth and power. The CO issue is an embarrassing part of an archaic past and is viewed as an out-of-touch kind of radicalism. As people of the tradition have become more wealthy, most have become right-wing Republicans, vigorously anticommunist, and supporters of a strong military. There is also a theological heritage at work. The C of C are one of the strictest traditions in the Baconian Enlightenment heritage. Ideas are put forth as propositions to be analyzed, argued, and debated. One must think rationally and logically in approaching Scripture. One's own prejudices, emotions, and experiences are to be hidden and kept out of sight in studying the Bible and Christianity; there is no legitimate place for experience or personal narrative. Consequently no stories of COs are told in church or in Bible study. When narrative, history, and tradition are devalued, events and experiences quickly recede in the collective memory. A new generation that does not know what went on before thus arises. Exacerbating this tendency in the C of C is the predominant view that the CO issue is a private matter, a choice of individual conscience, not a matter for the whole church. The CO has increasingly been the lone individual making his own idiosyncratic choice. The World War II COs of CPS are not "freak specimens of humanity" in the C of C today. Instead they are forgotten relics of a supposedly irrelevant past.

NOTES

I wish to thank the Pepperdine University Research Council for a research grant and the Seaver College Research Committee for reassignment that enabled me to conduct the oral history interviews. Note: All interviews cited in the notes were interviews with me.

1. Foy E. Wallace Jr. "The Christian and the Government," *Bible Banner,* Mar. 1942, p. 6; Dakin quoted in James P. Miller, "Two Letters," *Gospel Advocate,* Mar. 11, 1943, p. 220; E. LeRoy Dakin, "If It Were Your Boy," *Christian Leader,* July 6, 1943, p. 9; and Dakin to Russel Squire, Feb. 19, 1943, Jimmy Lovell papers (these papers to be given to the Center for Restoration Studies, Abilene Christian University, Abilene, Tex.; I thank Lovell's daughter Patsy Trowbridge for making them available).

2. U.S. Bureau of the Census, *Religious Bodies: 1906,* 2 vols. (Washington: U.S. Government Printing Office, 1906), 2:241–42.

3. Elmer T. Clark, *The Small Sects of America* (New York: Abingdon-Cokesbury, 1950), 214, declared that the C of C is "the largest Protestant group showing pronounced sectarian tendencies, though loudest in protestation that it is not a sect or 'denominational church' but the 'true Church of Christ,' conforming in every detail to the apostolic and scriptural pattern."

4. The CPS directory officially counted 199 men from the "Church of Christ," yet it listed only 196 names. From other sources I have determined that 204 CPSers, including one man converted to the C of C, were members of the

tradition. The number could have been as high as 216; several men who listed their denomination as "none" could have been C of C members, since many in the tradition reject denominationalism.

5. Clifford Geertz, *The Interpretation of Cultures* (New York: Basic, 1973), 6, 21, 24. On oral history method see James Hoopes, *Oral History: An Introduction for Students* (Chapel Hill: University of North Carolina Press, 1979). On the differences between oral and print cultures see Walter Ong, *Orality and Literacy: The Technologizing of the Word* (London: Methuen, 1982).

6. Michael Casey, "New Information on Conscientious Objectors of World War I and the Churches of Christ," *Restoration Quarterly* 34 (1992): 83–96.

7. One of the best accounts of the CPS is Mulford Sibley and Philip E. Jacob, *Conscription of Conscience: The American State and the Conscientious Objector, 1940–1947* (Ithaca, N.Y.: Cornell University Press, 1952), 110–331.

8. David Edwin Harrell Jr., "Disciples of Christ Pacifism in Nineteenth-Century Tennessee," *Tennessee Historical Society Quarterly* 21 (Sept. 1962): 263–74; Michael Casey, "From Pacifism to Patriotism: The Emergence of Civil Religion in the Churches of Christ during World War I," *The Mennonite Quarterly Review* 66 (July 1992): 376–90. Lipscomb was editor of the *Gospel Advocate,* the leading periodical of the Churches of Christ, from 1866 to 1912.

9. R. F. Duckworth, "Money-Mad Religion," *The Apostolic Way,* Feb. 1, 1920, p. 1; J. P. Watson, "A Note of Warning," *The Apostolic Way,* Mar. 15, 1921, p. 5. See also Larry Hart, "Brief History of a Minor Restorationist Group (The Non-Sunday School Churches of Christ)," *Restoration Quarterly* 22 (1979): 212–32; and Ronny Wade, *The Sun Will Shine Again Some Day: A History of the Non-Class, One-Cup Churches of Christ* (Springfield, Mo.: the author, 1989), 24–52.

10. R. F. Duckworth, "Something Definite," *The Apostolic Way,* Mar. 15, 1928, pp. 1–2. On the mainline churches and pacifism, see my "From Pacifism to Patriotism."

11. Shawn Perry, *Words of Conscience: Religious Statements on Conscientious Objection* (Washington: National Interreligious Service Board for Conscientious Objectors, 1980), 35–37; and Wade, *The Sun Will Shine,* 53–116, 153–57.

12. See Michael Casey, "Warriors against War: The Pacifists of the Churches of Christ in World War II," *Restoration Quarterly* 35 (1993): 159–74; it tells the story of the struggle of the pacifist tradition in the mainline C of C churches during World War II.

13. From this point onward I focus on the "inner facts" of the lives of the men. Oral history lends itself to exploring reasons and motives rather than dates and other minute details; see Hoopes, *Oral History,* 41, 47.

14. Interviews: Houston Martin at Kinston, Ala., Aug. 3, 1992; Phil Teague at Sweetwater, Tex., Dec. 27, 1990; Glen Stice at Garden Grove, Calif., May 13, 1991.

15. Interviews: Phil Himes at Villanova, Pa., Mar. 25, 1991; Carl Kessler at Wedowee, Ala., Aug. 1, 1992; Elton Wyly at Friona, Tex., May 23, 1992.

16. Interviews: Elton Wyly, May 23, 1992; Carl Kessler, Aug. 1, 1992; J. C. Eager at Lubbock, Tex., May 21, 1992. (On Davis see Alvah Davis, "War Time Persecutions," *The Apostolic Way*, June 15, 1925, p. 2; and Casey, "New Information," 85.) Interviews: Albert Strickland at Chattanooga, Tenn., July 31, 1992; R. W. Carter and Rayo Carter at Anniston, Ala., July 31, 1992. Albert and Clinton Strickland and R.W. and Rayo Carter were from Clay County.

17. [R. F. Duckworth], "Certificate for Military Exemption of Conscientious Objector of Church of Christ," copy in author's possession. Interviews: Elom Harbin at Plainview, Tex., May 21, 1992; J. C. Eager, May 21, 1991; Phil Teague, Dec. 27, 1990.

18. David Lipscomb, *Civil Government: Its Origin, Mission, and Destiny and a Christian's Relation to It* (Nashville, Tenn.: Gospel Advocate, 1889); the book had three reprintings: Nashville: McQuiddy Printing, 1913; Nashville: Gospel Advocate, 1957; and Wesson, Miss.: M. Lynnwood Smith, 1984. None of the men interviewed is politically active or attracted to politics. Often their exposure to Lipscomb's book depended on where they lived, with those from small, isolated rural churches quite unaware of Lipscomb and those with some connection to Christian colleges tending to know about *Civil Government*. Some preachers in the one-cup churches reprinted Lipscomb's book and circulated it among their congregations (interview, J. Ervin Waters at Malibu, Calif., Sept. 13, 1990).

19. Bales to author, Aug. 17, 1990; Bales to Mary Bales, Dec. 29, 1942; Bales to John S. Workman, Aug. 4, 1991; copies in author's possession. I thank Dr. Bales for making copies of these letters available. James D. Bales, *The Christian Conscientious Objector* (Berkeley: the author, [1943]), 211. Interview: James David Hamm at Valdosta, Ga., Aug. 3, 1992.

20. The exception to this was men from small rural churches dominated by local preachers who had limited contact with churches from other areas. Houston Martin of Kinston, Ala., is an example, in addition to the men who came from Clay County, Ala. Also there is a group of one-cup churches near Winston-Salem, N.C., that remain aloof from other one-cup churches. These churches sent several men to CPS (interview, J. Ervin Waters, Sept. 13, 1990).

21. Interview: Winfield Skinner at Athens, Ala., July 30, 1992; L. O. Sanderson, "Preacher Fails to Register," *Gospel Advocate* 84 (Apr. 16, 1942): 363.

22. On COs in the C of C in World War I, see my "New Information" (n. 7). On the Pepperdine students who were COs, sources are interviews: J. P. Sanders at Malibu, Calif., Apr. 25, 1991; and Russel Squire at Palm Springs, Calif., Sep. 7, 1991.

23. Phil Himes, Mar. 25, 1991.

24. Ibid.

25. Ibid.

26. Winfield Skinner, July 30, 1992. Charles Betterton of Atlanta, Ga., and James Roy Copeland and Julian Copeland of Valdosta, Ga., had similar experiences (interviews: Lucile Betterton at Alpharette, Ga., Aug. 2, 1992; James Roy

Copeland at Lake Park, Ga., Aug. 3, 1992; Julian Copeland at Lake Park, Ga., Aug. 3, 1992). Bill Harmon was denied his ministerial deferment by the Wichita Falls, Tex., draft board and forced into CPS (interview: Harmon at Abilene, Tex., July 24, 1991).

27. *Directory of Civilian Public Service* (Washington, D.C.: National Service Board for Religious Objectors, n.d.) and "The Mancos Directory," a mimeographed document listing names of men who served at Mancos and their religious affiliations, including thirty-four Jehovah's Witnesses and thirty-one C of C members. Eight more C of C men can be found on the ex-Mancosites' list of the "Mancos Directory," which does not give church affiliation. I do not know how many Jehovah's Witnesses are on the ex-Mancosite list, so the C of C may have been the second-largest religious tradition at Mancos.

28. Phil Teague, Dec. 27, 1990; Murray W. Wilson, "The Conscientious Objector to Combatant Service," *Firm Foundation,* June 2, 1942, p. 6; B. C. Goodpasture, "Concerning Conscientious Objectors," *Gospel Advocate,* Feb. 5, 1942, p. 124.

29. G. B. Shelburne Jr., "Editorial Comment," *Gospel Tidings,* Nov. 1941, p. 110; L. W. Hayhurst, "News and Notes," *Gospel Tidings,* Jan. 1942, p. 143; Ervin Waters, "Contributions for Conscientious Objectors," *Old Paths Advocate,* Jan. 1, 1943, p. 3.

30. Batsell Moore, "From a Civilian Public Service Camp," *Old Paths Advocate,* July 1, 1942, p. 7. Interviews: Bertram Jack at Friona, Tex., May 23, 1992; Hugh Coleman Boyd at Montgomery, Ala., Aug. 4, 1992; H. C. and Marie Welch at Abilene, Tex., Dec. 30, 1990. Gus Winter, "A Visit to Camp Magnolia," *Gospel Broadcast,* Sept. 13, 1943, p. 485.

31. Phil Teague, Dec. 27, 1990; Hugh Coleman Boyd, Aug. 4, 1992.

32. Interview: Landon Hatley at Nashville, Tenn., July 18, 1991; "Letters," *West Coast Christian,* July 1944, p. 3; interview: Hugh Coleman Boyd at Montgomery, Ala., Aug. 4, 1992; see also G. C. Brewer, "A Correction and a Citation," *Gospel Advocate,* Jan. 25, 1945, pp. 54–55.

33. H. C. and Marie Welch, Dec. 30, 1990.

34. Phil Teague, Dec. 27, 1990.

35. Phil Teague, Batsell Moore, Houston Martin, "The Viewpoint of Some Brethren in C.P.S. Camps," *The Truth,* June 1945, pp. 113–14; and "News and Notes," *Gospel Tidings,* Sept. 1945, p. 94.

36. Hugh Coleman Boyd, Aug. 4, 1992.

37. Ibid.

38. Sibley and Jacob, *Conscription of Conscience,* 249. Interviews: Bertram Jack, May 23, 1992; Clarence Eager at Abilene, Tex., Dec. 20, 1990; Clinton Strickland at Waco, Tex., July 23, 1991.

39. Clarence Eager, Dec. 20, 1990.

40. Bertram Jack, "Reports," *West Coast Evangel,* Feb. 1946, p. 5; Clarence Eager, Dec. 20, 1990; Julian Copeland, Aug. 3, 1992.

41. J. Ervin Waters, interview at Malibu, Cal., Sept. 13, 1990.
42. Glen Stice, May 13, 1991.

6

৵৹

AN UNCERTAIN VOICE FOR PEACE

The Church of God (Anderson) and Pacifism

৵৹

Merle D. Strege

War, said the Church of God paper *The Gospel Trumpet* in 1898, is an activity in which no Christian should participate:

> There is no place in the New Testament wherein Christ gave instruction to his followers to take the life of a fellow-man. In older times it was "an eye for an eye and a tooth for a tooth." "Love your neighbor and hate your enemy."
>
> In this gospel dispensation it is quite different. Jesus says: "But I say unto you, do good to them that despitefully use you," etc.—Matt. 5:44. "Avenge not yourselves." "If thine enemy hunger, feed him; if he thirst, give him drink"—not shoot him.[1]

Such was the *Trumpet*'s position on the eve of the Spanish-American War. Even as war talk escalated, the paper's editorial policy moved to an unpopular position in favor of pacifism. That policy continued during the "splendid little war" and throughout the first decade of the twentieth century. Thus in 1909 the paper printed a testimony that declared: "I should refuse to go to war or obey an officer's command to shoot anyone. We are followers of the 'Prince of Peace' and 'the weapons of our warfare are not carnal.'"[2]

This same attitude toward war predominated during the first years of World War I. Even after the United States entered that war, *The Gospel Trumpet* stated that the "general sentiment" among people of the Church of God movement was averse to the taking of human life in general and to war specifically.[3] Nevertheless, by the time of the armistice, both *The Gospel Trumpet* and the Church of God as a whole clearly had retreated from the paper's announced pacifism. After America had declared war, the paper had stated that although the church deplored the taking of human life, no person would be "un-Christianized" for going into battle. By 1918 the paper rationalized the buying of Liberty Bonds to support the war effort. The most detailed studies of the Church of God's response to war assert that the majority of the church's men rejected the pacifism that *The Gospel Trumpet* had said was the church's general sentiment.[4]

The Church of God (Anderson) appears later to have repented of that retreat from pacifism. During the 1920s and 1930s the church once again repeatedly disavowed war as an instrument of national policy. In 1932 its general ministerial assembly declared, "We will *never again* sanction or participate in any war." In the same resolution the assembly renounced "the whole war system" and stated its intention to withhold financial and moral support from any war.[5] In that same decade the newly organized International Youth Convention of the Church of God repeatedly issued statements disavowing participation in war. Also during the 1930s the Church of God Peace Fellowship was formed through the leadership of F. G. Smith, a former editor of *The Gospel Trumpet*; Adam W. Miller, executive secretary-treasurer of the missionary board; and Russell Olt, dean of Anderson College.

Of course during the 1930s pacifism enjoyed fairly broad support among other American Protestants. Then, after 1939, much of the nation's enthusiasm for pacifism evaporated. In this the Church of God movement closely followed the trend in the larger society. During World War II the percentage of Church of God men who declared themselves to be conscientious objectors was only a fraction larger than that for the population as a whole.[6] In 1941 only twenty Church of God men were in conscientious objector camps. The church's support of these men and of others who joined them during the war years was never very strong. The president of the church's executive council declared: "Our purpose is not to make conscientious objectors of our young men, but rather to give assistance to such as need assistance in obtaining this classification."[7] By 1945 the Church of God was $18,000 in arrears in its financial support of its men serving in Civilian Public Service camps.[8] Meanwhile the church's implicit support of the war effort increased. The Church of God began a military chaplaincy program, and by 1941 thirteen of the church's ministers were serving in it.[9]

In an earlier essay on the topic of pacifism in the Church of God (Anderson), I explored the disparity between published statements by Church of God leaders who supported the pacifist position and the military participation of the majority of men in the church.[10] Despite many strongly worded pacifist statements published in *The Gospel Trumpet* and elsewhere between 1895 and the conclusion of World War I, and despite even more strongly stated antiwar positions taken during the 1930s, a large majority of Church of God draftees (plus some volunteers) entered military service during World War II. The Selective Service System classified the Church of God as a peace church, yet the contrary behavior of so many men raises questions about the accuracy of that designation. I attempted to answer these questions by describing the early pacifism of some Church of God leaders as a well-intentioned but false start in the direction of becoming a peace church. In fact, during World War I some pacifist leaders in the Church of God undermined their own position, apparently by letting wartime propaganda influence them to grant to the state the use of violence.[11] Importantly, pacifist leaders took almost no steps to form the characters of succeeding generations toward nonviolence. Without the narratives of a peace church, I concluded, it is difficult to sustain pacifist commitments in the face of a powerful nationalist ideology. Despite published statements favoring pacifism, the absence of a pacifist narrative rendered ineffective the appeals and exhortations of the Church of God's pacifist leadership.

I now wish to test my earlier judgments in the light of the Church of God movement's response to a more recent episode of American militarism: the Vietnam War. Did the church's early pacifism resurface in the 1960s and 1970s? Did the church's attitude change in the light of a war that lacked the apparent justification of either World War I or II? Were the church's commitments to pacifism as tenuous during the unpopular Vietnam War as they had been during the world wars?

THE THEOLOGICAL AND SOCIAL LOCATION OF THE CHURCH OF GOD (ANDERSON)

Theologically the Church of God movement might fairly be described as a combination of Wesleyan soteriology and Free Church ecclesiology. The church came into being during the heyday of American revivalism, some of its earliest leaders having studied at Oberlin College during Charles G. Finney's tenure there. Rising out of the American Holiness movement in the early 1880s, early Church of God leaders were strongly committed to the doctrine of "entire sanctification," which promises a "second blessing" that frees believers from the power of sin in their daily lives. In fact, however, the movement's doctrine of entire sanctification stands logically subordinate to its doctrine of the church. Early leaders like D. S. Warner or Enoch E. Byrum had left the Churches of God of North America or the Brethren Church, respectively. With them they took a deep commitment to the idea of the church that people enter only through a profession of faith in Christ. In Warner's mind, only a church filled with entirely sanctified believers can be the restoration of the lost unity of the New Testament church. Christ alone rules this church and governs it through the distribution of the gifts of the Holy Spirit. In the true church of God no humanly devised rules or regulations are necessary, nor are they appropriate. Such commitments meant that the Church of God movement's polity would be radically congregational. No ecclesiastical authority would tell congregations how they must live or what they must believe, for as Church of God folk love to sing, "the Bible is our rule of faith, and Christ alone is Lord."

Historically the bulk of the Church of God's constituency has been rural and small-town folk of the American Midwest. With urbanization large African-American congregations developed in the inner parts of large cities, whereas white churches have commonly been located in outlying neighborhoods and the suburbs. Even now the majority of large white congregations are in small cities such as Springfield, Ohio; Wichita, Kansas; and Butler, Pennsylvania. Many other congregations are in small towns and rural areas. Politically the church's strong temperance position aligned it early on with the Republican party. Although some slight evidence suggests that some people in the Church of God movement favored a policy of separation from party politics and of refusing to vote in civic elections, in general Church of God folk have participated in the political process. Most commonly they have been Republicans, whether conservative or moderate.[12]

THE CHURCH OF GOD AND THE VIETNAM WAR

Early in 1960 *The Gospel Trumpet* ran an article entitled "Serving God in the Military Service," written by one Wayne Johnson, an Army retiree.[13] Johnson saw no inherent conflict between Christian discipleship and military service and argued that Christians in the military service encounter no greater difficulties than those "engaged in any other type of occupation."[14] He wished to allay the belief that military service undermined the morals of Christian men and women or corrupted their witness. According to him the military life held no greater temptations than those that Christians might encounter while "working or even while attending a non-Christian college or university."[15] Moreover, military service afforded Christians opportunities for evangelistic witness and lay ministry in the military bases' chapel programs. Johnson assumed that "in our present day and age it is almost certain that our young men will be required to serve a period in one of the branches of the military."[16] At no point did he question the appropriateness of Christians doing such service; apparently he gave no thought to Christian pacifism. His assumptions are one index of erosion of Church of God pacifism in the years following World War II and the Korean War.

Some pacifism still remained as a minority viewpoint within the Church of God, however, as became evident in the considerable response that Johnson's article provoked from *Gospel Trumpet* readers. Some readers expressed gratitude for an editorial policy broad enough to include opposing points of view concerning military service. Others hinted rather darkly that some Anderson College students were in college to escape the draft and that they were not regarded with good will. A few letters supported a pacifist position—the most outspoken being by Robert J. Hazen, pastor of a Church of God congregation in Lansing, Michigan. Hazen identified himself as one of "a very, very small minority in the Church of God who thinks with our Quaker and Friends [*sic*] brethren on the question of peace."[17] He pointedly asked whether the "peace minority" in the Church of God had become so small that military service was no longer controversial in the church.

The Lansing pastor requested permission to rebut Johnson's article. The editor obliged, and Hazen began his *Gospel Trumpet* piece by conceding that the church would be unjust indeed were it to "condemn and unchristianize" its young people who were in military service. After all, he reasoned, they came "from a society that glorifies war, a government that spends billions for armor, and a church that is silent on war and peace."[18] Having himself been a conscientious objector during World War II, Hazen appealed to the Sermon on the Mount and to Jesus' own submission to governmental authority in the Garden of Gethsemane as the basis for Christian pacifism. He challenged the consistency of the argument that makes the tax-paying Christian as responsible for war as is the weapons-bearing soldier.[19] Such were his arguments. At no point did he invoke or even mention the pacifist statements of early Church of God leaders. This notable absence tempts one to infer that the Church of God—at least that part of it with which Robert Hazen was familiar—had been quite silent about its own pacifist history.

While Hazen prepared his rebuttal, in an editorial for March 20, 1960, *Gospel Trumpet* editor Harold L. Phillips followed Johnson's prowar article with comment of his own. For Phillips just as for Johnson, the question of whether young people of the Church of God should enter the military was virtually moot. He estimated that two thousand Church of God men and women were currently in uniform and that thousands more would be so in the future. Phillips concluded with the rhetorical warning: "Let him who thinks he is without 'sin' (not guilty of any involvement in the military aspects of modern society) cast the first stone at the next Church of God boy who feels that the necessity is laid upon him to answer his country's call. Is the man who wears the uniform more 'guilty' than the man who buys it with his taxes?"[20]

Phillips did not have the final word. Hazen's article appeared, and then another by a Church of God minister named Ralph Adamson. Adamson's article took a middle position between Johnson's and Phillips's on the one hand and Hazen's on the other. During the Korean War Adamson had volunteered for duty as a chaplain in the United States Army. Where others saw clear New Testament teaching on the subject of pacifism and conscientious objection, Adamson found very little light. This led him to articulate the position that had become prevalent throughout the Church of God movement. The decision to be a pacifist, a noncombatant member of the military, or a combat soldier was personal, said Adamson, and each individual had to seek God's guidance and direction in the choice. "In each case, the final decision must rest with the individual on his knees before God."[21]

Like Hazen, Adamson made no appeal to historical statements on pacifism by the Church of God. One interested follower of the articles, another pastor by the name of Richard Woodsome, wrote a letter specifically mentioning the absence of church teaching on the subjects of pacifism and alternatives to military service. Woodsome could not "recall any pastoral counseling against military service."[22] The absence of appeal to earlier Church of God teaching and Woodsome's specific statement suggest that few people in the church knew of this earlier tradition or were affected by it. The fact that only ministers took up the defense of *their* pacifism raises the further question of whether, in the Church of God, conscientious objection had become an alternative primarily for men and women who were in, or preparing for, the ministry.

Early in the Vietnam War, then, the Church of God position on pacifism was as ambiguous as ever. The Selective Service System recognized the group as a peace church, while the group's ministers increasingly volunteered for the chaplains' corps. The Peace Fellowship published pamphlets quoting the pacifist statements of earlier generations of Church of God leaders, while large numbers of Church of God youth either enlisted or accepted induction into the military. Although *The Gospel Trumpet* espoused neutrality, its refusal to endorse pacifism had the effect of supporting those in the church who saw little contradiction between Christian discipleship and military service.

In late 1966 public debate on the Vietnam War began in the Church of God. As has been typical of the church, this debate was conducted first in the articles and letters published in the church paper *Vital Christianity* (renamed from *The Gospel Trumpet* in 1962). Subsequently it reached the floor of the church's general assembly.[23] In 1966 *Vital Christianity* published an article entitled "Viet Nam: My View." The article opened a debate. Perhaps predictably, opinion on the war varied widely. Interestingly the opening round of the debate turned on the suitability of war as an instrument of national policy. Those who opposed the war did so out of political conclusions about war and foreign policy; nobody had much to say about a theological commitment to pacifism as the way of Christian discipleship. In other words, the Church of God was conducting its debate in the categories employed in the nation. To enter into a discussion of the suitability of violence for foreign policy is in some sense to beg an important question: the approach determines the discussion's parameters before the debate begins. Church of God people who debated the Vietnam issue did so from the most broadly stated military and political perspectives. Apart from the tiny minority in the Peace Fellowship, they failed to establish a position on Christian pacifism before they entered the debate.

Those in the Church of God opposed to the Vietnam War scored an important victory in 1966 when they secured passage in the church's general assembly of the "Statement of Conviction on War and Peace."[24] In this statement the assembly noted "with deep concern the escalating military involvement and the conscription of our youth for military service. We believe," its statement continued, "that war represents our moral failures. We abhor the causes that lead to war. We stand by the teaching of our Lord who taught us and showed us the way of sacrificial love."[25] Nonetheless the assembly also expressed respect for each individual's right to follow the dictates of his or her own conscience. To those whose consciences called them to military service and to those whose consciences did not, the general assembly pledged equal support. Jesus may have shown his followers the way of sacrificial love, but individual consciences were permitted to decide for themselves whether they would follow him in that way.

An important center of Church of God opposition to the Vietnam War developed at the church's Anderson College after 1967. All through the war years Anderson students were divided in their attitudes. Mock elections on campus in 1968 resulted in students reelecting Richard Nixon over Eugene McCarthy and Robert Kennedy.[26] Nevertheless, editorials in the student newspaper, *The Andersonian,* and letters to the paper's editor spoke out against the war and the draft. Meanwhile, as in the case of opinion expressed in *Vital Christianity,* student debate at Anderson turned on the question of the approval of the particular war. Rarely did it rest on the question of pacifism, and only once was there much reference to early Church of God teaching on the subject.

The first large-scale formal campus discussion of the Vietnam War and the draft occurred in the spring of 1968. *The Andersonian* carried three guest columns that took different points of view on the conflict and on Americans' role in it. One student advocated selective objection to war. He stated his conscientious objection to the Vietnam War and his intention to use every means afforded by the Selective Service System to extend his deferment, which was about to expire. A second writer, a veteran of the war, expressed admiration for conscientious objectors who served as combat medics but disapproved of those who forsook military service altogether. The third writer took the position of the "New Left," as he himself described it, to argue for confronting the entire draft system. He thought the draft law should be opposed because "that law perpetuates the economic and educational inequalities of the youth of this country and implicitly propagates the myth that violence is a just option in seeking solutions to the problems of mankind."[27]

Both writers who opposed the war and the draft took a high moral tone. One of them perceived a moral irony in America's use of means that inevitably led to ends the nation abhorred.[28] In this largest and most closely reasoned student debate on the war to date, however, the writers couched their discussions in the most general of moral language; neither the Bible nor church tradition played any role in their remarks. The absence of any biblical note stands in sharp contrast to Church of God practice in most matters of public debate. The closest that theology came to appearing in any of the essays was one writer's observation that America was not the kingdom of God. Part of the student body at Anderson College strongly opposed the war and the draft, but the early Church of God position favoring pacifism appears to have played little or no role in shaping that opposition or providing its content.

Over the next several years opposition to the Vietnam War continued to grow among Anderson students, as it did among American university students in general and broadly in the nation. In 1969 students at Anderson formed the Student Mobilization Committee against War in Vietnam. The committee's purposes were fourfold: promoting student opposition to the war, encouraging conscientious objection among students, serving as a vehicle for the nonviolent expression of student dissent, and counteracting "all general apathy."[29] Renamed the Anderson Peace Committee, the group received the official endorsement of the college administration as a recognized campus organization. The preamble to the committee's constitution quoted a section of the general assembly's Statement of Conviction on War and Peace and expressly identified the committee's goals with the spirit of sacrificial love. Although the assembly's statement had been passed more than three and a half years earlier, this is the first and only public reference to that document in support of the student protest movement at Anderson College.

Debate over the Vietnam War and the military draft continued in the Church of God until the war began winding down. More voices added their support to those who criticized U.S. involvement in Southeast Asia. In 1970 *Vital Christianity* carried an open letter that endorsed every person's right to follow the dictates of conscience and also pledged its signers' support for those who elected conscientious objection.[30] Opposition to the war increased, but the church remained deeply divided. Moreover, although the number of voices in the opposition may have increased, the character of the debate remained unchanged. The discussion remained centered on questions about the use of violence in national polity, the morality of the Vietnam War specifically, and injustices in the United States spawned by the student protest movement. In other words, the Church of God thought about the Vietnam War and debated it according to the language and conventional wisdom on either side of the debate being conducted in American society as a whole. Little or no evidence exists to suggest that the early pacifist tradition in the Church of God contributed to the church's debate on the Vietnam War. Only the Peace Fellowship of the Church of God attempted to keep that early pacifism alive and give it a voice in the 1960s. Given the paucity of references to that tradition, it seems reasonable to judge that the Peace Fellowship's efforts largely failed.

A TENUOUS PACIFISM

Describing pacifism at an earlier moment in the life of the Church of God (Anderson), I concluded that the church had made a false start at becoming a peace church. Early leaders such as Enoch Byrum and F. G. Smith, along with second-generation leaders such as Adam Miller and Russell Olt, held deep and earnest convictions about pacifism as a necessary expression of the sanctified life of a Christian disciple. Their commitments were shared by others, and the early published statements of this committed minority in *The Gospel Trumpet* made their position appear to be the one generally held by the church at large. In the absence of formal creeds or binding doctrinal summaries, the paper served as the church's teaching authority. The fact that statements supporting pacifism appeared in the paper serves to strengthen an impression that these were generally held convictions within the Church of God movement. However, nonpacifist opinions expressed in *The Gospel Trumpet* during both World Wars, plus the military service of a large majority of Church of God men, belie that impression. Very few Church of God young people chose to become conscientious objectors in either of the two world wars, and there is reason to believe that among those who did, the large majority were either clergy or ministerial students. The pacifist tradition of the Church of God appears to have had little impact on the lives of laypeople during those wars.

It may be argued that pacifism's low degree of commitment in the Church of God was due to the enormous pressure of wartime propaganda, especially in World War I. In addition many pacifists of the 1930s reversed their commitments after the attack on Pearl Harbor. Nevertheless we are entitled to ask whether Mennonites, Brethren, or Friends succumbed to nationalism in World War I or the 1940s, and if they did not, what accounts for the difference between their behavior and that of men in the Church of God movement? It has also been observed that the Church of God's social location placed it among the segment of the American population most likely to have supported the Nixon administration's policy in Southeast Asia. Therefore the suggestion follows that the church's social location predisposed it to attitudes unsympathetic toward pacifism. But we are entitled to ask why similar social locations of Mennonites, Brethren, and Friends did not have a similar effect. That they did not compels us to look elsewhere for explanations of the Church of God's tenuous commitment to pacifism.

Even during the unpopular Vietnam War the Church of God's voice in support of pacifism and conscientious objection was uncertain. It could do no better than endorse the private judgments of both those whose consciences led them into battle and those who took the path of nonviolence. Moreover, such pacifist commitments as had once existed in the early decades of the Church of God played only an insignificant role in the thought of those who did oppose the Vietnam War. Opponents of the war couched their opposition in the language of the debate then raging in American society at large.

How are we to understand such a tenuous commitment to pacifism? Part of our answer to this question must be sought in the church's pietistic, Wesleyan, subjectivist individualism. Without creed or a judicatory to enforce it, the Church of God had no means or instrument for effective church discipline on ethical matters. A radically congregationalist polity coupled with an abiding respect for the individual's right to decide according to the dictates of his or her own conscience could lead only to divided opinion on pacifism, a subject on which Christians have often been divided.

Beyond matters of polity and respect for individual consciences, there remains the simple but important fact that, despite the deep commitment and influential voices of its minority of pacifist leaders, the Church of God (Anderson) simply has not carried on much discussion of pacifism. In this it seems to have followed the lead of the society of which it is a part. The discussions of pacifism and conscientious objection that surfaced in 1960 illustrate the point. Without a strong tradition of pacifism, the church could discuss it only in an uncertain voice, leaving its men and women to decide the matter for themselves.

NOTES

1. "Should We Go to War?" *The Gospel Trumpet,* Apr. 14, 1898, p. 4.

2. *The Gospel Trumpet,* Apr. 1, 1909, p. 4.

3. "Our Attitude toward War," *The Gospel Trumpet,* Apr. 26, 1917, p. 12.

4. Mitchell K. Hall, "A Withdrawal from Peace: The Historical Response to War of the Church of God (Anderson, Indiana)," *Journal of Church and State* 27, no. 2 (1985): 305.

5. Minutes of the General Ministerial Assembly of the Church of God, June 23, 1932.

6. Hall, "A Withdrawal from Peace," 308 n. 26.

7. Minutes, Executive Council of the Church of God, Jan. 6, 1941.

8. Ibid., June 13, 1945.

9. Ibid., 309.

10. Merle D. Strege, "The Demise (?) of a Peace Church: The Church of God (Anderson), Pacifism and Civil Religion," *The Mennonite Quarterly Review* 65, no. 2 (Apr. 1991): 128–40.

11. Of course some Christian pacifists have granted that God's permissive ethic for the kingdoms of the world, where governments must keep order among the unregenerate, allows governments to use "the sword," that is, legal, responsible, controlled violence. Such pacifists have seen pacifism as a higher ethic only for the regenerate, in the church, whose people are to live by the higher ethic of the kingdom of God—plus perhaps as an ethic against which to measure governments' behavior prophetically, calling governments to relatively more pacifism and relatively less violence in particular situations.

12. The Church of God traditionally has taken a strong position in favor of temperance. In the early twentieth century this position made Church of God folk the natural political allies of prohibitionist Republicans. A 1981 survey of the readership of *Vital Christianity* reported that 45 percent of Church of God retirees considered themselves politically conservative and another 42 percent, moderate; among pastors the figures were 69 percent conservative and 28 percent moderate; among working people the figures were 44 percent conservative and 46 percent moderate. Interestingly the same survey reported that the constituency of the Church of God equally *distrusted* Senator Edward Kennedy and television preacher Jerry Falwell (*Vital Christianity* Market Research Study Final Report, Mar. 10, 1981).

13. Wayne Johnson, "Serving God in the Military Service," *The Gospel Trumpet*, Feb. 14, 1960, pp. 9–10.

14. Ibid., 9.

15. Ibid.; apparently Johnson had an unusually high opinion of church-related colleges.

16. Ibid.

17. Robert J. Hazen, letter to the editor, *The Gospel Trumpet*, Mar. 20, 1960, p. 16.

18. Robert Hazen, "Should a Christian Bear Armor?" *The Gospel Trumpet*, July 3, 1960, p. 7.

19. "We pledge our allegiance to the government, the government licenses the sale of liquor, and we insist that we believe and practice total abstinence. The government levies taxes, builds for war and declares war. Let's be consistent and believe in personal abstinence from breaking the Sixth Commandment, "Thou shalt not kill" (ibid., 8).

20. Harold Phillips, "Should a Christian Bear Armor?" *The Gospel Trumpet*, March 20, 1960, p. 3.

21. Ralph F. Adamson, "I Was a Conscientious Objector," *The Gospel Trumpet,* July 31, 1960, p. 7.

22. Richard Woodsome, letter to the editor, *The Gospel Trumpet,* Aug. 7, 1960, p. 16. Woodsome quoted an entry from his diary, dated March 8, 1951: "I cannot dare to express my feeling of terror when I am taught whom to kill and whom not to kill; what to destroy and what not to destroy. This is not a Christian conflict, neither is it a war to protect the standards and freedoms of a Christian society. Can the way of Christ be protected by persons who are not of him, and by methods which he opposes, and on principles that are neither fundamentally or practically Christian?"

23. Mitchell Hall has written a fine survey of the Church of God's response to the Vietnam War; see "A Time for War: The Church of God's Response to Vietnam," *Indiana Magazine of History* 79, no. 4 (Dec. 1983): 285–304.

24. The statement first appeared in the *1967 Yearbook of the Church of God* and then in each subsequent volume through 1973. It has not been published in any volume since, and the *Yearbook* gave no reason for its disappearance.

25. *1967 Yearbook of the Church of God* (Anderson, Ind.: Executive Council of the Church of God, 1967), 151.

26. Hall, "A Time for War," 296.

27. Tony Wolfe, "Modern Issues Forum," *The Andersonian,* Mar. 22, 1968, p. 5.

28. Ibid.

29. *The Andersonian,* Sep. 26, 1969, p. 2.

30. Letter to the editor, *Vital Christianity,* Aug. 9, 1970, p. 22.

7

꒰

TESTING THE METAL OF PACIFISM

A Response to Michael W. Casey and Merle D. Strege

꒰

C. Leonard Allen

Michael Casey's account of conscientious objectors from the Churches of Christ in World War II and Merle Strege's retelling of pacifism in the Church of God (Anderson) are both narrow but important stories. The stories are valuable as significant pieces of historical recovery, and I found them to be enormously interesting in and of themselves. They are like short scenes in a long and intricately plotted drama, however, and we have walked in near the end of the drama. We find the scenes to be interesting, tantalizing, and perhaps even captivating—but also cryptic and puzzling. The drama calls for context, linkage, and interpretation, some of which I will try to give.

I have considerably more acquaintance with the story of the Churches of Christ than with that of the Church of God (Anderson). It seems to me, however, that both stories are of a similar genre, so that it is helpful to discuss the two of them together. The two groups have held much in common: strong restorationist appeals, strict congregational polity, a passionate concern for Christian unity, and a steady polemic against the evils of "sectarianism."

The Churches of Christ found their identity in Alexander Campbell's claim to have restored "the ancient gospel and order of things," an order long lost amid the "trash" of human tradition. They rejected the authority of all creeds and the elaborate vocabulary of traditional theology and sought to confine themselves to the "plain declarations recorded in the

Bible." The original New Testament pattern for the church, they believed, was clear and simple; and by putting aside all human inventions and additions, all believers could embrace that simple pattern and unite, thus eradicating the rancor and scandal of sectarian divisions.[1]

The Church of God (Anderson), which emerged out of the late nineteenth-century Holiness revivals, made similar claims. For example, an early twentieth-century leader claimed that in contrast to other nineteenth-century renewal movements, this movement was "a reformation which takes in full the [New Testament] characteristics defining the church in her wholeness." Thus, he said, the Church of God represented the "final reformation resulting in the restoration of all things to the Scriptural ideal." He reasoned that this was true because, unlike other restoration movements, the one behind the Church of God "recognizes the rule of the Holy Spirit in the organization and government of the church." Its only test of fellowship, he claimed, was "true Christianity possessed within the heart." Its platform was thus both as narrow and as broad as the New Testament.[2]

In 1922 another Church of God leader condemned all "human ecclesiasticism" and claimed that the Church of God movement "makes no demands except those made in the gospel; it lays down no rules that are not necessarily binding upon all Christians; it makes no requirements that God does not make." To him, those facts made the Church of God "fundamentally distinct from all sectarian institutions." The fundamental goal of the movement was to unify believers by abandoning "sectarianism" and depending on the work of the Holy Spirit. "The Apostolic Our Only Standard" became the rallying cry.[3]

Such restorationist groups of the nineteenth century arose out of a profound disenchantment with denominational divisions, bickering, and contamination of the biblical message with human doctrines. Sometimes that disenchantment found striking expression. Alexander Campbell could write, for example, that "on the subject of religion I am fully persuaded that nothing but the inspired scriptures ought ever to have been published." Regarding the Bible, he said, one must strive to read it "as if it had dropped from heaven into his hands alone."[4]

Much American Protestantism in the nineteenth century was marked by this kind of brash dismissal of tradition, but this spirit took a particularly virulent form in the collective mind of the Churches of Christ—a mind-set that persists, in many quarters, down to the present day. This has not only meant that the Churches of Christ simply discounted eighteen centuries of Christianity as at worst a diseased tumor or at best an instructive failure; it also has meant that they tended to dismiss even their own history as irrelevant. After all, they claimed to be New Testament Christians, nothing more and nothing less; attention to the past or the recognition of a tradition might well serve to distract them from their true calling.

The Churches of Christ of course developed their own strong—albeit clandestine—tradition. Because theirs was an antitradition tradition, however, and therefore mostly unrecognized and unadmitted, it could not provide a forthright and explicit resource for resisting cultural encroachment and erosion. For example, influential leaders such as Alexander Campbell and David Lipscomb advocated pacifism, but they could neither draw persuasively on the long tradition of the peace churches nor establish an enduring pacifist tradition of their own. In other words, the Churches of Christ could not perpetuate the strong narratives necessary to maintain the sharply countercultural pacifist stance. Campbell and Lipscomb both exercised considerable influence with their pacifist views, but Campbell's position was derailed by the Civil War, and (as Casey's story shows) Lipscomb's barely survived World War I.

Strege's story of the Church of God suggests a similar dynamic. The Church of God, like the Churches of Christ, was profoundly restorationist, and both groups suffered the lack of history that has tended to beset American-born restorationist groups. As a result both groups have been unable to sustain the necessary moral tradition in the face of growth, prosperity, and the relentless pressure to accommodate with American civic ideals.

This trait, I think, provides one important clue to the fate of pacifism in these two movements. But there seem to be other, even more significant clues at which these two essays barely hint. I share Strege's sense that we must look beyond such social factors as the pressures of wartime propaganda and the influence of social location. These factors test the metal of all pacifist groups, staining and corroding that metal to varying degrees. What interests me, however, is not so much the corrosive acids as the metal itself. Of what is the group made? What is the theological metal that embodies its shape and substance? What are the ingredients of the alloy in the casings? Where are the hidden fault lines?

In other words, what was the theological substance that allowed an explicit pacifism to be erected but that provided it such unsteady grounding among the Churches of Christ and the Church of God (Anderson)? Why, as Casey has suggested, was there only a small and obscure remnant of full-fledged conscientious objectors among Churches of Christ by 1940? And why, as Strege has argued, did so few Church of God young people conscientiously refuse military service during America's three twentieth-century wars?

There seem to have been two especially crucial elements in the theological metal. Each group, the Churches of Christ and the Church of God (Anderson), was marked—each in a somewhat different way—by (1) a narrowed and privatized ethic or understanding of Christian discipleship in the world and (2) an eschatology that was inadequate to sustain an enduring pacifism.

First, each group reflects a narrowed and privatized understanding of Christian discipleship. For the Churches of Christ, we must begin with Alexander Campbell. For Campbell, restoring the true church basically meant getting the original Christian ordinances back in place and fine-tuning the "ancient order of things." The movement thus rested on a scientifically precise, Baconian reconstruction of the New Testament church more than on the nature and demands of discipleship. For Alexander Campbell and many of his disciples, the marks of the true church were primarily doctrinal and formal, not ethical and communal.[5] They held up a precise New Testament blueprint or model for structuring the church, not a vision of a radically transformed kingdom community. They proclaimed believers' baptism by immersion as a formal ordinance required for salvation and church membership—not as a symbol of entry into a community formed by trust in and radical obedience to a Christ who walked the way of the cross yet triumphed mightily over all the principalities and powers.

Campbell thought that baptism should be followed by the "Christian life" and growth in grace, but he did not see the life of discipleship as particularly odd. After all, he and his followers were living in an especially propitious time, a blessed time when a democratic, Protestant-dominated, providentially prepared nation stood poised to usher in the great millennial age. Discipleship thus remained a somewhat tame and culturally acceptable proposition, not a path especially marked by oddness or dislocation—and certainly not a path of persecution. In response to a preacher who in 1859 insisted that Christians must "take up their crosses and bear them" after Christ, Alexander Campbell wrote: "There is now no cross under our [American] government. In other words there is no persecution in our country. . . . Hence no man in the United States has to carry a cross for Christ's sake."[6]

Such pronouncements strongly suggest that Alexander Campbell failed to see the extraordinary nature of Jesus' ethic or the fuller significance of the confession that Jesus, not Caesar—that Jesus, not American democratic institutions—is Lord. Throughout much of his career Campbell could mount strong defenses of pacifism based on the Sermon on the Mount, but his accommodationist ethic kept that pacifism flaccid. As long as the gospel and Anglo-Saxon culture formed such a happy marriage, as long as the postmillennial march of freedom, peace, and prosperity continued, opposition to all war made sense. Indeed, violence seemed almost impossible under the exhilarating march of progress. The U.S. Civil War dashed such postmillennial hopes, however, and dashed them most rudely, so that the pacifism aligned with such hopes receded. It seems that few if any draft-age Disciples of Christ registered as conscientious objectors to avoid serving in the Union army. Alexander Campbell's oldest son served in the Confederate cavalry. Among the northern Disciples of Christ, where Alexander Campbell's influence was greatest, pacifism virtually disappeared—so much so that Disciple of Christ peace activist Kirby Page could confess that he had never come across "an informed and determined pacifist" before 1914.[7] Behind this development, I suggest, was a narrow and privatized ethic, an ethic that lacked any adequate christological and ecclesiological grounding.

Apparently the Church of God (Anderson) was also marked by an overly privatized ethic, but for a quite different reason. This restoration movement, quite unlike Campbell's, focused on the work of the Holy Spirit in sanctifying the believer and in drawing believers together in unity. As Strege points out, the church has been characterized by a "pietistic, Wesleyan, subjectivist individualism." Here one could easily come to dwell in the inner temple of experience. The church did not give much emphasis to an idea of a visible, disciplined community confessing Christ's lordship over all things in a way that would demand following him in a politically charged way of the cross. In the inner temple the Christian may seek the private sweetness of the Spirit's caresses rather than the public buffetings of Christ's odd way. One may well claim that the Spirit's sanctifying work brings purity of life and "empowerment for service," but that life and that service may easily be defined in narrow and individualistic ways. The pacifist commitment, whatever its private springs, is a public and usually an odd commitment, especially in times of war fever. From Strege's data, it seems that the strong pacifist rhetoric in the early days of the Church of God (Anderson) flew in the face of the movement's strong, pietistic individualism. Consequently, among the rank and file, pacifism simply did not take hold.

The second (and closely related) problem in the theological metal of these two restorationist groups is the inadequacy of its eschatology. The Christian ethic is grounded in a bold eschatological claim—the claim that in Jesus' death and resurrection the "powers" of this present age have been disarmed and defeated. The claim is that God's kingdom has broken into history and that for the believer, it has brought an end to all other kingdoms. In Jesus' victory and in this new kingdom the believer sees the end of history and knows how history will turn out. While the worldly powers seem to rage, the believer knows that they are doomed—finished. Knowing this, the disciple can follow Jesus in all things, even in those things that seem to be utterly impractical and unworkable to those who do not know what Christians know. The Christian way of nonresistance and nonviolence is grounded in just such an eschatological claim.

From an admittedly sparse reading of early theological writings among the Church of God (Anderson), I did not see much evidence that this kind of eschatological claim functioned as a basis for Christian social ethics. Writers showed a strong aversion to premillennial eschatology, with its emphasis on a literal earthly kingdom, but what they put in its place was a highly spiritualized kingdom—a kingdom equated with personal and private salvation from sin. It seems to me that the Church of God (Anderson) may have lacked an eschatology able to sustain a wide pacifist conviction.

The Churches of Christ in the nineteenth century showed a similar tendency. They tended increasingly to identify the kingdom of God with the precisely restored church as Alexander Campbell had defined it. *Church* and *kingdom* became virtually synonymous terms. As this happened, the kingdom lost its eschatological tension. It became an institution fully present in the restored church, not an expansive, eschatological reality only partially realized in the church. As a result the sense of conversion as inauguration into an eschatological community diminished. The call to a radically transformed, eschatological lifestyle easily became an admonition to "be good" as defined by conventional, civic morality. That ethic fit nicely with the cultural status quo.

Given this, it is not surprising that the most robust pacifism among the Churches of Christ arose from the influence of David Lipscomb of Nashville, Tennessee. Although deeply shaped by Alexander Campbell's theology, Lipscomb held a very different eschatology. He believed that all human government represented the rebellion of humankind against God's sovereign rule and the transferring of allegiance to the kingdom of Satan. As a result of this rebellion against God's government, the earth, which was once a paradise, became "a dried and parched wilderness" where sin and suffering permeated everything. Under human governments, it became a place of "confusion, strife, bloodshed, and perpetual warfare."[8]

Christ came, Lipscomb said, to rescue this world and to restore it to its "primitive and pristine allegiance to God." Christ mightily engaged Satan's rule and succeeded in reestablishing God's kingdom. This kingdom in its present churchly form is not the "everlasting kingdom," however, but rather the kingdom in "a lower state of growth and development."[9]

But the time will come, Lipscomb believed, when Christ will "put down all rule, and all authority and all power." Through Christ, God's kingdom "shall break in pieces and consume all the kingdoms of earthly origin." Then Christ will deliver up the kingdom to the Father, and God will rule "in and through his restored kingdom on earth." When that occurs, Lipscomb stressed, peace will reign: "the will of God will be done on earth as it is in heaven, and all things in the world will be restored to harmonious relations with God."[10]

For Lipscomb, God's kingdom remained a transcendent reality that alone should claim Christians' allegiance. Because Christians are citizens of that kingdom, they should place little hope in human governments, with all their might and force. God's kingdom, he believed, is a kingdom of peace and can never be shaken—indeed, it will one day fill the whole earth.

As Mike Casey and Richard Hughes have shown in recent articles, pacifist views like those of David Lipscomb remained fairly strong among southern Churches of Christ until World War I.[11] With that war, however, Churches of Christ increasingly cast off pacifism and rejected its call for radical discipleship. They usually replaced their earlier views with a rigid form of Campbell's biblical patternism and an exclusivism that more and more identified the Churches of Christ as the one true restored kingdom of God. By the time of World War II, David Lipscomb's strict pacifism was almost forgotten. The 200 conscientious objectors whom Casey studied were among a small remnant who remembered.

Among both the Churches of Christ and the Church of God (Anderson) the theological metal was tested by the acids of culture. That metal gave way not because the acids were new and more potent but rather because the alloy itself was missing some necessary ingredients.

NOTES

1. See Alexander Campbell's long series "A Restoration of the Ancient Order of Things," beginning in the *Christian Baptist* 2 (Feb. 1825).

2. Andrew L. Byers, *Birth of a Reformation* (1921), excerpted in Callen, ed., *A Time to Remember: Teachings,* Church of God Heritage Series (Anderson, Ind.: Warner, 1978), 76, 77.

3. Albert Gray, "A Universal Posture," *The Gospel Trumpet,* Feb. 23, 1922, excerpted in Callen, *Time to Remember,* 79.

4. Alexander Campbell, "Prefatory Remarks," *Christian Baptist* 4 (Aug. 7, 1826): 3; *Millennial Harbinger Extra* 3 (Aug. 6, 1832): 343.

5. Campbell could write that the "distinguishing characteristic [of the current reformation] is, A RESTORATION OF THE ORDINANCES OF THE NEW INSTITUTION TO THEIR PLACE AND POWER" ("The Ordinances," *Millennial Harbinger,* new ser., 7 [Jan. 1843]: 9).

6. Alexander Campbell, "Opinionisms—No. 1," *Millennial Harbinger,* 5th ser., 2 (Aug. 1859): 436–37.

7. Cited by Peter Brock, *Freedom from War: Nonsectarian Pacifism, 1814–1914* (Toronto: University of Toronto, 1991), 151–52.

8. David Lipscomb, "The Ruin and Redemption of the World," in *Salvation from Sin* (Nashville: Gospel Advocate, 1950 [1913]), 109–28.

9. David Lipscomb, *Civil Government: Its Origin, Mission, and Destiny and the Christian's Relation to It* (Nashville: McQuiddy, 1889), 44–93; Lipscomb, "The Kingdom of God," *Gospel Advocate* 45 (May 21, 1903): 328.

10. Lipscomb, "Kingdom of God," 328.

11. Michael W. Casey, "From Pacifism to Patriotism: The Emergence of Civil Religion in the Churches of Christ during World War I," *The Mennonite Quarterly Review* 66 (July 1992): 376–90; Richard T. Hughes, "The Apocalyptic Origins of the Churches of Christ and the Triumph of Modernism," *Religion and American Culture* 2 (Summer 1992): 181–214.

PART 3

MORMONISM, ADVENTISM

8

꙳

PACIFISM AND MORMONISM

A Study in Ambiguity

꙳

Grant Underwood

A famous verse of Mormon scripture exclaims "renounce war and pro-claim peace."[1] That this seemingly pacifist injunction is embedded in a revelation explaining the conditions under which defensive war is per-missible suggests the complexity of the Mormon experience with paci-fism. Pacifism, of course, is many things to many people. For some, fol-lowing the "Lamb of God" demands not only total abstinence from the use of force under any conditions but also separation from people and societies that do use it. At the other end of the spectrum are those, some-times calling themselves "pacifists," who decry any war of aggression but yet condone genuinely defensive wars conducted along "Christian prin-ciples." Mormons—and here I am referring to members of the Church of Jesus Christ of Latter-day Saints (LDS)[2]—tend to be located toward the latter position, although with a history of declarations from points all along the spectrum.

As will be seen, a major theme in the history of LDS attitudes toward peace is that the outer limits of pacifist expression have usually been drawn at the point where pacifism clashes with legal and civic duty. To the degree that pacifism commits Mormons to loving their personal enemies, returning good for evil, praying for antagonists, turning the other cheek, and seeking peaceful solutions to interpersonal problems, LDS preaching has been consistently pacifist. Early on, however, Mor-mons affirmed their allegiance to civil authorities. In words that would become canonized as an LDS Article of Faith, they declared their belief "in being subject to kings, presidents, rulers, and magistrates, in obeying, honoring, and sustaining the law."[3] Particularly in the twentieth century this came to mean that when a president declares war, obedience to civil authority takes precedence over pacifism, and Mormons will support the call to arms. Another fascinating aspect of the Mormon attitude toward pacifism is the way in which ideas expressed in the group's semitheocratic circumstances of the nineteenth century came to be understood and applied in the pluralist twentieth century.

Any discussion of Mormon attitudes and ideals must begin with the Prophet Joseph Smith himself. Clearly he called for personal or private pacifism: "wise men ought to have understanding enough to conquer men with kindness . . . and it will be greatly to the credit of the Latter-day Saints to show the love of God, by now kindly treating those who may have, in an unconscious moment, done wrong; for truly said Jesus, Pray for thine enemies. Humanity towards all, reason and refinement to enforce virtue, and good for evil are so eminently designed to cure more disorders of society than an appeal to arms, or even argument untempered with friendship."[4] The Prophet, of course, tried to practice what he preached. After one of many episodes of legal harassment, he told his friends, "I have had the privilege of rewarding them good for evil. They took me unlawfully, treated me rigorously, strove to deprive me of my rights, and would have run with me into Missouri to have been murdered, if Providence had not interposed. But now they are in my hands; and I have taken them into my house, set them at the head of my table, and placed before them the best which my house afforded."[5]

Smith, however, drew the pacifist line where life, liberty, or limb was at stake. The same Joseph Smith who taught long-suffering and love is also credited with declaring, after the Mormons had suffered repeated depredations at the hands of mobs, "I call God and angels to witness that I have unsheathed my sword with a firm and unalterable determination that this people shall have their legal rights, and be protected from mob violence, or my blood shall be spilt upon the ground like water, and my body consigned to the silent tomb. While I live, I will never tamely submit to the dominion of cursed mobocracy. I would welcome death rather than submit to this oppression . . . any longer."[6]

Part of the explanation for this change in rhetoric lies in a revelation that was received early in the church's history and has continued to be important for Mormons to the present day. The missive offered a sort of midrash on biblical teachings regarding war and peace by discussing the law on which "all mine ancient prophets and apostles" supposedly operated. It was that "if any nation . . . should proclaim war against them, they should first lift a standard of peace unto that people . . . and if that people did not accept the offering of peace, neither the second nor the third time, they should bring these testimonies before the Lord. Then I, the Lord, would give unto them a commandment, and justify them in going out to battle against that nation, tongue, or people." Despite the broadening phrase, "behold, this is an ensample unto all people, saith the Lord your God, for justification before me," the revelation presumed a people theocratically situated.[7] Nineteenth-century Mormons, who saw themselves as modern Israel, a separate "people," almost a nation within a nation, felt these verses were directly applicable to themselves. The national scene, of course, was another matter. Andrew Jackson and other presidents of the United States had little intention of bringing peace proclamation "testimonies before the Lord" or of waiting until they received "a commandment from God" to engage in war.

Toward the end of Joseph Smith's life, after years of trying to avert violence in the spirit of this revelation, the Prophet declared:

If Missouri will not stay her cruel hand in her unhallowed persecutions against us, I this day turn the key that opens the heavens to restrain you no longer from this time forth. I will lead you to the battle; and if you are not afraid to die, and feel disposed to spill your blood in your own defense, you will not offend me . . . bear untill they strike you on the one cheek; then offer the other, and they will be sure to strike that; then defend yourselves, and God will bear you off, and you shall stand forth clear before his tribunal.[8]

As Joseph summarized it, "the time has come when forbearance is no longer a virtue."[9]

The city council in Mormon Nauvoo agreed:

We have done good for evil long enough, in all conscience. We think that we have fulfilled the Scriptures every whit. They have smitten us on the one cheek, and we have turned the other, and they have smitten that also. We have also fulfilled the law, and more than fulfilled it. And for sake of peace, when we knew that we had violated no law, nor in anywise subjected ourselves to persecutions, we have endured the wrong patiently, without offering violence or in anywise injuring those heartless wretches. . . . The time, however, is now gone by for this mode of proceeding, and those vagabonds must keep within their own borders and let peace-able citizens alone, or receive the due merit of their crimes.[10]

As a Mormon apostle summarized it later in the century, "We delight not in the shedding of blood"; "we are for peace, but we intend to have it, if we have to fight for it."[11]

Such attitudes were reinforced by the degree to which the Mormons continued to find the Hebrew Scriptures central to their self-image, ty-pologically and theologically. As modern Israel, they expected their ex-perience to parallel that of ancient Israel. "If oppression comes," pro-claimed Joseph Smith, "I will then shew them that there is a Moses and a Joshua amongst us."[12] The effort to rear a temple in Nauvoo remind-ed them of what had happened in Nehemiah's day. "We want to build the Temple in this place," they declared, "if we have to build it as the Jews built the walls of the Temple in Jerusalem, with a sword in one hand and the trowel in the other."[13] Their close identification with Israel reinforced the acceptability of war under certain conditions.

Occasionally brandishing with the theocratic rhetoric of the Old Testament led to the Mormons' being misrepresented as advocates of "holy war." Far from ever declaring a *jihad,* however, the Mormon *Mil-lennial Star* editorialized: "We wish it distinctly understood that the in-terpretation given . . . as to the Latter-Day Saints drawing the sword against others who may differ from them in religious belief is without shadow of truth, being contrary to the whole spirit of the Christian re-ligion, which they (the Saints) profess. . . . The Latter-Day Saints never did draw the sword except in defence of their lives and the institutions and laws of their country, and they never will."[14] Moreover, Mormons recognized that they lived in a secular world and needed, whenever possible, to work within the country's legal system. In an important early statement entitled "Of Governments and Laws in General" and later canonized, LDS leaders wrote, "We believe that men should appeal to the civil law for redress of all wrongs and grievances, where personal abuse is inflicted or the right of property or character infringed, where such laws exist as will protect the same; but we believe that all men are justified in defending themselves, their friends, and property, and the government, from the unlawful assaults and encroachments of all per-sons in times of exigency, where immediate appeal cannot be made to the laws, and relief afforded."[15]

Arms were to be a last resort in preserving peace. Even examples of total nonresistance can be found in LDS scripture. The Book of Mormon tells of a group who "took their swords, and all the weapons which were used for the shedding of man's blood, and they did bury them up deep in the earth." When attacked "they would lie down and perish, and praised God even in the very act of perishing under the sword."[16] This so impressed the attackers that over a thousand converted to Christ. Latter-day Saints themselves, however, never invoked this strategy in the nineteenth century, perhaps because the normative Mormon position was elsewhere expressed as: "Inasmuch as ye are not guilty of the first offense, neither the second, ye shall not suffer yourselves to be slain by the hands of your enemies. And again, the Lord has said that: Ye shall defend your families even unto bloodshed."[17] Still, in the second half of the twentieth century conscientious objection became more common among Latter-day Saints, especially during the Vietnam War. When it did, some young Mormons sought legitimation for their positions in the nonresistance of these Book of Mormon pacifists.[18]

Following the death of the Prophet Joseph Smith, Mormons continued to face persecution and harassment and continued to affirm both the need for personal pacifism and their right to defend themselves, if necessary. They also had to face a situation that had not existed during Smith's lifetime. What would they do when the United States officially declared war? Their early responses can be characterized as cool at best. The "civic duty" argument did surface on these occasions, but in the case of the "Mormon Battalion" raised to assist in the Mexican War, the Latter-day Saints, who were in the midst of their exodus to Utah, were motivated more by the prospect of receiving the much-needed financial boost that army pay would provide than by their support of governmental war aims.

As for the Civil War, the Mormons simply refused to get involved. Coming as it did on the heels of the "invasion" of Utah by the U.S. Army under General A. Sidney Johnston, the Civil War seemed to Mormons like God's promised vengeance on their wicked persecutors. This was not *their* war. They had "come out" of "Babylon," and it was ripe for destruction. Brigham Young also spoke favorably about those non-Mormons "who are peaceably disposed" and who came west to escape service in the Civil War. Said he, "I think they are probably as good a class of men as has ever passed through this country; they are persons who wish to live in peace. . . . As far as I am concerned I have no fault to find with them."[19] In the years following the Civil War a Republican-dominated Congress sought to crush the Mormon theocracy in the West just as it had the slavocracy in the South. Had there been any wars during those

years, it is doubtful either that the U.S. government would have requested Mormon troops or that the Latter-day Saints would have been willing to respond.

This history provides helpful background for understanding the
seemingly contradictory expressions of church leaders. Brigham Young
sounds very pacifist in the following statement regarding international
conflict: "[American] traditions have been such that we are not apt to
look upon war between two nations as murder; but suppose that one
family should rise up against another and begin to slay them, would they
not be taken up and tried for murder? Then why not nations that rise
up and slay each other in a scientific way be equally guilty of murder?"[20]
On the other hand, he took a wholly different attitude when it came to
religious wars in which God's people stood in need of defense. He explicitly rejected nonresistance, asking, "What ground have we to hope
this [will work]? Have I any good reason to say to my Father in Heav-
en, 'Fight my battles,' when he has given me the sword to wield, the arm
and the brain that I can fight for myself? Can I ask him to fight my battles and sit quietly down waiting for him to do so? I cannot. . . . To ask
God to do for me that which I can do for myself is preposterous to my
mind."[21] For the Mormons, there was a significant difference between
taking up the sword under God's direction to protect family and faith
in the group's mountain retreat and participating in some erstwhile-
persecuting potentate's bloody pursuit of power or prestige.

All this began to change in the 1890s, however. With its citizens dis-
franchised, its property escheated, and itself on the verge of dissolution
as a legal entity, the Mormon church realized that to stay alive it would
have to surrender some of its cherished ideals and institutions, including a theocratic orientation. In exchange it hoped to regain its rights and
properties and eventually to gain statehood. This occurred in 1896. Two
years later, when the United States commenced a war with Spain, the
Mormons were compelled to approach the matter of war and peace as
part of the nation rather than as a semiautonomous people.

George Q. Cannon of the First Presidency helped to make the transition by applying item 98 of the LDS *Doctrine and Covenants* (D&C)
canon to national politics. "The Lord says we should lift up a standard
of peace. . . . That is the duty of this nation. That is the duty of the Latter-day Saints. . . . We must proclaim peace; do all in our power to ap-
pease the wrath of our enemies; make any sacrifice that honorable people can to avert war. . . . It is our duty, I say, as a nation." Cannon
admitted that "it is scarcely to be expected" that the U.S. government

would follow D&C 98 and bear testimony of their peace proposals to God or await his direction to engage in battle, but he did encourage the Latter-day Saints to use their "influence for this purpose." "Our prayers," he declared, "should ascend to God; our petitions should ascend to the government of our nation to do everything that honorable people can to avert war."[22] Realizing this might sound too pacifistic for some, Cannon explained, "One man may say, 'is it not our duty to defend our country and our flag?'. . . Certainly it is," he responded. But, he reminded LDS members, "it is no part of cowardice to take the plan that the Lord has pointed." In this situation, "if war should come, it will no doubt come because of the determination of Spain to force it upon us." In that case, "let us do the best we can under the circumstances."[23]

War did come, although many did not see it as "forced" on the United States. Nonetheless, the Mormon response was that "war has been declared, and we have to meet it," as the First Presidency declared. "Our citizens are called upon to enlist, and Utah is asked to furnish cavalry and batteries of artillery approximating 500 men. We trust that the citizens of Utah who are Latter-day Saints will be found ready to respond with alacrity to this call which is made upon our state."[24] As one historian has noted, "from 1898 onward, the official position of the First Presidency would be to decry war, but to support any declaration of war by the government and to urge Church members to support the conduct of war."[25] The "civic duty" argument loomed larger and larger in the twentieth century as Latter-day Saints bent over backward to prove their loyalty to the United States and their genuine assimilation into the larger body politic. Mormons continued to "renounce war and proclaim peace," but once a final decision had been made by the U.S. government to enter a war, LDS belief in being "subject" to kings, presidents, and rulers took precedence.

America's entry into World War I occurred only twenty years after Utah became a state and while the Latter-day Saints were still being lampooned in the national press. Mormons keenly felt the need to prove their patriotism. B. H. Roberts, who himself served as a chaplain in the war, reflected, "Had Utah failed as a state in filling up the full measure of her duty, the [Latter-day Saints] would have been held—and justly— responsible for any delinquency in duty of the state." On the other hand, Utah's "promptness in action and the spirit" in which it "did [its] part" demonstrated its "patriotism" and the "intensity" of its "Americanism."[26]

With the arrival of World War I, the Latter-day Saints began to develop a more detailed philosophical position on matters of war and peace. President Joseph F. Smith, nephew of the founding prophet and head of the Mormon church from 1901 to 1918, was the first church leader to consider the matter at length. He made four key points. First, he re-affirmed that war and genuine Christianity were antithetical. If nations "really possessed the Spirit of the living God—could this condition ex-ist?" he asked. "No; it could not exist, but war would cease, and conten-tion and strife would be at an end." He said world leaders lacked "the spirit of the true Shepherd sufficiently to govern and control their acts in the ways of peace and righteousness."[27]

Second, Smith warned about the evils of a permanent military estab-lishment. Although it is "righteous and just for every people to defend their own lives and their own liberties, and their own homes, with the last drop of their blood," and though "it has been held that peace comes only by preparation for war; the present conflict should prove that peace comes only by preparing for peace, through training the people in righ-teousness and justice."[28]

Given that the Mormons felt obliged to support the U.S. president in his call to arms, Smith found the gospel to be most fruitful in help-ing to guide the morality of the soldiers rather than in deciding the morality of the conflict itself. Here he painted a picture of what he hoped LDS soldiers would be like by recalling a Book of Mormon account of 2,000 "stripling" warriors: "pure young men that abjured war and the shedding of blood, lived pure and innocent, free from the contaminat-ing thought of strife, of anger, or wickedness in their hearts; but when necessity required, and they were called to go out to defend their lives, and the lives of their fathers and mothers, and their homes, they went—not to destroy but to defend, not to shed blood but rather to save the blood of the innocent and of the unoffending, and the peace-lovers of mankind." Smith's concern was whether the Mormon men from Utah would do likewise. "Will they go out as men, in every sense—pure men, high-minded men, honest men, virtuous men, men of God? That is what I am anxious about."[29]

Finally, Smith felt the need to articulate a position on the culpability of the soldier in taking life. "Should [soldiers] be required," he an-nounced, "in the defense of the principles for which they go to war, to shed the blood of any among the contending forces, it shall not be a sin, and the blood of their enemies shall not be required at their hands." Those responsible would be the leaders "who place their people in jeop-ardy, and demand their life blood for their maintenance in position of prominence and power."[30]

During the second quarter of the twentieth century, Mormon senator Reed Smoot of Utah wielded considerable influence on Capitol Hill, and a nationally recognized LDS businessman, Heber J. Grant, was at the helm of the church. Any likelihood that Mormons would ever again need to defend themselves physically receded into the past. Thus, LDS discussions of war and peace almost entirely presumed a secular conflict. During the period between the world wars, pacifism among Latter-day Saints received some impetus from the pronounced mood of isolationism prevalent in the country. This was especially prominent in a key church leader, J. Reuben Clark, although he also credited the pacifism of his Quaker and Dunkard ancestors.[31] A successful eastern lawyer, Clark had served in the earlier years of the century as undersecretary of state and later as ambassador to Mexico. In the mid-1930s he was called into the church's First Presidency, where he served for the next thirty years.

By the late 1930s Clark was becoming active in national pacifist causes. In 1939 he accepted membership in the National Advisory Council of the American Peace Society; in 1944 he became a member of its board of directors, a position he held until he died in 1961. A staunch isolationist, he wrote to the director of the U.S. Defense Bond program shortly before Pearl Harbor was bombed to declare that "we do not believe that aggression should be carried on in the name and under the false cloak of defense."[32] During World War II President Clark occasionally encouraged young men who sought his counsel to serve a mission instead of joining the armed forces. He also monitored the treatment of a handful of Latter-day Saints who were placed in CPS camps, and after the war he arranged for the church to reimburse the peace churches for the expenses of maintaining those LDS conscientious objectors.[33]

Clark also vigorously opposed the use or further development of weapons of mass destruction. At the October 1946 General Conference Clark declared that for him, dropping the atomic bomb on Japan was "the crowning savagery of the war," and he described the latest developments in chemical warfare as being "the most savage, murderous means of exterminating peoples that Satan can plant in our minds." "God will not forgive us for this," he warned. "As one American citizen of one hundred thirty million, as one in one billion population of the world, I protest with all of the energy I possess against this fiendish activity, and as an American citizen, I call upon our government and its agencies to see that these unholy experimentations are stopped, and that somehow we get into the minds of our war-minded general staff and its satellites, and into the general staffs of all the world, a proper respect for human life."[34]

Clark was eloquent against the war and its conduct, then, but other important leaders who more openly supported World War II were at least far from hawkish. David O. McKay, Clark's functioning companion in the three-man First Presidency (by 1941 Heber J. Grant had become largely incapacitated through a stroke), thoroughly agreed that war was the antithesis of Christianity: "War impels you to hate your enemies. The Prince of Peace says, love your enemies. War says, curse them that curse you. The Prince of Peace says, pray for them that curse you. War says, injure and kill them that hate you. The risen Lord says, do good to them that hate you. We see that war is incompatible with Christ's teachings. The gospel of Jesus Christ is the gospel of peace. War is its antithesis and produces hate. It is vain to attempt to reconcile war with true Christianity." Despite this eloquent renunciation of war, however, McKay also felt compelled to affirm the LDS duty to support governing authorities. Admitting that his statements might seem "inconsistent," he nonetheless declared, "I uphold our country in the gigantic task it has assumed in the present world conflict and sustain the Church in its loyal support of the government in its fight against dictatorship."[35]

For McKay, there were two conditions "when entrance into war is justifiable, and when a Christian nation may, without violation of principles, take up arms against an opposing force." "Paramount among these reasons," he declared, is "the defense of man's freedom. To deprive an intelligent human being of his free agency is to commit the crime of the ages. So fundamental in man's eternal progress is his inherent right to choose that the Lord would defend it even at the price of war."[36] Mormon apostle and sometime secretary of agriculture Ezra Taft Benson explained: "The only real peace—the one most of us think about when we use the term—is a peace with freedom. A nation that is not willing, if necessary, to face the rigors of war to defend its real peace-in-freedom is doomed to lose both its freedom and its peace! These are the hard facts of life."[37] McKay's second condition was the one that had long been expressed by church leaders: loyalty to country. "With other loyal citizens," he wrote, "we serve our country as bearers of arms, rather than to stand aloof to enjoy a freedom for which others have fought and died."[38]

The most detailed of all official Mormon discussions of war and peace came in April 1942 from the combined efforts of Clark and McKay. That discussion represents the high-water mark of such discourse in the LDS community. As recently as the 1970s the First Presidency was still refer-ring inquirers to its contents with the declaration that the church's "at-titude has not changed."[39] "Christ's Church should not make war," de-clared the Presidency, "for the Lord is a Lord of peace. . . . Thus the Church is and must be against war. It cannot regard war as a righteous means of settling international disputes; these should and could be set-tled—the nations agreeing—by peaceful negotiation and adjustment. But," continued the statement, "the Church membership are citizens or subjects of sovereignties over which the Church has no control. When, therefore, constitutional law, obedient to these principles, calls the man-hood of the Church into the armed service of any country to which they owe allegiance, their highest civic duty requires that they meet that call." Support of governmental authorities, theoretically in place during the nineteenth century, had become the cardinal rule of the twentieth cen-tury. "Obedient to these principles, the members of the Church have always felt under obligation to come to the defense of their country when a call to arms was made."[40]

The Presidency also addressed the morality of taking life during a war. They reaffirmed what President Smith had said a generation before, explaining: "If in harkening to that call and obeying those in command over them [soldiers] shall take the lives of those who fight against them, that will not make of them murderers, nor subject them to the penalty that God has prescribed for those who kill." Continuing, they empha-sized "that sin" is "to the condemnation of . . . those rulers in the world who in a frenzy of hate and lust for unrighteous power and dominion over their fellowmen, have put into motion eternal forces they do not comprehend and cannot control. God, in His own due time, will pass sentence upon them."[41] The bottom line was that "it would be a cruel God that would punish his children as moral sinners for acts done by them as the innocent instrumentalities of a sovereign whom He had told them to obey and whose will they were powerless to resist."[42] This lat-ter statement highlights Mormon pragmatism. Better to be alive and able to practice some of your ideals than to be dead and capable of practic-ing none of them. If the Latter-day Saints were willing to give up po-lygamy—long considered as central to Mormonism—to stay alive, both institutionally and individually, they certainly would do the same with pacifism, which in fact did not occupy top priority in a list of moral principles. Mormons have never espoused an ethic of martyrdom.

By the 1940s Mormonism was reasonably well established through-out Europe. This, along with Clark's strict "just-war" views, tempered an unabashed nationalism or moral triumphalism. "This Church is a world-wide Church," read the statement. "Its devoted members are in both camps. They are the innocent war instrumentalities of their warring sovereignties. On each side they believe they are fighting for home, and country, and freedom. On each side, our brethren pray to the same God, in the same name, for victory." Nonetheless, echoing St. Augustine's declaration that no earthly order is free from sin and that therefore none dare equate itself unambiguously with "the good" or "the just," the First Presidency wrote, "Both sides cannot be wholly right; perhaps neither is without wrong. God will work out in His own due time and in His own sovereign way the justice and right of the conflict, but [returning to the culpability theme] He will not hold the innocent instrumentalities of the war, our brethren in arms, responsible for the conflict."[43]

God would, however, hold them responsible for what they could control—their own personal morality. "To our young men who go into service, no matter whom they serve or where, we say live clean, keep the commandments of the Lord, pray to Him constantly to preserve you in truth and righteousness, live as you pray, and then whatever betides you the Lord will be with you and nothing will happen to you that will not be to the honor and glory of God and to your salvation and exaltation." Since the church could not control global politics, it directed its counsel toward what it could control. "How great will be your happiness," it promised, "whether you be of the victors or of the vanquished, that you have lived as the Lord commanded." This each soldier could do. "You will be looked up to and revered as having passed through the fiery furnace of trial and temptation and come forth unharmed."[44]

Mormon interaction with world war may have produced conscientious soldiers, but it also produced conscientious objectors. For the first time, the issue was mentioned in public, and although never encouraged, it was not disparaged either. One young inquirer asked, "Can I feel that my Church understands and recognizes the validity of my being a conscientious objector, or am I repudiated, as a matter of Church policy, in my stand?" Clark replied that the church had no policy regarding conscientious objection and that it did not censure Latter-day Saints who were conscientious objectors.[45] In an editorial in the church's *Deseret News* just after V-J Day, the editor remarked: "the earnest, sincere, loyal conscientious objector, who, because of his religious convictions, asked to be relieved of military service which would necessitate his taking the life of a fellowman, is entitled to his opinion just as much as the man who felt that poison gas should be used and the enemy annihilated completely. And the chances are that the objector would prove to be the better citizen of the two."[46]

In the late 1940s the administration of U.S. president Harry Truman strongly advocated a one-year "universal military training" program. Although a Gallup poll reported that nearly 80 percent of the country's citizens supported the proposal, the First Presidency were vehemently opposed. "We had hoped," the Mormon leaders remarked, "that mature reflection might lead the proponents of such a policy to abandon it"; and they offered seventeen reasons why the plan was folly. Among their arguments was the idea that preparation for war would "invite and tempt the waging of war against foreign countries." Building a "huge armed establishment" would "belie our protestations of peace and peaceful intent and force other nations to a like course of militarism." In the end, "we shall make of the whole earth one great military camp whose separate armies, headed by war-minded officers, will never rest till they are at one another's throats in what will be the most terrible contest the world has ever seen." As a result of their pacifist concerns, the First Presidency urged Mormon legislators to "do your utmost to defeat any plan designed to bring about the compulsory military service of our citizenry." "What this country needs," they concluded, "and what the world needs, is a will for peace, not war. God will help our efforts to bring this about."[47]

Unfortunately that will for peace was not demonstrated over the next twenty years. With each new conflict the church supported the formal call to arms even as it continued its proclamation of peace and its toleration of the few LDS men who chose the path of conscientious objection. As it did with other groups in the United States during the Vietnam era, the war in Southeast Asia spawned an agonizing variety of responses among the Mormons.[48] Once the U.S. government committed itself militarily to Vietnam, however, the church's position was familiar: "We believe our young men should hold themselves in readiness to respond to the call of their government to serve in the armed forces."[49] At the same time church leaders privately reaffirmed that conscientious objection was a personal matter that in no way affected one's standing in the church. The secretary to the First Presidency wrote: "As [church leaders] understand it, the existing law provides that men who have conscientious objection may be excused from combat service. There would seem to be no objection, therefore, to a man availing himself on a personal basis of the exemption provided by law."[50]

One of the most common strategies for young Mormons applying for I-O (conscientious objector) status was to interpret D&C 98 literally. In that way they could claim opposition to all United States conflicts (since none was divinely decreed) and thus eliminate the legal objection that they were selective objectors (not qualified for I-O classification) who were trying to avoid participation only in the Vietnam War.[51] When draft boards denied applications, draftees who persisted in their refusal to enter the service found themselves afoul of the law. Here the Mormon COs took comfort from the examples of earlier Latter-day Saints who had become "prisoners for conscience sake" over polygamy. They also drew moral strength from the early LDS statement "Of Governments and Laws in General" (D&C 134) and its strong affirmation of freedom of conscience. And they were inspired by a declaration of Apostle Rudger Clawson (made in response to antipolygamy legislation of the 1880s): "I very much regret that the laws of my country should come in conflict with the laws of God; but whenever they do, I shall invariably choose the latter. If I did not so express myself, I should feel unworthy of the cause I represent."[52]

As tension mounted in America during the war, a "love it or leave it" mentality prevailed among some conservative Latter-day Saints, and some began to question whether "Mormon conscientious objector" was not an oxymoron. The First Presidency issued a statement clarifying that the worthiness of Mormon COs was not necessarily in question. After specifying that conscientious objectors, if worthy on other counts, could hold various church positions, the church's leaders bluntly concluded that "it would be contrary to Church policy to disfellowship men because they have conscientious objections regarding participating in military combat activities."[53] Firm in its decision not to decide the morality of any given war or to provide authoritative interpretation of civil or political matters generally, the church made no official statements against the war. It encouraged its young men to serve in the military as their civic duty at the same time that it kept the door open to conscientious objection for those so inclined.

Since the Vietnam War church members have continued to serve in the military at all levels, and church leaders continue to focus most of their attention on ministering to those who have already made their personal choices about participation rather than on attempting to shape such choices to begin with. By that formula the church's leaders support those in the armed forces and yet have not forgotten their divine mandate to "proclaim peace."

One of the best examples of that dual approach was the leaders' formal response in the early 1980s to the proposal on the basing of the MX missile. The First Presidency began by expressing dismay over the "terrifying arms race" and declared that they "deplore[d] in particular the building of vast arsenals of nuclear weaponry." In the first place, "enough such weaponry" already existed to cause "suffering and misery of incalculable extent." And even though MX planners considered the system to be defensive in concept, the First Presidency were not convinced. "History," the group declared, "indicates that men have seldom created armaments that eventually were not put to use." Above all, however, the presence of missiles in the Mormon heartland seemed too inconsistent with the ideals and image that the Mormons wished to cultivate. The Presidency explained that "our fathers came to this western area to establish a base from which to carry the gospel of peace to the peoples of the earth. It is ironic, and a denial of the very essence of the gospel, that in this same general area there should be constructed a mammoth weapons system potentially capable of destroying much of civilization."[54]

Although church leaders realize that sometimes war may be the only way for Christian love to protect one's own family, country, or neighboring nation from oppression, still they do not celebrate war. Recent church president Spencer Kimball summed up well what historically has been the gist of the Mormon position: "We do not favor war. We do not like the blood of war, the stench of war, the suffering of war, the deprivations of war, the cruelty of war, the degradation of war. We hate war, but there are considerations that must be kept in mind."[55] In short, Mormons have attempted to render their due both to Christ and to Caesar.

NOTES

1. A large number of the revelations received during the early years of Mormonism have been compiled and canonized by the church as *The Doctrine and Covenants of the Church of Jesus Christ of Latter-day Saints,* or more simply, the *Doctrine and Covenants.* Throughout the remainder of this study, the standard convention of referring to this volume as "D&C" will be followed. Unless the wording has been significantly changed from the original, the most recent edition (Salt Lake City: Church of Jesus Christ of Latter-day Saints, 1981) will be cited.

2. Dean C. Jessee, ed., *The Personal Writings of Joseph Smith* (Salt Lake City: Deseret Book, 1984), 219–20.

3. Article of Faith no. 12, *Pearl of Great Price* (Salt Lake City: Church of Jesus Christ of Latter-day Saints, 1981), 61. The "Articles of Faith" originally were part of a March 1842 letter that Joseph Smith wrote to John Wentworth, editor of the *Chicago Democrat,* describing the history and faith of the Latter-day Saints. They are reproduced in original form in Jessee, *The Personal Writings of Joseph Smith.* Today they constitute part of the LDS volume *The Pearl of Great Price,* which has canonical status.

4. Joseph Smith Jr., *History of the Church of Jesus Christ of Latter-day Saints,* 2d ed., rev., 7 vols. (Salt Lake City: Deseret Book, 1964), 6:219–20.

5. Ibid., 5:467.

6. Ibid., 6:499.

7. D&C 98:33–43.

8. Andrew F. Ehat and Lyndon Cook, eds., *The Words of Joseph Smith: The Contemporary Accounts of the Nauvoo Discourses of the Prophet Joseph* (Provo, Utah: Brigham Young University Religious Studies Center, 1980), 218.

9. Ehat and Cook, *Words of Joseph Smith,* 217.

10. Smith, *History of the Church,* 6:111–12.

11. *Journal of Discourses,* 26 vols. (London: Latter-day Saints' Book, 1855–86), 10:153–54. The *Journal of Discourses* is a collection of discourses given by LDS church leaders from the 1850s to the 1880s.

12. Ehat and Cook, *Words of Joseph Smith,* 129.

13. Smith, *History of the Church,* 7:256.

14. *Millennial Star* 2 (July 1841): 43.

15. D&C 134:11.

16. Like the Bible, the Book of Mormon consists of a series of books bearing the names of ancient and, in this case, American prophets. Citation follows the biblical pattern. Hence the quotation is from Alma 24:17–23.

17. Alma 43:45–47.

18. The very existence of Gordon C. Thomasson, ed., *War, Conscription, Conscience and Mormonism* (Santa Barbara: Mormon Heritage, 1971), suggests that there was a minority of young Latter-day Saints during the Vietnam era who wished to see themselves as both committed Mormons and committed pacifists. Although Thomasson, then a graduate student in religious studies at University of California, Santa Barbara, recognized that pacifist "convictions are at variance with the majority of his community," he hoped that any draftable Mormon male who read his work and chose conscientious objection would "realize that he is still part of both the LDS community and the Church of Jesus Christ, and that many of his brothers, today as in the past, share his feelings and attitudes while maintaining themselves in full faith and fellowship with the Church" (title page).

19. *Journal of Discourses,* 10:248.

20. Ibid., 7:137.

21. Ibid., 12:240–41.

22. *Conference Report of the Church of Jesus Christ of Latter-day Saints* (Salt Lake City: n.p., 1898), 86.

23. Ibid., 88.

24. James R. Clark, ed., *Messages of the First Presidency*, 6 vols. (Salt Lake City: Bookcraft, 1965–73), 3:299.

25. D. Michael Quinn, "Conscientious Objectors or Christian Soldiers?" *Sunstone* 10 (Mar. 1985): 18.

26. B. H. Roberts, *A Comprehensive History of the Church of Jesus Christ of Latter-day Saints, Century I*, 6 vols. (Salt Lake City: Deseret News Press, 1930), 6:455.

27. Joseph F. Smith, *Gospel Doctrine* (Salt Lake City: Deseret News Press, 1919), 416–17.

28. Ibid., 419, 421.

29. Ibid., 423.

30. Ibid., 427.

31. The best treatment of Clark's views is the chapter entitled "They That Take the Sword," in D. Michael Quinn, *J. Reuben Clark: The Church Years* (Provo, Utah: Brigham Young University Press, 1983), 197–219.

32. Cited in Quinn, *J. Reuben Clark*, 207.

33. Quinn, *J. Reuben Clark*, 208, 210.

34. J. Reuben Clark, "Demand for Proper Respect of Human Life," *Improvement Era* 49 (Nov. 1946): 689, 740.

35. David O. McKay, *Conference Report*, April 1942, p. 71.

36. Ibid., 72

37. Ezra Taft Benson, *An Enemy Hath Done This* (Salt Lake City: Parliament, 1969), 161–62.

38. McKay, *Conference Report*, 73.

39. Joseph Anderson, secretary to the First Presidency, to "Dear Brother," March 20, 1970. This form letter was sent out during the presidency of Joseph Fielding Smith in response to those who asked about the church's position "regarding war and conscientious objectors"; it is reproduced in *Dialogue: A Journal of Mormon Thought* 3 (Spring 1968): 8.

40. *Message of the First Presidency, April 6, 1942* (Salt Lake City: Church of Jesus Christ of Latter-day Saints, 1942), 32; his message was issued as a pamphlet and distributed to church members.

41. Ibid., 35, 39–40.

42. Ibid., 34–35.

43. Ibid., 35–36.

44. Ibid., 40–41. A volume by Denny Roy, G. Paul Skabelund, and Ray C. Hillam, *"A Time to Kill": Reflections on War* (Salt Lake City: Signature, 1990), is a collection of excerpts from oral histories of Mormon servicemen during the twentieth century. The book's great value is that its recollections show that ordinary Mormons seemed to have absorbed and endorsed the attitudes toward

the war that were coming from the church leaders. In particular, the chapters "Going to War" and "Killing and Being Killed" demonstrate this.

45. Cited in Quinn, *J. Reuben Clark*, 210.

46. *Deseret News* (Sept. 11, 1945), cited in Quinn, "Conscientious Objectors," 20.

47. "Letter of the First Presidency," *Improvement Era* 49 (Feb. 1946): 76–77.

48. See the roundtable discussion in *Dialogue* 2 (Winter 1967): 65–100; and Knud S. Larsen and Gary Schwendiman, "The Vietnam War through the Eyes of a Mormon Subculture," *Dialogue* 3 (Fall 1968): 152–62, which reports a survey of Mormon students. See also Thomasson, *War, Conscription, Conscience and Mormonism*.

49. First Presidency Statement, *Church News*, May 24, 1969, p. 12, cited in Quinn, "Conscientious Objectors," 21.

50. As reproduced in Thomasson, *War, Conscription, Conscience and Mormonism*, 5.

51. See samples of applications reported in ibid., 29–87.

52. Thomasson's collection illustrates how these ideas and aspects of the Mormon heritage helped LDS conscientious objectors feel they were in good Mormon company. The Clawson quotation is cited on p. 86. Clawson's life is examined in David S. Hoopes and Roy Hoopes, *The Making of a Mormon Apostle: The Story of Rudger Clawson* (New York: Madison, 1990).

53. Cited in Quinn, "Conscientious Objectors," 22.

54. "First Presidency Statement on Basing of MX Missile," in *Ensign* 11 (June 1981): 76. See also Steven A. Hildreth, "The First Presidency Statement on MX in Perspective," *BYU Studies* 22 (Spring 1982): 215–25. In addition to recognizing a pacifist motivation for the First Presidency's proclamation, some also, or even primarily, see self-preservation as a factor. See Matthew Glass, *Citizens against the MX: Public Languages in the Nuclear Age* (Urbana: University of Illinois Press, 1993).

55. Edward L. Kimball, ed., *The Teachings of Spencer W. Kimball* (Salt Lake City: Bookcraft, 1982), 414.

9

꽃

ADVENTISM AND MILITARY SERVICE

Individual Conscience in Ethical Tension

꽃

George R. Knight

The Seventh-day Adventist Church has opted to take the uncomfortable middle ground between pacifism and armed combat participation in the military. In other words, although the denomination frowns on military conflict and believes that war is certainly an unmitigated evil, it still recommends that its young people serve their country in uniform. But Adventism holds that uniformed service by Christians should seek to save life rather than destroy it. Consequently the denomination strongly recommends that its young people not bear arms; rather, they should work in hospitals or in other humanitarian endeavors. The stated policy of the Seventh-day Adventist Church is thus one of *conscientious cooperation.* In the terminology of the military draft, however, its members are defined as a variety of conscientious objector.

Conscientious cooperation is the recommended position of the denomination, the large majority of its young people have selected that option, and the denomination has gone to great expense to train its young people to be prepared for that choice; Adventism nonetheless holds that the individual conscience must decide the issue as it grapples with ethical responsibility. As a result, although most young Adventists throughout the denomination's history have been conscientious cooperators, others have opted either for other pacifist positions or for combatant service.

The roots of Seventh-day Adventist policy on military service go back to the U.S. Civil War. Before that war the young church had no occasion to take a stand on the issue. Having arisen out of the Millerite movement of the 1840s, Sabbatarian Adventists did not even organize as a denomination until the early 1860s. The year 1861 saw the formation of their first state conference, and May 1863 witnessed the banding together of the several state conferences into the General Conference of Seventh-day Adventists. Before that time the movement had been held together by its foremost journal, the *Adventist Review and Sabbath Herald,* and by occasional meetings of like-minded believers. Thus the young denomination had just barely organized before the circumstances of war *forced* it to take a stand on military service.

Actually the discussion about military service had begun—with great exuberance—about eight months before the denomination was organized. "In the case of drafting," James White had penned in August 1862, "the government assumes the responsibility of the violation of the law of God, and it would be madness to resist." White believed that "he who would resist until, in the administration of military law, he was shot down, goes too far." Such a person took "the responsibility of suicide."[1]

Those controversial words, penned by the acknowledged leader of the Sabbatarian Adventists, set the stage for avid discussion among the incipient denomination's members and clergy. The Civil War had been under way for nearly sixteen months, and its escalation, with an ever-growing number of casualties, was producing a great deal of emotional pressure and tension for Adventism from both within and without.

TENSIONS WITHIN AND WITHOUT

The internal tensions centered on the issue of loyalty to government versus loyalty to God. That tension is not an especially difficult one for those who see earthly governments as either redeemed or redeemable; but the Sabbatarian Adventists had imbibed their view of government from the great, panoramic prophecies of Daniel and the Book of Revelation. Daniel in particular viewed earthly governments as unregenerate beasts that tear, devour, and persecute God's people. To make matters worse, Adventists taught that these earthly powers often are aided and abetted in their work by the debauched women of John's Apocalypse, the apostate churches.[2]

Still more damning in the eyes of patriotic onlookers must have been preaching that pictured the Adventist denomination as the faithful, commandment-keeping, end-time "remnant" of Rev. 12:17 and 14:12 that would clash with the beastly powers of Revelation 13. Both Adventism's theological understanding and its prophetic viewpoint led it to see the last great issue in world history as that of loyalty to God—especially as demonstrated by keeping the Ten Commandments, including the fourth (the seventh-day Sabbath), which was the only one that nineteenth-century Protestants disputed. In interpreting Revelation 12–14 the Adventists believed that at some time in the future, they, the commandment-keeping remnant, would be pitted against both world Catholicism (the beast of Rev. 13:1–7) and, eventually, the United States of America. Thus they preached that the United States was the lamblike beast of Rev. 13:11–17. Just prior to the Second Coming of Christ, the United States would reject its principles of religious liberty, learn to speak like a dragon, and promulgate a decree of death for those remaining faithful to God's commandments.

In the light of that widely preached evangelistic message, it was easy to interpret Adventists as being negative toward earthly government in general and the United States in particular. Although such a message may have aroused opposition in time of peace, in time of war it could be seen at best as disloyalty and at worst as treason. That would be especially true if the message came from a religious body supplying no men for military service. Thus the tension from without.

There was tension also from within, from at least two sources. First, believing in the New Testament's injunctions that Christians ought to obey and honor earthly rulers as the "ministers of God . . . for good," ministers who were sent by God for the "punishment of evildoers,"[3] Adventists felt impelled to serve their nation in time of crisis. Second, and closely related, Adventist believers, as members of a reform movement, were in harmony with the principles of the North. Not yet having spread to the South, Adventism was almost unanimous in viewing slavery as being under God's curse and as a moral evil to be destroyed.

On the other hand, standing against these strong ethical convictions to obey the government and to stamp out slavery were the Ten Commandments, especially the command not to kill. Beyond that, most Adventists realized that it would be nearly impossible to keep the Sabbath properly in the wartime military.

The ethical tensions facing the Adventists in the early 1860s appeared to be unsolvable, since noncombatant options were as yet unavailable. For which set of principles should they stand? That was an important point, since abdication of either side of the dilemma seemed to be a betrayal of the faith. Fortunately for the groping Adventists, up through 1862 there was no compulsory draft. Church members could simply avoid military service. That avoidance allowed Adventist believers to escape violating the Ten Commandments. Amid the charged emotions of war, however, it did not make the developing denomination very popular.

THE TENSION RAISED TO CONSCIOUSNESS

It was in the explosive context of the internal and external tensions facing the Adventists that James White penned his controversial editorial of August 1862. Part of the immediate historical background to the editorial seems to have been events that James and his wife had experienced recently in Iowa. A group of Adventists there had come under suspicion as secessionists because they had taken an aggressively pacifist position. These members, in the words of James's wife, "mistook zeal and fanaticism for conscientiousness" and "were ready to become martyrs for their faith." The Iowa crisis, plus the general tenor of the times, set the stage for White's opening of public discussion on the topic of military service among Seventh-day Adventists.[4]

Obviously on the defensive, White began his article by noting that "for the past ten years the Review has taught . . . that slavery is pointed out in the prophetic word as the darkest and most damning sin upon this nation." The Adventists' antislavery stance, he cautioned, had made circulation of the denomination's publications "positively forbidden in the slave States." He closed his opening paragraph by pointing out that those Adventists who had cast ballots in the 1860 election "to a man voted for Abraham Lincoln. We know of not one among Seventh-day Adventists who has the least sympathy for secession."[5]

Having established the all-important point of Adventist loyalty to the North, White went on to discuss the incongruence between keeping God's commandments and the necessities of war. "The position which our people have taken relative to the perpetuity and sacredness of the law of God contained in the ten commandments," he penned, "is not in harmony with all the requirements of war. The fourth precept of that law says, 'Remember the Sabbath day to keep it holy'; the sixth says, 'Thou shalt not kill.'"[6]

Up to that point James probably had most of his brothers and sisters in the faith agreeing with him. In his next sentence, however, he dropped a verbal bomb: he implied that a Christian should not resist the draft too far, since "the government assumes the responsibility of the violation of the law of God" for draftees. Adventists, White reminded his readers, should render to Caesar his due. "Those who despise civil law, should at once pack up and be off for some spot on God's foot-stool where there is no civil law."[7]

Near the close of his August 12, 1862, editorial White pointed out that according to the Adventist interpretation of Revelation 13, a time will come when believers will have to stand against the government and risk martyrdom. But that time had not yet arrived. In the present crisis, "for us to attempt to resist the laws of the best government under heaven, which is now struggling to put down the most hellish rebellion since that of Satan and his angels, we repeat it, would be madness."[8] The tension between duty to God and duty to nation permeates White's editorial. He left both his Adventist and his non-Adventist readers quite clear as to the patriotism of Adventists, but readers must not have found much certainty concerning a person's proper relationship to military service.

CORPORATE TENSION

The 1862 editorial set off a barrage of opinionating on the topic. Two weeks after its publication White reported that some of the brethren had reacted to it "in rather a feverish style," for they had essentially charged him "with teaching Sabbath-breaking and murder." He added that if any of the Adventist draft resisters chose "to have a clinch with Uncle Sam rather than to obey," they could try it. James claimed that he had no wish to contend with them, "lest some of you non-resistants get up a little war before you are called upon to fight for your country." Then, significantly, he added that "any well-written articles, calculated to shed light upon our duty as a people in reference to the present war, will receive prompt attention."[9]

That invitation brought forth a flood of articles. Their number and vigor demonstrate that the tension in James White's value system as he faced the ethical dilemma brought about by the Civil War also permeated the larger Adventist community. The next four months witnessed quite a debate in the pages of the evolving denomination's major periodical. Writers raised nearly every possible option.

At one extreme some respondents held that Adventists should bear arms. M. E. Cornell, for example, was upset with those who would "get up Daniel in the lion's den, and the three Hebrew worthies in the fiery furnace, as parallels to being drafted." That might do, he added, "if the war was against Seventh-day Adventists." Following what he perceived to be White's lead, Cornell supported military-imposed commandment breaking by referring to the Hebrew slaves in Egypt, who could not be held responsible for Sabbath-keeping because of their servitude. He went on to suggest that "what is called civilized warfare" may not always imply breaking the sixth commandment. In the Old Testament even God had commanded warfare.[10]

Even more aggressive was Joseph Clarke. During the previous winter, he claimed, he had suffered "the war fever so high" that it had "injured" him "somewhat." Clarke wanted to see the "treason" of the South "receive its just desserts." Dreaming of "Gideons, and Jepthas, and fighting Davids," he put the war in covenant perspective. He fancied "a regiment of Sabbath-keepers [who] would strike this rebellion a staggering blow, in the strength of Him who always helped His valiant people when they kept His statutes."[11] In a second article Clarke used the epistle to the Romans and the example of the centurion Cornelius as a soldier devoted to and accepted by God. The Cornelius story showed that Christians could participate in a "just war." Clarke went on to point out that there was war in heaven when Satan was driven out. He could not conceive of it being murder "to hang or shoot a traitor." Rather, such activity was Christian duty. Therefore, Clarke concluded, "let us lay aside fanaticism and act like men."[12]

At the other extreme Henry E. Carver took the pacifist position. White's August 1862 article had "astonished and grieved" him. Although admitting to the emotional pull of Clarke's regiment-of-Sabbath-keepers argument, Carver had concluded that "under no circumstances was it justifiable in a follower of the Lamb to use carnal weapons to take the lives of his fellow-men." White's argument, Carver claimed, was an abdication of moral responsibility. After all, what did Daniel do "when he knew the decree was signed? Did he throw the responsibility on the government and neglect prayer?"[13]

Meanwhile, White and others were urging caution. In September 1862 White suggested that one purpose of his original editorial had been "to check the fanatical rashness which many are liable to run into, and disgrace the cause of truth." More important, he had wanted to raise the issue for discussion before a draft began. Now was "the time in a God-fearing manner to search out the truth, and learn our duty, and be ready to act unitedly."[14] A few weeks later White expressed regret that Adventists had not thought through the problems of war when they had had more time. "The crisis is upon us," he wrote, "and we are poorly prepared to meet it."[15]

J. H. Waggoner also urged caution. "One freak of fanaticism, at such a time as this," he wrote, "would work more injury to the cause than could be undone in years." Although the brethren had "generally desired to be as harmless as doves," he suggested that in the present crisis they also needed "to be as wise as serpents."[16]

Ellen White, the prophetic thought-leader of the Adventists and the only prominent female among them, had remained largely silent on the topic of military service—although in early 1862 she had spoken in no uncertain terms, saying that God would "punish the South for the sin of slavery, and the North for so long suffering its overreaching and over-bearing influence." Her first remarks on military service were in a private letter penned a week after her husband's controversial 1862 editorial. The letter basically backed her husband's counsel of obedience to the laws of the nation. Nonetheless, she admitted that she was "not fully settled in regard to taking up arms."[17]

In January 1863 Ellen White broke her public silence on military service. Publicly, in print, she supported her husband's editorial. Adventists in some places showed little interest in the war, she observed, and so in the emotional heat of the times they "were looked upon as sympathizing with the Rebellion." She also regretted that some had "moved very indiscreetly in regard to the article mentioned. . . . Some [had] seized the pen and jumped hastily at conclusions which would not bear investigation." She was particularly upset with those who, in their extreme and aggressive pacifism, "were ready to become martyrs for their faith."[18]

On the other hand, in the same article Ellen White also claimed that "God's people . . . cannot engage in this perplexing war, for it is opposed to every principle of their faith. In the army they cannot obey the truth and at the same time obey the requirements of their officers. There would be a continual violation of conscience." "I saw," she wrote, "that it is our duty in every case to obey the laws of our land, unless they conflict with the higher law which God spoke with an audible voice from Sinai. . . . The wisdom and authority of the divine law are supreme."[19]

Thus Ellen White both felt and expressed the same ethical tension in relation to military service that her husband expressed and that had split Adventist thinkers on the topic. Her counsel, however, lined up with the implication of her husband's; that is, Adventists had no business volunteering for military service and putting themselves in an untenable position.

ENUNCIATING A DENOMINATIONAL POSITION

In the meantime the nature of the challenge facing Adventism was changing. The military draft that had been talked about in August 1862 became
a reality in March 1863. The draft "noose" had not yet completely tightened, however. Although the 1863 law made no provision for noncombatants, it did allow them a way out if they could furnish a substitute or pay
a maximum of $300 for procuring one. The provisions for substitution
were open to anyone and did not require religious convictions.[20]

The next major turning points came on February 24 and July 4, 1864.
On those two dates Congress amended the 1863 draft law to revoke the
$300 exemption option, except for those "conscientiously opposed to the
bearing of arms" on the basis of religious conviction. In addition the revision provided that such conscientious objectors might be declared "noncombatants." If drafted, such noncombatants would "be assigned by the
Secretary of War to duty in the hospitals, or to the care of freedmen [ex-
slaves]."[21] The revised law forced the newly organized (May 21, 1863) denomination to take an explicit stand in relation to war and combatancy.

The first step was to get approval of Adventism's noncombatant convictions from the governors of those states wherein most of the Adventist members resided. On August 2, 1864, the denomination's general
conference committee wrote to the governor of Michigan, the state in
which the general conference headquarters were located. In their letter
the denomination's leaders claimed, with a great deal of exaggeration,
that Seventh-day Adventists "are unanimous in their views" that the
Bible's "teachings are contrary to the spirit and practice of war; hence
they have ever been conscientiously opposed to bearing arms. . . . In
none of our denominational publications have we advocated or encouraged the practice of bearing arms." The letter concluded with a petition
that their denomination's members be included in the noncombatant
provision of the 1864 draft law revision.[22]

Although that letter stretched the truth regarding the unanimity of
Adventists, it did represent the denomination's first formal stand on the
issue of military service. Moreover it secured the endorsement of Austin Blair, the governor of Michigan, on August 3, 1864. For the first time
a government formally recognized Adventists as conscientious objectors
and noncombatants. The next few weeks saw similar endorsements from
the chief executives of Wisconsin, Illinois, Pennsylvania, and other
states.[23] By the end of August John Nevins Andrews, a leading Adventist minister, had met with the provost marshal general of the United

States in Washington, D.C., and had obtained federal recognition for the noncombatancy of Seventh-day Adventists.[24]

The 1864 draft regulations marked a major turning point both in Adventism and in United States history as it relates to noncombatancy. Some Adventists still paid the $300 exemption fee, but others (who might not have been able to pay the fee or who actually desired to serve as a way to help others) could now serve as recognized noncombatants.

Legal recognition did not solve all the problems for Adventist draftees, however. Some field commanders refused to abide by the law. For example, after presenting his papers C. F. Hall was put under guard, cursed by his commander, and accused of being a rebel. "The opposition to non-combatants in the army is so great," wrote Hall in January 1865, "that one of the commanding officers said that if it was in his power he would hang me in a minute."[25]

Still other Adventist young men enlisted as combatants. These men were disfellowshipped. The *Review* of March 7, 1865, reported two such cases. That of Enoch Hayes reads: "As voluntary enlistment into the service of war is contrary to the principles of faith and practice of Seventh-day Adventists as contained in the commandments of God and the faith of Jesus, they cannot retain those within their communion who so enlist. Enoch Hayes was therefore excluded from the membership of the Battle Creek [Michigan] church, by a unanimous vote of the church, March 4, 1865."[26]

The Civil War ended a few weeks later. In May 1865, a month after the completion of the war, the Adventists' annual general conference session adopted a resolution on its people's duty to the government. The church leaders recognized civil government as being ordained of God to maintain peace and order and acknowledged their duty to serve the government as enjoined by the New Testament—but to serve only as long as the government's requirements did not violate the law of God. However, their resolution continued, "we are compelled to decline all participation in acts of war and bloodshed as being inconsistent with the duties enjoined upon us by our divine Master toward our enemies and toward all mankind."[27]

In a similar vein the 1868 general conference session passed a resolution declaring that church members should abstain from worldly strife. "War," the resolution proclaimed, "was never justifiable except under the immediate direction of God." Since such conditions did not presently exist, "we cannot believe it to be right for the servants of Christ to take up arms to destroy the lives of their fellow-men."[28]

THE TENSION LIVES ON

The 1868 general conference resolution makes it appear that Seventh-day Adventists had reached unanimity on the military question, but such was not the case. The problem of divided opinion showed up in relation to a position paper requested on the topic. The 1865 general conference session resolved that an article should be prepared to set forth the denomination's viewpoint. The 1866 session assigned the church's leading scholar, John Nevins Andrews, to the task. Two years later Andrews reported to the 1868 session that the job was much more complex than he had anticipated and that he was not yet finished with it.[29]

To treat all sides of the topic fairly, Andrews apparently canvassed the opinions of the leading Adventist thinkers. One of those contacted was George I. Butler, who would be elected to the general conference presidency in 1871. Butler replied on November 24, 1868. His letter removes all doubt as to whether the Adventists had achieved unanimity on military service. Butler was overjoyed that Andrews had been given the assignment; Andrews would look at all the arguments, Butler wrote, whereas if the other chief contender for the task had been chosen, "we would have been treated to a rehash of non-resistant theories, with no consideration of the other side at all." In his vigorous style Butler urged Andrews on with the task but also argued at length for combatant participation in a just war—even though he claimed not to be fully satisfied with his own position.[30]

Unfortunately Andrews never completed his assignment. Adventism thus entered the twentieth century without a thorough and well thought-out argument undergirding its official position on the topic of military service. That lack would contribute to difficulties in implementing a consistent approach in World War I.

Meanwhile we need to go back to 1865 and the disfellowshipping of Adventists who had volunteered for military service. Related to that topic, C. S. Longacre (the leader in Adventist religious liberty work from 1913 through 1936) reported that S. N. Haskell (one of the pioneers of Adventism) had advised him that Ellen White had disagreed with the disfellowshipping of the volunteers. According to Haskell, reporting a half-century later, White had said in substance regarding one of the cases: "The young man evidently did what he considered was his patriotic duty and followed his conscience in the matter. You must not sit in judgment upon him and be conscience for him. You must not discipline him nor disfellowship him for doing what he had done in defense of his country and in following his conscience."[31]

That purported conversation is plausible in the light of the tensions in conscience that appeared among the Adventists throughout the Civil War. The statement itself, however, is open to serious question as to its authenticity. Haskell claimed to have heard Ellen White's words at a meeting of the Battle Creek church board, yet he apparently had never been to Battle Creek before 1870.[32]

On the other hand, even if apocryphal, the statement seems to be quite true to the conscience-based approach that Ellen White espoused in relation to ethical dilemmas. For example, in the 1890s she wrote: "In matters of conscience the soul must be left untrammeled. No one is to control another's mind, to judge for another, or to prescribe his duty. God gives to every soul freedom to think, and to follow his own convictions. 'Every one of us should give account of himself to God.'. . . In all matters where principle is involved, 'let every man be fully persuaded in his own mind.' Rom. 14:12, 5."[33]

Whether or not Haskell's report is accurate, its repeated retelling by Longacre over three decades undoubtedly helped to keep the Adventist position on military service from hardening into pacifism. It also undoubtedly contributed to a broadness in the denomination's position that may not have been there otherwise.

Throughout the twentieth century the repeatedly expressed denominational ideal has been one of conscientious cooperation. Unfortunately that ideal has at times fallen short in practice, especially in Germany in World War I.[34]

Even though all official pronouncements of the denomination's general conference in the twentieth century have been for noncombatancy and conscientious cooperation, there were some leading ministers in the 1920s who argued that Adventism should move to pacifism. On the other hand, as the clouds of war formed in the 1930s, there were major voices against the pacifist position.[35]

The most significant move toward denominational support for conscientious cooperation is found in the development of the Medical Cadet Corps under Everett Dick, a professor of history at Union College in the late 1930s. It had been discovered in the Civil War and in World War I that the best way for Adventist young people in the military to avoid bearing arms and breaking the Sabbath was to work in medical activities, since medics performed acts of mercy and did not need to carry weapons. Thus young Adventists working as medics could serve both God and their country and thereby at least partly resolve the ethical tension that lay at the foundation of their dilemma.

As war became more probable in the late 1930s, the denomination, under the urging of Professor Dick and others, decided to make it easier for Adventists to obtain medical positions. Its method was to give them extensive training along medical and military lines through the denominationally developed Medical Cadet Corps. The church provided the training at its colleges and secondary schools in place of physical education. By this method thousands of young Adventists in World War II and the Korean conflict found an easier road into acceptable military service than had their predecessors.[36]

In 1954 the U.S. Army, recognizing the contributions of programs like the Medical Cadet Corps, set up its own program for the training of conscientious cooperators. For the program the army established a special basic training camp at Fort Sam Houston in Texas. The training at "Fort Sam" had two advantages. First, it removed noncombatants from the basic training of regular infantry units, where their unwillingness to carry arms had been a source of constant perplexity. Second, the new training was specifically aimed at providing noncombatants with the medical skills needed to equip them to be agents of healing rather than of destruction. One authority reports that more than half the men who went through basic training at Fort Sam Houston were Seventh-day Adventists. It was a program engineered for the needs of conscientious cooperators.[37]

Meanwhile, throughout the twentieth century, the official position of the church has remained that of discouraging enlistment, since volunteers give up certain rights through the very act of volunteering.

INDIVIDUAL CONSCIENCE IN ETHICAL TENSION

Adventism's latest official action regarding military service reflects both the ethical tension related to a Christian's responsibilities to God and Caesar and the fact that Christians must make moral decisions based on their individual consciences. Thus an action taken in 1972 emphasizes that "genuine Christianity manifests itself in good citizenship and loyalty to civil government." On the other hand, the action states, the emergency of war "in no way alters the Christian's supreme allegiance . . . to God or modifies his obligation to practice his beliefs and put God first." The action reiterates that Seventh-day Adventists "advocate a noncombatant position, following their divine Master in not taking human life, but rendering all possible service to save it."[38]

Even though noncombatancy is the officially voted Adventist ideal, the resolution stated clearly that "the above statement is not a rigid position" that binds church members. Rather, the resolution's idea is to provide guidance, "leaving the individual member free to assess the situation for himself." Although the statement encourages Adventists to select the noncombatant option, it promises to stand behind those who opt for "civilian alternative service in lieu of military service." It even promises denominational support for "those who conscientiously choose," with pastoral guidance, to serve as combatants, "since the Church refrains from passing judgment on them."[39]

Thus the Seventh-day Adventist Church, in facing the tensions involved in military service, has come to a conscience-based position. It is a position that leaves the final choice to individuals as they struggle with convictions relating to their responsibilities toward both the kingdom of God and kingdoms of the present world. Officially the church takes the uncomfortable middle ground in an ethical area that naturally tends to polarize individuals and groups. Bypassing the "clear" choices of unlimited military participation and absolute refusal to participate, Adventism has opted for conscientious cooperation.

NOTES

1. James White, "The Nation," *Review and Herald*, Aug. 12, 1862, p. 84.

2. See especially Daniel 7–8 and Revelation 12–14. For an early Adventist treatment of the topic, see Uriah Smith, *Thoughts, Critical and Practical, on the Book of Revelation* (Battle Creek, Mich.: Seventh-day Adventist Pub. Assn., 1867); and Smith, *Thoughts, Critical and Practical, on the Book of Daniel* (Battle Creek, Mich.: Seventh-day Adventist Pub. Assn., 1873).

3. Rom. 13:4; 1 Pet. 2:13, 14; 1 Tim. 2:1, 2.

4. Ron Graybill, "Thoughts on Seventh-day Adventists and the American Civil War," unpublished research paper [ca. 1970], doc. file. 320, E. G. White Estate vault, Andrews University, Berrien Springs, Mich. (hereinafter EGW vault); James White, "Western Tour," *Review and Herald*, Aug. 19, 1862, p. 92; J. H. Waggoner, "Report from Bro. Waggoner," *Review and Herald*, Sep. 9, 1862, pp. 118, 119; Ellen G. White, *Testimonies for the Church*, 9 vols. (Mountain View, Calif.: Pacific, 1948), 1:356, 357; Fred Albert Shannon, *The Organization and Administration of the Union Army, 1861–1865*, 2 vols. (Cleveland: Arthur H. Clark, 1928), 1:275–77.

5. James White, "The Nation," *Review and Herald*, Aug. 12, 1862, p. 84.

6. Ibid.

7. Ibid.

8. Ibid.

9. James White, "The Nation," *Review and Herald,* Aug. 26, 1862, p. 100.

10. See letter from M. E. Cornell in James White, "To Correspondents," *Review and Herald,* Sept. 9, 1862, p. 118.

11. Joseph Clarke, "The War! The War!!" *Review and Herald,* Sept. 23, 1862, p. 134.

12. Joseph Clarke, "The Sword vs. Fanaticism," *Review and Herald,* Sept. 23, 1862, p. 135.

13. Henry E. Carver, "The War," *Review and Herald,* Oct. 21, 1862, pp. 166, 167.

14. James White, "Our Duty in Reference to the War," *Review and Herald,* Sept. 16, 1862, p. 124.

15. James White, "Letter to Bro. Carver," *Review and Herald,* Oct. 21, 1862, p. 167.

16. J. H. Waggoner, "Our Duty and the Nation," *Review and Herald,* Sept. 23, 1862, pp. 132, 133.

17. E. G. White, *Testimonies,* 1:264; Ellen G. White to Sister Steward, Aug. 19, 1862, letter file, EGW vault.

18. E. G. White, *Testimonies,* 1:356, 357.

19. Ibid., 1:361.

20. Edward Needles Wright, *Conscientious Objectors in the Civil War* (New York: A. S. Barnes, Perpetua Edition, 1961), 64–65.

21. *The Views of Seventh-day Adventists Relative to Bearing Arms Together with the Opinion of the Governor of Michigan* (Battle Creek, Mich.: Seventh-day Adventist Pub. Assn., 1864), 3, 4; Wright, *Conscientious Objectors,* 82–86 (quotations are from the language of the February amendment as reproduced on 82–83).

22. General Conference Committee to Austin Blair, Aug. 2, 1864, in *The Views of Seventh-day Adventists Relative to Bearing Arms, as Brought before the Governors of Several States and the Provost Marshal General* (Battle Creek, Mich.: Seventh-day Adventist Pub. Assn., 1865), 6–7.

23. Ibid., 8–14.

24. J. N. Andrews, "Seventh-day Adventists Recognized as Noncombatants," *Review and Herald,* Sept. 13, 1864, pp. 124, 125.

25. C. F. Hall, "Something Wrong," *Review and Herald,* Jan. 24, 1865, p. 70.

26. "Notice," *Review and Herald,* Mar. 7, 1865, p. 112.

27. John Byington and Uriah Smith, "The Conference," *Review and Herald,* May 23, 1865, p. 197.

28. J. N. Andrews and Uriah Smith, "Business Proceedings," *Review and Herald,* May 26, 1868, p. 356.

29. Byington and Smith, "The Conference," 197; John Byington and Uriah Smith, "Fourth Annual Session of General Conference," *Review and Herald,* May 22, 1866, p. 196; Andrews and Smith, "Business Proceedings," 356.

30. George I. Butler to J. N. Andrews, Nov. 24, 1868, doc. file 320, EGW vault.

31. Statement of S. N. Haskell to C. S. Longacre, n.d., doc. file 320, EGW vault.

32. Roger Guion Davis, "Conscientious Cooperators: The Seventh-day Adventists and Military Service, 1860–1945" (Ph.D. diss., George Washington University, 1970), 99.

33. Ellen G. White, *The Desire of Ages* (Mountain View, Calif.: Pacific Press, 1940), 550.

34. See Daniel Heinz, "Service or Resistance: The Response of German Adventism to Conscription in World War I" (research paper, Andrews University, 1985).

35. *Our Youth in Time of War* (Washington, D.C.: Review and Herald, 1934), 5–6; Davis, "Conscientious Cooperators," 174–76.

36. Everett N. Dick, "The Adventist Medical Cadet Corps: As Seen by Its Founder," *Adventist Heritage* 1 (July 1974): 18–27.

37. Davis, "Conscientious Cooperators," 222.

38. *Annual Council of the General Conference Committee* (Takoma Park, Md.: General Conference of Seventh-day Adventists, 1972), 42–43.

39. Ibid.

10

❧

PROPHETIC PACIFISM IN THE AMERICAN EXPERIENCE

A Response to Grant Underwood and George R. Knight

❧

William E. Juhnke

The essays by Grant Underwood, "Pacifism and Mormonism: A Study in Ambiguity," and George R. Knight, "Adventism and Military Service: Individual Conscience in Ethical Tension," offer us a glimpse of pacifism in two church traditions born in the American experience. Both Mormonism and Adventism came out of the religious ferment of the second quarter of the nineteenth century. Both have been characterized as sectarian movements, and in that sense, especially in their early years, they are like the historic peace churches. To themselves and to others, both Adventists and Mormons have seemed to be outside the mainstream of American religion. Often because of persecution and ridicule, they developed doctrines and practices less influenced by assimilationist pressures of American society than by their own internal dynamics and creative intelligence. Further, both groups were strongly shaped by individuals whose interpretations had the force of prophecy; those interpretations indelibly marked the character of their movements. (The ghosts of Joseph Smith and Ellen G. White hover over their traditions in more immanent ways than, for example, the personages of George Fox, Menno Simons, and Alexander Mack hover over the historic peace churches.) The similarities between Mormonism and Adventism may be part of the reason for placing these two essays in the same section. Moreover, these similarities may heighten our interest in their respective experience with pacifism and peace issues.

How have these two groups, each of which was sure that it embodied the one true way—and neither of which had the remotest connections to the historic peace churches' organization, doctrines, or history—responded to the realities of war and violence in modern society? What can they teach us about the opportunities and dilemmas of pacifism in the American experience? I do not know the authors of the two essays personally, but I surmise from their points of origin, Andrews University Theological Seminary and Brigham Young University of Hawaii, that to some degree the authors reflect as insiders on their traditions. Despite or perhaps because of their connections, they have presented us with two very fine essays. I myself am a member of the General Conference Mennonite Church teaching at a Reorganized Latter Day Saints school. Partly because of that fact, it might be helpful if I reflect on recent peace developments in the Reorganized Latter Day Saints church after I comment on the Adventist and Mormon essays.

At its outset Professor Knight's essay on Adventism, military service, individual conscience, and the ensuing ethical tension does a particularly fine job of identifying the Adventist position as one of "conscientious cooperation." This form of pacifism is best seen against the backdrop of the Civil War—the precise moment, Knight explains, when the Adventist church was taking shape. The story of church leaders' dilemmas and the debate in church publications during the Civil War was the most complete and compelling part of the essay. Is it moral to volunteer to become a killer on behalf of a cause even if the cause appears to be just? Is it sane to insist on "radical pacifism" to the point of suicide? Is it an "abdication of moral responsibility" to hide behind state compulsion? What are the limits of citizens' responsibilities? All these questions were wrestled with by a church convinced of the ultimate depravity of larger society and the imminence of a second Advent. The solution, "conscientious cooperation," appears ingenious and seems to have served the denomination extremely well over the years. Peter Brock, author of *Pacifism in the United States*, has noted that "apocalyptic pacifists" such as the Seventh-day Adventists have produced a "high proportion of conscientious objectors" in the wars of the twentieth century.[1] Historic peace church people might take special note.

In studying the emergence of the Adventist position, it might be worthwhile to pursue more fully the "apocalyptic pacifism" angle. To what extent did the apocalyptic outlook open the door for Adventists' pacifist position? Perhaps societal groups need such a cataclysmic vision to sustain an antisocietal position such as pacifism. And how has apocalypticism affected Adventist attitudes to war and peace issues in more recent times? In 1960 Booton Herndon, an Adventist apologist, proclaimed that there were only "minutes to midnight"—an interpretation verified, he thought, by the doomsday clock featured in the *Bulletin of the Atomic Scientists.* He wrote of the approaching nuclear nightmare as a blessing brought about by God's hand and looked "to the future with ever increasing joy."[2] Was Herndon typical for the 1960s? In the nuclear age, what sort of response did the Adventist have in general to war and peace?

Further, as apocalypticism in the Adventist church has been muted somewhat over the years (years in which, if I read Gary Land's *Adventism in America*[3] correctly, the church has moved from sect to denomination), has the pacifist message been enlarged or diminished? In this changing environment did the Vietnam War present any problems or opportunities for the Adventist church? Unfortunately, although perhaps inevitably given the limitations of space, Professor Knight treats Adventist pacifism in the twentieth century much less fully than he treats its nineteenth-century origins.

What of the Adventist's biblical basis for opposition to combatant military service? In Knight's treatment the Adventists emphasized Old Testament legalism, namely, the commandments "thou shalt not kill" and "keep the Sabbath holy," both of which the Adventists found to be impossible to obey in combatant service. When Adventists turned to the New Testament, they seemed to read mainly its injunctions to obey the higher authorities. What shall we make of this? Certainly the historic peace church traditions have emphasized more the words and spirit of Christ, particularly those in the Sermon on the Mount. To what extent is Adventist "conscientious cooperation" enriched by Matthew 5? Have Adventists refused to kill primarily because doing so dishonors God, particularly if done on the Sabbath, or primarily because it is blessed to make peace and practice love even to one's enemies? And if Adventists have emphasized the Old Testament, have there been practical effects?

Finally, and perhaps this should have been firstly, there is a question of definition. For the purposes of Knight's essay and perhaps of this entire volume, pacifism is understood in its negative sense: the refusal to take human life. It has been a narrow question of war—to kill or not to kill. It would have been interesting to have more on pacifism in its broader sense of peacemaking, the sense of building a culture of peace and fostering reverence for life. In that broader sense, what has been Adventists' experience? Has their apocalyptic and premillennial theology predominated? To what extent do Adventists look outward not only to invite converts but also to foster justice and a sustainable peace in an imperfect and unregenerate world? For that matter, have Adventists practiced internal peacemaking? To what extent have they had a peaceful church polity? Have they fostered peaceful conflict resolution among themselves?

Perhaps it is a testimony to the success of Knight's essay that I am discussing mainly a piece he did not write rather than the one he did. His picture of the Adventist tension between pacifism and armed combat is valuable in its own right.

Professor Underwood does a stimulating job introducing us to some ambiguity within the Mormon tradition regarding issues of war and peace. Having personally viewed the Mormon tradition as one of the most aggressive and militant in the American religious experience, I was not prepared for the picture that he drew. I had not imagined that there was so much pacific rhetoric coming from Mormon leaders. The witness of thirty-year Latter-day Saints (LDS) leader J. Reuben Clark even in the midst of World War I, his condemnation of the atomic bomb, and the First Presidency's opposition in 1981 to the MX missile program all took me by surprise. In addition, where words and actions were militant, Professor Underwood has offered insights that help us to put them into perspective. I find his positing of a dichotomy between personal pacifism and collective militancy to be valuable, as is his emphasis on the Mormon experience of persecution as a context for the early militant revelations and justification of violence in self-defense. And again in this tradition, as Professor Underwood points out, an Old Testament orientation seems to be a key to understanding the attitudes toward war and peace. Another helpful observation was the practical need to demonstrate patriotic loyalty in return for acceptance as good American citizens after 1890.

I have only a few questions, and I offer them tentatively. First, definition. Does the essay stretch the meaning of pacifism too far, in order to include under its banner the "just-war" position? Is not radical pacifism at one end of a spectrum of ethical attitudes toward participation in war and just-war theory at the other? Verbal opposition to war but practical full participation in any and all wars hardly seems to qualify as pacifism. But this may be a quibble over words.

Beyond that, I remain uneasy about modifying too quickly the essential aggressiveness and militancy of Mormonism, particularly in its early years. Professor Underwood has given hints of this image by pointing to

Joseph Smith's "unsheathed sword" revelation and God's promise to wreak vengeance on the church's enemies. My apologies to Mormon leader George Cannon, but the Lord's promise to join the Latter-day Saints' battle until vengeance had been taken on all their enemies to the third and fourth generations does not sound like a hallmark revelation of restraint leaving no room in LDS hearts for revenge. Even just-war doctrine would hardly contemplate punishment to the third and fourth generations. Such an attitude is more in the tradition of Old Testament holy war or the Muslim *jihad*. Additional militant images might include the picture of Joseph Smith in full military regalia heading the Nauvoo Legion. Then, too, there were the Danite bands, spawned among Mormons in time of persecution to seek not only revenge but also blood atonement. Finally there is the image of Brigham Young in the aftermath of the Mountain Meadows Massacre, where Mormons killed "Gentile" immigrants and not vice versa. Young proposed that the epitaph on the gravestone of Mountain Meadows should read, "Vengeance is mine, and I have taken a little."[4] The point is not to condemn Mormon militancy; their persecution was unprecedented in America, and they were violent largely in response to violence. Instead, the point is to emphasize that their response in the nineteenth century was hardly pacifistic.[5] Perhaps the focus should be to analyze why Mormons were persecuted and to ask whether other, more pacifistic alternatives were possible in their situation.

Then there is a question of divisions within the LDS church itself. A 150-year survey of church attitudes toward war and peace can hardly trace every internal controversy, but did the divisions involve any debates over pacifism? What was the church's response to Clark's opposition to atomic-bomb development or his response to the First Presidency's objection to the MX missile? Underwood analyzed matters at the level of church leadership. At that level there seem to have been no arguments going on, but were there none elsewhere? Have pacifist issues not been part of the Mormon dialogue in church publications or among Mormon intellectuals? Have those issues been treated as largely uninteresting or as settled? Or does the LDS church have little literature of controversy of any kind?

Finally, as with the Adventist essay, I am interested in the broader picture of peace within the LDS church tradition. How are conflicts handled? Have the preachments of pacifism at the personal level, which Professor Underwood noted as traditional in the LDS church, left a mark on individual actions within and without the church? Has the church polity been peaceful? Are peace and harmony a function of imposed or self-imposed homogeneity, or are they the product of conflict resolution among a richly diverse people?

· · ·

Professor Underwood commented that as a teacher at a Reorganized Latter Day Saints (RLDS) school, I might draw some comparisons between the pacifist experience of the Reorganized Latter Day Saints (essentially the Mormons who stayed behind) and the Utah Latter-day Saints, the much larger group with whom his essay deals. This is an interesting prospect. Sharing the same new scripture, the Book of Mormon, the same founding prophet, Joseph Smith II, and many of Smith's revelations, the two churches' stories with regard to pacifism are understandably much the same. Nonetheless there is one recent development among the RLDS that seems interesting in this context.

At the RLDS biennial world conference in 1968, the church's president, W. Wallace Smith, gave a remarkable prophecy: a call to build a temple. Although such a call was not unusual for Utah Mormons, it was unprecedented for the RLDS. The RLDS had not followed the pattern of the early Restoration, which had seen temples built at Kirtland, Ohio, and at Nauvoo, Illinois. Even more interesting in this context was the purpose of the RLDS temple as revealed to Wallace B. Smith in 1984. Said the Prophet President: "The temple shall be dedicated to the pursuit of peace. . . . It shall be a place in which the essential meaning of the Restoration as healing and redeeming agent is given new life and understanding."[6] This revelation followed a "peace resolution" adopted at the 1982 conference two years earlier. That resolution was every bit as extraordinary as the call for the temple, for it stated a peace position for the church and urged the members to become actively engaged in peace efforts. It declared:

> We, as a church, oppose all forms of destructive violence, such as national and international conflict, war, withholding of food, terrorism, and mental and physical abuse. . . . We, as a church, urge nations toward responsible reduction of the instruments of mass destruction. . . . We, as a church, emphasize that peace is not attained by mere nonparticipation in violence. The best form of Christian witness strives to promote peace and remove the causes of aggression. These causes are removed from society by the application of the gospel of Jesus Christ in the lives of individuals and the community. To support our belief in the value of peace, we proclaim again that we shall do all within our ability to make the gospel of peace an incarnate reality.[7]

In the aftermath of the resolution and the revelation, church publications, curriculum materials, and priesthood training programs have emphasized peace issues as never before.[8] The RLDS founded a creative "relief and release" agency, Outreach International, which grew and was successful. The church's colleges adopted peace studies programs. The temple was built at the "centerplace" of the RLDS church, Independence, Missouri, and was formally dedicated in 1994 after a cost of $60 million. As it takes form, the precise meaning of its purpose—"the pursuit of peace"—has begun to be more clear. A myriad of temple programs, all still in development, include a peace pavilion, a hands-on children's peace museum, a significant peace prize regularly awarded, a peace-education center with a library and multimedia peace programs, regular peace colloquies that draw international participation, and perhaps a conflict-resolution training center.[9] Now to be sure, the RLDS "peace-church-in-the-making" has not turned the faithful into instant Quakers or Mennonites. Nor, apparently, does peacemaking in the temple mean radical pacifism. For example, the RLDS church leaders endorsed the Gulf War,[10] and there are some among the rank and file who ask skeptically where all this peace stuff is leading. Nevertheless, apparently the RLDS church is taking on a mission to become, in a phrase common in the current environment, "an ensign of peace unto the world."

How did this come about, given the common history with the Latter-day Saints church, the defensive militancy born of persecution, and an Old Testament frame of reference? How did it happen, since the RLDS church's founder, Joseph Smith III, a son of the prophet, was a great antislavery, pro-Lincoln partisan and once gave an impassioned, spontaneous recruitment speech in 1861 that netted seventeen volunteers for Lincoln's army from an erstwhile passive crowd in Quincy, Illinois?[11] How does a church get from recruiting soldiers for war to fashioning its mission as an ensign of peace in the world?

To attempt a full answer would be to go beyond my role as responder. But four points might help to explain.

First, there was the persistence of the prophetic tradition. The presidents of the RLDS church since its beginning have not been as bold as Jeremiah, Amos, or Hosea of the Old Testament or as prolific as the Restoration founder Joseph Smith Jr. Nonetheless, they have continued to assert the power of revelation. Today's RLDS president is a *prophet* president. Words of the prophet president, presented as a preliminary document to the quorums of a world conference, are considered, if approved by the faithful, to have the authority of divine inspiration. Although it has not always been the case, the persistence of the institution of prophecy in the RLDS church can be a powerful instrument for change. It is difficult to imagine the current rush of peace thinking, planning, and activity without the continuance of this prophetic tradition.

Second, there was the modernization of the RLDS movement. By the 1980s the RLDS church had largely completed the transformation from sect to denomination. Although not a member of the World Council of Churches, it has many ecumenical ties. Its worldwide missionary program, partly because it has not been as wildly successful as the missionary program of the Utah church,[12] has brought the RLDS church into contact with divergent cultures in ways that enhance a respect for diversity. Moreover, since the 1960s church appointees have been encouraged to seek theological and ministerial training; because the RLDS church has not had its own seminary, future church leaders have received education at Union, St. Paul's, and numerous other theological schools reflecting the American religious mainstream. This modernization is bringing the church's leadership and its active lay priesthood into mainstream, contemporary currents of religious and ethical thought. Inevitably that development has led to ecumenical reflection on issues of war and peace—an important context for the developments of the last decade.

Third, there was an identity crisis. With modernization and movement from sect to denomination, an identity crisis was inevitable. If the RLDS church was no longer the one true church, what was the reason for its separate existence? In the nineteenth century a central organizing principle of RLDS identity was the assertion that its members were not Utah Mormons. And although in the beginning the RLDS had much in common with their Utah brethren, a hundred years later the religious-culture gap between them had widened to a chasm. If they were not Mormons, however, what were they? If older distinctions were no longer so salient, why not pack it in and join the Methodists, Baptists, or Presbyterians? The identity crisis provided an opportunity for prophecy.

Fourth, there was an attempt to resolve the identity crisis through creatively bringing together tradition and the contemporary challenge. In Section 156, the latter-day revelation that called for temple building, the prophet took a traditional symbol, the temple, which for many of the faithful still had much lure, and fused it with a contemporary issue of critical relevance—building a culture of peace. Many RLDS members, particularly the more conservative ones, had dreamed of having their own temple. Yet few in the church were enamored with the exclusive rites, such as baptism of the dead, that characterized LDS temple practice. The 1984 revelation captured the traditional symbol for a contemporary mission.

Nor in fact was the 1980s interest in peace entirely new, alien to the RLDS, or grafted onto a hostile tradition. In fact there are pacifist themes in the RLDS tradition. Grant Underwood has identified some in the LDS experience that the RLDS shared, but some were unique to the RLDS, also. Note, for example, that the symbol the RLDS church adopted at the time of its formation in 1860 was a symbol of peace: a lion, a lamb, and a child. Perhaps the symbol has been largely ignored in practice, but its meaning has been contemplated often in the church, and it is an originative part of the RLDS identity. Moreover, the RLDS revised Bible, called by the faithful "The Inspired Version," has as its largest and most distinctive addition a story of Enoch, which outlines a community order—a Zion—where justice and peace prevail.[13] Finally, one may view the Book of Mormon itself as the story of failing attempts to recover a 200-year Golden Age of Peace. The currently evolving RLDS peace mission thus can be seen as a creative recovery of the church's peace tradition. To be sure, many of the original references to peace, including the peace symbol, hint of the church's apocalyptic and millenarian origins. In the early days the image of lion, lamb, and child symbolized the peaceable kingdom that would arrive with Christ's reign, just as the drive for building a just and peaceful (albeit exclusive) Zion was the great act of preparation for the Second Coming. Some people may see a creative, prophetic genius in the recovery of these symbols to promote a view of the world in less hostile, apocalyptic terms—a world richly diverse, interesting, and salvageable. That view may provide the vital RLDS vision and identity in the twenty-first century.

This assessment is tentative and perhaps premature. The RLDS church may not adopt peace as its organizing principle. As a Mennonite and historian who would like to see the world recover a peace heritage and become more peaceful, I may be seeing in the RLDS church too much of what I would like to see. But there you have it: in my view this is one of the more interesting peace stories developing today.

NOTES

    1. Peter Brock, *Pacifism in the United States* (Princeton, N.J.: Princeton University Press, 1968), 948.
    2. Booton Herndon, *The Seventh Day* (New York: McGraw-Hill, 1960), 267.

3. Gary Land, "Coping with Change," in Land, ed., *Adventism in America,* 208–30 (Grand Rapids: Eerdmans, 1986).

4. Juanita Brooks, *The Mountain Meadows Massacre* (Norman: University of Oklahoma Press, 1962), 182–83.

5. William Juhnke, "Anabaptism and Mormonism: A Study in Comparative History," *The John Whitmer Historical Association Journal* 2 (1982): 38–46.

6. W. Wallace Smith, "Doctrine and Covenants 156," *Saints' Herald,* May 1984, p. 195.

7. Charlene A. Gleazer, "Peace As a Way of Life," *Saints' Herald,* Apr. 1984, p. 153.

8. Sandra L. Colyer, ed., *Basic Leadership Curriculum, Temple School: TL 101—The Temple Ensign of Peace* (Independence, Mo.: Temple School Division, RLDS Church, 1990); Elbert Dempsey Jr., *Blessed Are the Peacemakers* (Independence, Mo.: Herald, 1990); *Preparing for the Temple, A Selection of Herald Articles* (Independence, Mo.: Herald, 1989); Diane Henderson, "Embodying the Temple," *Saint's Herald,* Oct. 1992, p. 13.

9. Wayne Ham, "Temple Ministries Division Report," *World Conference Reports, 1992* (Independence, Mo.: Herald, 1992), 78–81.

10. Editorial, *Saint's Herald,* Feb. 1991, p. 3.

11. Richard Howard, ed., *The Memoirs of Joseph Smith III* (Independence, Mo.: Herald, 1979), 89.

12. Keith Henry, "RLDS Mission in Japan & Its Effects upon RLDS Mission in North America" (Senior Seminar Paper, Graceland College, 1979).

13. Gen. 7:35–79, in Joseph Smith's new translation of the Bible.

PART 4

≈

INTERWAR PROTESTANT PACIFISTS,
VIETNAM-ERA METHODISTS

≈

11

🙚

THE LIBERAL PROTESTANT PEACE MOVEMENT
BETWEEN THE WORLD WARS

A Realist Critique

🙚

William R. Marty

On questions of war and peace, Christians have acted within three broad traditions: pacifism, just-war theory, and the crusade. Scholars have long held that pacifism is the earliest of these three traditions, although recent scholarship strongly challenges that view.[1] Paul Ramsey, a noted Christian ethicist who accepted the earlier view, provided a list of reasons for that early pacifism.[2] The list included the exemption of Jews from Roman military service, the avoidance of military service to avoid idolatrous emperor worship,[3] anti-imperialism, the association of military service with devotion to the things of this world, the separation of early Christians in a large empire from positions of political power and responsibility, and the expectation of the imminent return of Christ.[4]

Ramsey's list also included the early Christians' desire to act in accordance with what they understood to be the implications of Christian love. Those implications were inevitably a matter of interpretation, however, since the Gospels do not provide a set of legalistic commands on the subject. Thus the historian Roland Bainton (who was sympathetic to pacifism) agreed with Ramsey (who was sympathetic to just-war theory) that pacifism was an attempt to *interpret* and apply the meaning of Christian love, not simply a clear commandment of the Gospels. As

Bainton put it: "The rejection of military service on the part of the early church was not however derived from any explicit prohibition in the New Testament. The attitude of the Gospels to the soldiers' calling was neutral. The centurion was commended for his faith rather than for his profession, but was not called upon to abandon his profession."[5]

THREE TRADITIONS: PACIFISM, JUST WAR, AND CRUSADE

Pacifism is one interpretation of the implications of Christian faith and love. Although it has always been the stance of some Christians, it did not remain the stance of most. By A.D. 177 Christians fought under Marcus Aurelius.[6] A decisive change occurred when Constantine converted to Christianity, however. Before then Christians were ruled; they did not have the responsibility of rule. They had been enjoined to "render unto Caesar what is Caesar's," but they had never had the burden of *being* Caesar or the responsibilities that being Caesar entails for protecting peace and good order or for restraining humans burdened with a fallen nature. In assuming the burdens of rule, Christians reassessed the implications of Christian love. As they did, most abandoned pacifism. Some have considered the change to have been a betrayal and a fall, but most have not. Most Christians have thought instead that (in Ramsey's words) "The change-over to just-war doctrine and practice was not a 'fall'. . . . [but rather] a change of tactics only. The basic strategy remained the same: responsible love and service of one's neighbors. . . . Christians simply came to see that the service of the real needs of all the men for whom Christ died required more than personal, witnessing action. It also required them to be involved in maintaining the organized social and political life in which all men live."[7]

Christians with the burden of political responsibility would allow armed forces for police and military duties—to preserve order and justice, to preserve the community and protect one's neighbor, and to protect the innocent from the guilty. Early versions of the just-war doctrine did not allow personal self-defense, however. Christians would fight to defend neighbors or the community but not to defend their own lives against violent attack.[8] The object of using force was to "vindicate justice and restore peace," and the "motive must be love."[9] Like pacifism, just-war theory was an attempt to discern and do what love requires, and as Christians assumed the responsibilities of rule, it became for many centuries the dominant interpretation. Only in recent years has that interpretation come under much challenge.

The third tradition with regard to war and peace in the Christian community is that of the crusade, or holy war. Drawing the distinction between just war and crusade, Catholic scholar George Weigel has noted that "in the crusade tradition, war is a positive moral good" that "expresses the will of God in the world," "punishes the heathen," "cleanses the world of sin," and "advances the claims of the Gospel." By contrast the "just-war tradition . . . views war as a moral tragedy"—"unavoidable, in certain circumstances, but a moral tragedy nonetheless." In this view war is never "a positive good" but at best "the lesser of evils."[10]

According to Bainton the differences among the three traditions—pacifism, just war, and the crusade—are not different views of God or even of fallen human nature; instead the disagreements are about how to deal with human depravity and the relationship of the church and the world. Bainton noted that "pacifism has commonly despaired of the world and dissociated itself either from society altogether, or from political life, and especially from war." Meanwhile, in the just-war view, "evil can be restrained by the coercive power of the state." In that view "the Church should support the state in this endeavor and individual Christians as citizens should fight under the auspices of the state." Bainton continued that the third position, belief in crusade, "belongs to a theocratic view that the Church, even though it be a minority, should impose its will upon a recalcitrant world." Therefore, Bainton noted, pacifism is "often associated with withdrawal, the just war with qualified participation, and the crusade with dominance of the Church over the world.[11]

Bainton's is a fair summary of the traditional understanding. In this century, however, many pacifists have adopted a fundamentally altered stance toward the world.

PACIFISM: FROM WITHDRAWAL TO ENGAGEMENT

Christian pacifism has traditionally been the province of those who withdraw, to some degree and in some manner, from the struggles of the world. In Roman Catholicism it was the position only of those who withdrew to monasteries or of others in religious vocations. In Protestantism it was restricted mainly to churches or sects that withdrew completely or, as in the case of early American Quakers, to some who participated in politics but tried, not always successfully, not to help raise and use military forces.[12] Traditionally, then, to be a pacifist or a member of a traditional peace church was to withdraw, at least in part, from the world. In the twentieth century the pattern changed greatly, however. Both here and in certain other democracies, such as Great Britain, pacifism spread broadly beyond the traditional peace churches, into the liberal Protestant denominations. The new pacifism was most notable for wanting to be effective in the world.[13] It aimed not only to witness to love but also to lead in establishing peace in the world. It is thus worth looking at the efficacy of the measures that the new pacifists advocated.

Between the world wars pacifism spread rapidly and extensively among the churches. Partly the churches were repenting from their too-uncritical support for the Allies during World War I. In retrospect the Allies seem not to have been so virtuous. Church people felt they had been manipulated by clever but unprincipled war propaganda and, worst of all, that they and their churches had too easily given up their scruples about war to sanctify an unholy crusade.[14]

Also, the new pacifism was born of a conviction that modern, technological, mass war was simply too terrible, bringing slaughter all out of proportion to any rational purpose. Modern war seemed immoral and unthinkable under any circumstances. In this view just-war theory seemed no longer defensible because the horrors of modern war could not be brought within its terms. Thus historian Donald Meyer has written that the new pacifists (and the neutralist churchmen) always reconciled their divisions by agreeing that "war gained nothing, war was worse than anything, always."[15] There were changes, too, in ideas about the potential for establishing God's kingdom in this world and about the possibilities for peace. At the least, some of these Christians hoped for more in this world than most Christians had hoped for in many centuries.

The turn to pacifism among a number of the Protestant churches was led by those who met in a number of umbrella organizations, most notably the Fellowship of Reconciliation (FOR), and it was backed by influential journals such as *Christian Century* and *The World Tomorrow*. In 1931 Kirby Page and *The World Tomorrow* polled about 53,000 ministers, of whom some 19,372 responded. In a startling rejection of traditional just-war theory, 62 percent of the respondents believed that the churches should go on record "as refusing to sanction or support any future war."[16] The poll had not covered Jews, Roman Catholics, Lutherans, Southern Baptists, or Southern Methodists. Nonetheless it did reveal that more than 12,000 ministers in mainline denominations wanted their churches to withhold support from any future war. Pacifism had broken the bounds of the traditional peace churches.

In 1934 the poll was repeated. This time 67 percent of the more than 20,000 respondents opposed their churches' supporting any future war.[17] Two years later, in 1936, a Methodist bishop, James Baker, obtained parallel results. He got those results even after Hitler had seized absolute power, invoked anti-Semitic laws, and openly rearmed in violation of treaties—and after Mussolini had invaded Abyssinia. In 1936 Hitler invaded the Rhineland and Spain dissolved into civil war, yet 56 percent of the 13,000 who responded to Baker still said they would refuse to support any future war.[18] Pacifism had become a significant position, at least among mainline Protestant ministers.

Some observers thought pacifism had become more than that. Robert Miller said it had become, even by the early 1920s, the "'party line' of liberal Protestantism."[19] Walter Van Kirk, after assessing the official statements of denominations that were members of the Federal Council of Churches, asserted in 1934 that religion had renounced war.[20] The council itself had passed a resolution in 1932 proclaiming that "the church as an institution should neither sanction nor bless war." There were only one or two dissenting voices among the four hundred delegates.[21]

For many Protestant church leaders and organizations between World Wars I and II, if not for the Protestant laity, Christianity entailed pacifism in the sense of refusal to sanction or participate in any war. Even in 1941, after France and much of Europe had fallen to the furious German onslaught and British forces had been driven from the Continent, some of this sentiment remained. Bainton has reported that "the Episcopalians were ready to support Britain; the Presbyterians were of divided counsels; [and] the Disciples were noninterventionist." Meanwhile the Methodists and the Congregationalists remained strongly pacifist, and even as war loomed, Lutherans were abandoning their traditional just-war doctrine. "As for Catholics, a poll of 54,000 students disclosed 97 percent opposed" entry into World War II.[22]

THE NEW PACIFISM: STRATEGIES AND CRITIQUES

The strong movement away from just-war theory among Protestant church leaders and organizations between the wars was not a movement away from engagement in the world. Quite the contrary. The new pacifists energetically attempted to mobilize opinion and influence government policies so as to bring an end to war. Therefore it is appropriate to examine the policies these pacifists preferred. Did the new politically engaged pacifism effectively refute the older Christian understanding that, in a world of fallen humans, pacifism can be a way for only a few individuals seeking perfection or for a sect that withdraws? Did it show that pacifism is a way to live in the world with political responsibility?

How was war to be avoided? Donald Meyer has written that for these church people, "the way to eliminate war was to support every policy consistent with absolute peace, oppose every policy and measure that accepted even the possibility of war."[23] Perhaps Meyer overstated the case, but let us examine the views of two leaders of the church peace movement, Kirby Page and Charles Morrison. Page served for a time as secretary of the Fellowship of Reconciliation and from 1926 to 1934 was chief editor of *The World Tomorrow.* He was for "American membership in League and World Court, American support for the outlawing of war, abandonment of all military and political imperialism in Latin America and Asia, freedom for the Philippines, reduction and if necessary cancellation of war debts both Allied and German, reduction of tariffs, [and] disarmament led by America."[24] Page qualified any support for the League of Nations because he had "reservations against the League's power to apply sanctions."[25] Sanctions could lead to war. Charles Chatfield, in summing up Page's policies, has described him as a leader in the "antipreparedness cause."[26]

Charles Morrison, editor of the *Christian Century,* the leading journalistic voice of liberal Protestantism by the mid-1930s, was also a leader in the peace movement and a politically engaged pacifist. He helped to lead the battle for the Kellogg-Briand Pact of 1928, which outlawed aggressive war.[27] His journal fought conscription, rearmament, the destroyers-for-bases deal, lend-lease, entanglement with Britain or France, aid to Britain, and any other breach of neutrality. He himself called for negotiated settlements of differences, and when a Belgian statesman put forward a plan for economic rearrangements in Europe, soon dubbed the "Van Zeeland proposals," Morrison led a fight for its adoption. He was instrumental also in getting first the Federal Council of Churches and then the World Council of Churches to agree to some type of international meeting to try to arrange concessions and a negotiated settlement. Referring to that meeting of churches, Donald Meyer has written that "thirty-four persons . . . collected in the Europe of July, 1939, to discuss reallocation of the world."[28] They did produce a statement, but by then war had broken out. In May 1940 Morrison proposed that President Roosevelt send a delegation to all the neutral capitals in Europe to assemble a peace conference for devising a radically new Europe. The idea was widely discussed. Unfortunately, as Meyer noted, by then there were "fewer neutral capitals."[29]

Page and Morrison, FOR, the *Christian Century* and *The World Tomorrow*, the Federal Council of Churches, many individual church organizations, and the religious peace movement all intended to be effective. They put pressure on government leaders. They put faith in international organizations (the League of Nations), in outlawing war (the Kellogg-Briand Pact), in agreements to settle conflicts without war (the Locarno Pact of 1925 and others), in either unilateral disarmament (opposition to military appropriations) or agreements to limit arms (the Washington and London conferences), in finding just economic settlements that would resolve what were thought to be the economic causes of war, and in noninvolvement and neutrality. Many of their proposals were sound as far as they went, but their pacifist commitment itself prevented them from going far enough. Consider how pacifism undermined the effectiveness of the peace effort.

The new pacifism was in principle internationalist; for example, it supported the League of Nations. That support was vitiated by a fatal flaw, however. Although the movement supported international condemnation of aggression, it tended to oppose all serious sanctions, for sanctions might lead to war. For example, in the case of Italy's invasion of Abyssinia, the league threatened sanctions. Italy's Fascist leader Mussolini rejected them, however, and then league members, afraid that serious sanctions might involve them in war, deliberately imposed sanctions that they knew would not seriously impede Mussolini's plans.[30] As Britain's great leader Churchill later caustically noted, under pacifist restrictions sanctions must not lead to war; therefore the league "proceeded to the rescue of Abyssinia on the basis that nothing must be done to hamper the invading Italian armies."[31]

For the new pacifism, this was not a good beginning. Theologian Reinhold Niebuhr asked, "Is it really 'Christian,' is it God's will, never to call the bluff of a bully for fear that you might be involved in violence? Then we had better prepare for the complete victory of the barbarism that is spreading over Europe."[32] The conquest of Abyssinia graphically illustrates the traditional failing of an engaged, political pacifism. If one is interested in achieving a degree of justice and order in the world, then one must be willing, if necessary, to resist armed aggression with force. Without that will, collective condemnation of Mussolini's aggression came to nothing.

Support for the League of Nations without support for the actions necessary to make the league meaningful was characteristic of the new pacifism and the peace movement that dominated the democracies between the wars. Thus the Kellogg-Briand Pact, which outlawed aggressive war, was hailed with enormous enthusiasm. Morrison and Page had campaigned hard for it. Kellogg, the U.S. secretary of state, proclaimed, "We have made peace at last." Briand, the French foreign minister, believed that this "marked a new day in the history of mankind." Nearly everyone signed. Still, and characteristically, the treaty lacked enforcement provisions. As historian Barbara Tuchman dryly noted: "In short, it was empty."[33]

The story was similar with the Locarno Treaties of 1925. These agreements tried to bind nations by solemn commitment to settle matters by arbitration. Germany bound itself to "pursue the course of arbitration in any disputes with Belgium, France, Poland or Czechoslovakia."[34] Nevertheless, each nation bound to Germany in this "binding" agreement—Belgium, France, Poland, and Czechoslovakia—soon found itself betrayed, and conquered, by Germany.

The new pacifism was not wrong in trying to establish commitments to the peaceful settlements of disputes. But binding agreements are futile without the will and the means to enforce them. As Churchill later observed, "no foreign policy can have validity if there is no adequate force behind it and no national readiness to make the necessary sacrifices to produce that force."[35] Unfortunately, neither the peace movements in the democracies nor the religious peace movement in the United States displayed the will, or supported creation of the necessary military strength, to enforce treaties such as the Kellogg-Briand and Locarno agreements. Instead they depended entirely on the good will and good faith of the other side. There came a day when that good will and good faith were not there.

In fact, those who hoped for peace had a touching faith in the power of the promise. It was a faith that produced an avid quest for signatures on pieces of paper. Speaking of British prime minister Neville Chamberlain's famous accord with Hitler at Munich in 1938, the First Lord of the Admiralty, Duff Cooper, resigning in protest, was contemptuous that Chamberlain had "confidence in the good will and the word of Herr Hitler." Cooper pointed to a string of solemn international agreements that Hitler had already made and then broken. "Still," he complained, "the Prime Minister believes that he can rely upon the [German dictator's] good faith."[36]

Cooper delivered his speech, to the British House of Commons, just

after Chamberlain had returned from Munich telling a euphoric public: "This is the second time there has come back from Germany to
Downing Street peace with honor. I believe it is peace in our time."[37] Of
course this promise also produced neither peace nor honor. Nor was
there much excuse for such naïveté on the part of those committed to
peace. History is replete with examples of broken promises. One need
look no further back than World War I, when Germany dismissed its
earlier pledge to honor Belgium's neutrality as merely "'*ein Fetzen Pa-
pier*' ('a scrap of paper')."[38] Securing promises from dictators while lack-
ing the will or power to enforce them—such lack being characteristic
of the new pacifism and of the pacifistic democracies between the
wars—did not prove a fruitful path to peace.

But perhaps arms themselves were the problem. Page had argued that
by "aggressive good will" before World War I, Germany's neighbors
could have shown Germany that no harm was intended it; he had argued further that the German public, relieved of its fears, would have
removed the German militarists from power, thereby securing peace.[39]
The implication was that nations arm from fear and that by unilateral
reduction or elimination of arms, fear would be removed, thus producing peace. Neither history nor the 1930s served this theory well, however. There no doubt are wars fought out of fear, but there are also wars
fought for revenge, for domination, for gain and glory, for pride and
honor, for the sake of a master race or the purposes of the proletariat,
or for empire and dominion. Moreover, disarmament—for example, in
the face of a nation seeking revenge—may not be a path to peace. Certainly reduction of arms in the face of the Nazis did not lead to peace.

Closely related to the idea that arms themselves are the problem was
the notion that democracies should refuse to engage in an arms race
because arms races "always lead to war." Here and abroad pacifists fierce-
ly resisted engaging in an arms race with the dictators. In Great Britain
between the wars the Labour party was led for years by George Lans-
bury, a pacifist[40] and, in the description of Reinhold Niebuhr, a saintly
Christian.[41] Later it was led by Ramsey MacDonald, all his life a pacifist.[42]
True to his faith, MacDonald was proud of rapidly dismantling England's armed forces.[43] He thoroughly opposed rearmament, sanctions
that might lead to war, and collective security that might require intervention on behalf of allies. Clement Attlee, a third Labour party leader,
was an equally strong proponent of pacifism and disarmament.[44] Under such leadership the Labour party, helped by the Liberal party, stead-
fastly resisted all attempts at military preparedness.[45] The refusal to race

while one's deadly enemies raced on was an ill-conceived strategy, however. When war began, it cost dearly.

Another notion held strongly at that time was that a major cause of war was the munitions makers' desire for profits. "Take the profits out of war!" cried the new pacifists. Munitions makers were "merchants of death." No matter that wars had long predated capitalism. Here and in the other democracies the peace movement tried to remove the profits from the arms industry. In the U.S. Senate the "Nye Committee" caused a national sensation with charges that munitions makers were responsible for World War I,[46] and the Senate itself ratified an international convention designed to reduce the arms trade.[47] It is true that the German war industries made great profits, but it was hardly in the democracies' interests to refuse to match them in arms out of fear that they might give profits to their own industrialists. The democracies did not recognize this fact until too late, however. By then most of the democracies of Europe had been conquered, and a nearly disarmed Britain was struggling alone—saved only by the English Channel and a very few brave British airmen.

Churchill, who led Britain in a deadly war against the most terrible odds, later wrote forcefully on the effect of another pacifist hope, arms-limitation agreements. He noted that the effect of the Anglo-German treaty of 1935 (sought because Germany had built larger warships than earlier treaties had allowed, and in spite of German violations of those and other treaties) had been to allow "Germany a Programme of new construction which would set her yards to work for at least ten years."[48] The general effect of such treaties, he observed, had been to allow both Germany and Japan to build for years as furiously as they could and not run afoul of the democracies (which were adhering to treaties); to allow both Germany and Japan, for a variety of reasons, to build larger ships with larger guns; and to allow Germany, at least, the additional advantages that accrued to those who cheat. Already in 1936 Churchill had objected furiously that "we alone are injured by treaties."[49] When World War II came in 1939, he was well-situated to assess the impact of the interwar arms-limitation pacts. Treaties, he observed, bind only those who do not cheat—and his nation's deadly enemies had cheated.

In fact the problem with arms limitation runs deeper than mere cheating. Once again, Churchill expressed it well: "It is the greatest mistake to mix up disarmament with peace. When you have peace you will have disarmament."[50] But Churchill's was not the only voice. After long experience Salvador de Madariaga, chairman of the League of Nations

Disarmament Commission, concluded that "the trouble with disarmament is that the problem of war is tackled upside down and at the wrong end. . . . Nations don't distrust each other because they are armed; they are armed because they distrust each other. . . . To want disarmament before a minimum of common agreement on fundamentals is as absurd as to want people to go undressed in winter."[51]

Arms-limitation treaties gave the democracies a false sense of security, but they did not prevent the interwar dictators from building furiously in preparation for their conquests. The pacifists and the pacifistic democracies seriously underestimated the gravity of the situation and proposed ineffective measures. Conversely they resisted the very measures that might have cowed and deterred their enemies.

Two additional strategies commended themselves to the new pacifists. One was the attempt to avoid war by eliminating the injustices leading to war. The interwar pacifists especially emphasized economic injustices. For example, Morrison of the *Christian Century* zealously advocated the Van Zeeland proposals for economic rearrangements in Europe and pushed for that meeting of churchmen for the "reallocation of the world."[52] It is hard to see the moral logic of such efforts, however. If it was wrong for Britain to colonize India, then how could it be right to try for peace by allocating Germany its share of illicit empire? If injustice leads to war, then how could giving Germany its share of unjust empire produce peace? Is the world to be redivided each time an excluded power is denied a share? Is that not an invitation to become a power and then make demands? And what if there is no agreement on what the allocation is to be? What, in fact, would have satisfied Hitler—or the Japanese? The questions expose a muddle, not the least a moral muddle. As the Allies were to discover, each appeasement of Hitler whetted his appetite for more and caused him to respect and fear them less. This was not an effective strategy for peace.

The attempt by pacifists and the peace movement in the United States to avoid war by avoiding U.S. entanglement also failed. In effect the pacifists ended up as allies of the isolationists, the America Firsters, the Fortress America crowd. It was an odd alliance, one that sought peace through neutrality. For some countries this strategy worked. Sweden, which supplied much of the iron ore for the Nazi war machine, was allowed to remain neutral while nations all around it, also hoping to remain neutral, were conquered and occupied. Switzerland also escaped. But trying to stay neutral did not work for Holland, Belgium, Denmark, or Norway, and in the end it did not work for the United States. Staying out of war depends, finally, on others, on whether they wish to war on you and whether they believe they have the strength to do it. Thus the efforts of Holland and Belgium to remain neutral failed, if for no other reason, because Germany found that the best way to conquer France was to drive through these two nations. Thus America's attempt to remain neutral failed when the Japanese decided to bomb Pearl Harbor (our nonviolent sanctions against the Japanese having in fact provoked them), and Hitler, scorning what he thought was a flabby democracy, honored his alliance with Japan. The U.S. desire to stay neutral failed because America's enemies disregarded it.

Finally, Christian pacifism views itself as the proper expression of Christian love. Nevertheless, it is hard to see how standing by without doing anything to help while one nation after another is conquered by fascist dictators is an expression of love. This indeed was Reinhold Niebuhr's charge—that to be neutral in such a contest is a loveless choice that sacrifices the innocent neighbor.[53] This was also the criticism that Dean Shailer Mathews of the University of Chicago Divinity School had made of Page's pacifism in 1918. It was, he said, "as if the Good Samaritan, if he had come down a little earlier, had waited until the robbers had finished with the traveler before he assisted him."[54]

THE NEW PACIFISM: A FAILED HYBRID

The period between the world wars was a time of great shift in religious opinion. New developments in theology, new attitudes toward what was possible and necessary, and a revulsion against the horrors of the Great War produced a new, politically engaged pacifism that intended to influence governments to avoid and prevent war. Earlier pacifists had mainly withdrawn from this sinful world. They had not expected wars to cease, nor had they tried, at least directly, to influence the powers of this world. Instead, as monastics or sectarians, those earlier pacifists had stood as a reproach to this world and a testimony in favor of the next. They refused the things that were Caesar's. The older pacifism, in rejecting political power, rejected political responsibility or left it to others acting according to different standards.

The traditional alternative to the pacifism of withdrawal was some form of just-war theory. Those who accepted political responsibility—and most Christians over the whole span from the time of Constantine until the present have accepted such responsibility as a duty of Christian love—accepted, as well, a responsibility to use force on occasion.

They accepted it precisely as a necessary deduction of what Christian love requires if the neighbor is to be protected. The use of Caesar's power is legitimate because we *are* our brother's keeper, and in this world to accept that responsibility is to accept the necessity of force.

The new pacifism, which spread broadly in Protestant churches between the wars, was a hybrid. It took from traditional pacifism the refusal to accept violence or engage in war, and it took from traditional just-war theory the appropriateness of acting in the world, accepting political power, and using that power for the goal of peace and protection of the neighbor. But does such a hybrid make sense? Can one be fully committed to peace under all circumstances and also be committed to effective action in the world to protect the innocent neighbor?

The experience between the wars strongly supports the traditional positions of pacifism and just war but not the new hybrid. The engaged political pacifism of the interwar period, both religious and secular, was quite effective in influencing the policies of the great democracies, especially those of Great Britain and the United States. Nonetheless, those great pacifistic democracies failed to deter war. Most of the European democracies were conquered. Britain was saved only by the Channel, the heroism of its pilots and the British people, and German blunders in its air war. What in particular was wrong with the hybrid? The simple answer is that it disarms those who would resist evil.

The new pacifism remained pacifism. It refused to fight. That refusal undermined the effectiveness of nearly every one of its own policies for pursuit of peace. The newly engaged pacifism supported international organizations such as the League of Nations and the World Court, but it had a reservation. It was pacifist; it would not support war; therefore it would not support sanctions that carried a risk of war. The new pacifism accepted responsibility for the neighbor in the world, but when the dictator chose to conquer the neighbor, the new pacifism sacrificed the neighbor rather than fight the dictator. This was neither an effective way to preserve peace nor an obvious expression of love for, say, the Abyssinian neighbor.

The new pacifism also put much energy into seeking international treaties and promises. Some of its efforts would have had merit, had there been the will and the power to enforce these agreements and promises. The new pacifism was still pacifism, however, and thus it shrank from using violence to enforce anything. Moreover, unlike the traditional pacifism, it led the battle to ensure that its nonpacifist fellow citizens also were denied the military force levels they would have needed to enforce these treaties and promises. Consequently the new pacifism was reduced to begging dictators for promises to behave. When the dictators did not behave, there was no recourse but to beg them again. Thus encouraged, the dictators became quite fearless. In effect, then, the new pacifism helped to produce invasions, war, conquests, and the deaths of some tens of millions.

If one accepts the mantle of Caesar—the responsibility for enforcing a degree of harmony and order in the world, of protecting subjects and citizens—then love requires serious consideration of how fallen humans behave in this world and of what is necessary to restrain them from gratifying their worst desires. The new engaged hybrid pacifism failed those tests.

PACIFISM AND VIOLENCE

Pacifism, even when it offers total nonresistance and capitulation in order to secure peace, does not necessarily secure an end to violence, either against the pacifists themselves or against others. Pacifists should be reflectively aware that avoiding a war or ending it will not necessarily mean avoiding violence or terrible slaughter of innocents. The Nazis set about to kill *all* the Jews and Gypsies in the nations they dominated—men, women, children, babies, old, young, healthy, infirm—all. As they invaded and conquered various countries, they killed approximately 6 million of the 9 million Jews of Europe, plus millions of other people. Just-war theory may presume that there are times when surrender is imperative[55] if the violence of war is out of proportion to the violence that may follow surrender; even as it makes that point, however, it leaves open the possibility that in some cases the opposite will be true. Surely fighting the Nazis was a case of the opposite: the killing of Jews and others stopped only when the Nazis were defeated in battle. But pacifists do not concede such cases.

Had the Nazis conquered the United States, or had we surrendered to avoid the horrors of war, then we must assume that the Nazis would have set about killing every single Jew and Gypsy in the United States as they had in Europe. Moreover, we should recall that Nazis considered not only Jews to be subhuman; they thought the same of Africans. Of course it is not imaginable that the Nazis would have tried to exterminate all Americans of African descent, but neither had it been thought imaginable that they would try to exterminate the whole "race" of Jews. Yet they did try, and they nearly succeeded. Neither appeasement of an enemy, nonviolent resistance, nor nonresistance and surrender ensure an end to violence and the slaughter of innocents. In some cases it just marks the beginning.

Nor were the Nazis an aberration. "Progressive" communist regimes have proved to be equally deadly to those in their power. Indeed, they performed some of the great slaughters of history. One could elaborate on the great slaughters in the Soviet Union, which began immediately in 1917–18 and by the 1930s had reached 40,000 per month.[56] One could mention those in "progressive" China: Peter Berger has cited an estimate of "no more than ten million, no less than five million" outright executions (plus many who died less directly) during the collectivization and "rectification" campaigns of 1945–55.[57] Neither the Soviet Union nor communist China compared in horror to Cambodia and Pol Pot's Khmer Rouge, however.[58] In Cambodia in the 1970s whole categories of people were exterminated: members of the former government; army personnel; "intellectuals"; and many ethnic groups, such as Indians, Chinese, and Vietnamese. David Hawk, an anti–Vietnam War activist and a past executive director of Amnesty International, USA, has recounted an interview with a man whose wife was of Vietnamese descent. "He told me," Hawk wrote, "that the Khmer Rouge had killed not only her, but five of their sons, three of their daughters, three of their grandchildren, and sixteen other members of his wife's family."[59] Religious people too were attacked, as they had been at times by the Soviets and the Chinese.[60] Only the intervention of Vietnamese military forces halted this slaughter of the innocents.

Thus even if pacifism were able to secure the avoidance of war, that would not itself stop violence or the slaughter of innocents. This presents an interesting point. Just-war theory is often condemned because modern war leads to the killing of innocent noncombatants. In fact, however, pacifist refusal to use force to stop terrible tyrannies itself leaves those tyrannical regimes free to torture, starve, kill, and slaughter every age and condition of humankind—men, women, children, and babies. It is certainly not clear that the refusal to use force to stop even monstrous evil is what love requires. Certainly it is not what most Christians through the centuries, including the "Age of Faith," have thought love requires.

One could, of course, argue that Christians cannot use force because Christians are enjoined to "resist not evil." If one takes that as a commandment applicable to all circumstances, however, then it forbids the new pacifism as well as the old just-war theory. The new pacifism, the politically engaged pacifism, engages in a whole range of techniques of nonviolent resistance, all intended to resist evil and to do so effectively. After all, nonviolent resistance is still resistance. The interpretation that allows "resist not evil" to become "resist evil, but nonviolently," can as easily become "resist evil, even sometimes with force, if that is what love requires."[61]

If we judge on the basis of the experience between the wars,[62] we find that a politically engaged pacifism, by its commitment to pacifism, undermines the very strategies it proposes for avoiding war. It proves to be incapable of securing peace, a cessation of violence, or an end to the slaughter of innocents. It sacrifices justice. It needlessly sacrifices the brother and sister. There is no reason, then, to suppose that it is an acceptable alternative to the traditional pacifism of withdrawal (as witness), on the one hand, or, on the other, the traditional willingness to use force under some circumstances, if political responsibilities are accepted.

NOTES

Professors Theron F. Schlabach and Richard T. Hughes were generous in accepting this essay criticizing the view informing this book. I appreciate their largeness of spirit. I would like to thank Glenn Chafetz, Carl Gibeaux, and Martin E. Marty for their comments and suggestions and Professor Schlabach for his careful editing. This essay augments and refines the arguments of an earlier essay, "The Role of Religious Organizations in the Peace Movement between the Wars," in Barbara M. Yarnold, ed., *The Role of Religious Organizations in Social Movements* (New York: Praeger [an imprint of Greenwood Publishing Group, Inc., Westport, Conn.], 1991), 45–70, 113. This research was funded by the United States Institute of Peace. The opinions, findings, and conclusions or recommendations expressed in this essay are those of the author and do not necessarily reflect the views of the Institute.

Realism can have many meanings. As used in the title of this essay, it means only the difference between pacifism and the just-war view.

1. Paul Ramsey has noted the traditional view that the earliest Christians were pacifist; see his *War and the Christian Conscience: How Shall Modern War Be Conducted Justly?* (Durham, N.C.: Duke University Press, 1961), xv. A wealth of evidence to challenge and modify that view is provided by John Helgeland, Robert J. Daly, and J. Patout Burns in *Christians and the Military: The Early Experience* (Philadelphia: Fortress, 1985). Professors Martin E. Marty and James L. Guth drew my attention to the later scholarship. This essay's argument does not hinge on which of the two views is correct, however.

2. Ramsey, *War and the Christian Conscience*, xv ff.

3. See also Geoffrey Nuttall, *Christian Pacifism in History* (London: Blackwell and Mott, 1958).

4. Ramsey, *War and the Christian Conscience*, xv ff.; cf. Roland H. Bainton, *Christian Attitudes toward War and Peace: A Historical Survey and Critical Reevaluation* (Nashville: Abingdon, 1960), 66ff.

5. Bainton, *Christian Attitudes toward War and Peace*, 53.

6. Ramsey, *War and the Christian Conscience*, xvi; Bainton, *Christian Attitudes toward War and Peace*, 68–69.

7. Ramsey, *War and the Christian Conscience*, xvii.

8. Ibid., xvii–xviii; Bainton, *Christian Attitudes toward War and Peace*, 97–98.

9. Bainton, *Christian Attitudes toward War and Peace*, 14.

10. George Weigel, *Peace & Freedom: Christian Faith, Democracy and the Problem of War* (Washington, D.C.: The Institute on Religion and Democracy, 1987), 38; cf. George Weigel, *Tranquillitas Ordinis: The Present Failure and Future Promise of American Catholic Thought on War and Peace* (New York: Oxford University Press, 1987), 38–41.

11. Bainton, *Christian Attitudes toward War and Peace*, 14–15.

12. See, for example, A. J. Beitzinger's account of the Quaker experience in Pennsylvania in *A History of American Political Thought* (New York: Dodd, Mead, 1972), 80–84.

13. There are other understandings of pacifism. Stanley Hauerwas, for example, insists that "My pacifism, which is based upon christological presuppositions, does not look on our disavowal of war as a strategy to make the world less violent" (Stanley Hauerwas and Richard John Neuhaus, "Pacifism, Just War & the Gulf: An Exchange," *First Things* 13 [May 1991]: 39; see also Hauerwas, *The Peaceable Kingdom: A Primer in Christian Ethics* [Notre Dame, Ind.: University of Notre Dame Press, 1983]). This statement seems to express a pacifism of withdrawal, but Hauerwas has refused this understanding, writing: "Christian commitment to non-violence does not require withdrawal from the world and the world's violence. Rather it requires the Christian to be in the world with an enthusiasm that cannot be defeated" (Hauerwas, *Should War be Eliminated? Philosophical and Theological Investigations* [Milwaukee: Marquette University Press, 1984], 57). Hauerwas does engage in public debate about policies of war and peace and makes recommendations. His pacifism, despite its being a form of discipleship rather than a strategy to reduce violence, is a politically engaged pacifism and on that level is subject to the type of critique made in this essay.

14. See Ray H. Abrams, *Preachers Present Arms: The Role of the American Churches and Clergy in World Wars I and II, with Some Observations on the War in Vietnam* (Scottdale, Pa.: Herald, 1969). Cf. Patrick Glynn, former special assistant to the director of the Arms Control and Disarmament Agency, who

provides a critical review of the period leading up to World War I insofar as myths about that period provided "the historical and intellectual origins of arms control theology" (Glynn, "The Sarajevo Fallacy: The Historical and Intellectual Origins of Arms Control Theology," *The National Interest* 9 [Fall 1987]: 3–32). In many respects Glynn's analysis amounts to a "realist" critique of many of the assumptions that underlay the strategies adopted by the peace movement between the world wars (and after).

15. Donald Meyer, *The Protestant Search for Political Realism, 1919–1941* (Berkeley: University of California Press, 1960), 353.

16. Charles Chatfield, *For Peace and Justice: Pacifism in America, 1914–1941* (Knoxville: University of Tennessee Press, 1971), 127–28.

17. Ibid., 128.

18. Meyer, *The Protestant Search for Political Realism*, 354.

19. Robert Miller, *How Shall They Hear without a Preacher? The Life of Earnest Fremont Tittle* (Chapel Hill: University of North Carolina Press, 1971), 403.

20. Walter Van Kirk, *Religion Renounces War* (Chicago: Willett, Clark, 1934).

21. Quoted in ibid., 44.

22. Bainton, *Christian Attitudes toward War and Peace*, 219.

23. Meyer, *The Protestant Search for Political Realism*, 352.

24. Ibid., 155.

25. Ibid., 352.

26. Chatfield, *For Peace and Justice*, 146.

27. Meyer, *The Protestant Search for Political Realism*, 53.

28. Ibid., 373.

29. Ibid.

30. Winston S. Churchill, *The Gathering Storm*, vol. 1 of *The Second World War*, 6 vols. (Boston: Houghton Mifflin, 1948), 174–76.

31. Ibid., 176.

32. Reinhold Niebuhr, "The Will of God and the Van Zeeland Report," in D. B. Robertson, ed., *Love and Justice: Selections from the Shorter Writings of Reinhold Niebuhr*, 168–72 (Glouster, Mass.: Peter Smith, 1976), 170–71.

33. Barbara W. Tuchman, "The Alternative to Arms Control," *New York Times Magazine*, Apr. 18, 1982, p. 93.

34. Ibid.

35. Churchill, *The Gathering Storm*, 376–77.

36. Quoted in ibid., 325–26.

37. Cited in Churchill, *The Gathering Storm*, 318.

38. William Manchester, *The Last Lion: Winston Spencer Churchill; Alone, 1932–1940* (Boston: Little, Brown, 1988), 63.

39. Meyer, *The Protestant Search for Political Realism*, 157.

40. Churchill, *The Gathering Storm*, 67.

41. Reinhold Niebuhr, *Christianity and Power Politics* (New York: Scribner's, 1940), 102; Robertson, *Love and Justice*, 167.

42. Manchester, *The Last Lion,* 77.

43. Ibid., 95.

44. Ibid., 87.

45. Churchill, *The Gathering Storm,* 114, 355–56; Manchester, *The Last Lion,* 142, 220.

46. Charles DeBenedetti, *The Peace Reform in American History* (Bloomington: Indiana University Press, 1980), 126.

47. Chatfield, *For Peace and Justice,* 164–67.

48. Churchill, *The Gathering Storm,* 138.

49. Ibid., 13–14; see also 134, 137, 139–142, 160–61, 163, 237, 360, and 464.

50. Ibid., 102.

51. De Madariaga quoted in Tuchman, "The Alternative to Arms Control," 98.

52. Meyer, *The Protestant Search for Political Realism,* 373.

53. Ibid., 396–97.

54. Mathews quoted in Chatfield, *For Peace and Justice,* 45–46.

55. John Howard Yoder has emphasized that aspect of just-war thinking in "Surrender: A Moral Imperative," *The Review of Politics* 48 (Fall 1986): 577.

56. Aleksandr I. Solzhenitsyn, *The Voice of Freedom* (Washington, D.C.: AFL-CIO, 1975), 9.

57. Peter Berger, *Pyramids of Sacrifice: Political Ethics and Social Change* (Garden City, N.J.: Doubleday/Anchor, 1976), 94–95.

58. David Hawk, "The Killing of Cambodia," *New Republic* 15 (Nov. 1982): 17.

59. Ibid., 20.

60. Ibid., 19–20.

61. See Niebuhr, *Christianity and Power Politics,* 1–32, for the "realist" position on pacifism and 9–10 on this point; see also John H. Hallowell, "Pacifism—The Way to Peace?" *Crozer Quarterly* 26 (Jan. 1949): 30–40, for a defense of a nonpacifist Christian view in the nuclear era.

62. For accounts of pacifism after World War II, see Guenter Lewy, *Peace & Revolution: The Moral Crisis of American Pacifism* (Grand Rapids, Mich.: Eerdmans, 1988); for various views on Lewy's work, including some from pacifists and some from nonpacifists, see Michael Cromartie, ed., *Peace Betrayed? Essays on Pacifism and Politics* (Washington, D.C.: Ethics and Public Policy Center, 1990). (The pacifist responses include essays by Charles Chatfield, John Swomley, Charles Fager, Stanley Hauerwas, John Richard Burkholder, and others.)

12

སྒྲ

FREE (BUT NOT HELPED) TO BE PACIFIST

Methodist COs in the Vietnam Era

སྒྲ

S. Ronald Parks

This essay investigates the development and expression of the pacifist ethic among 491 United Methodist conscientious objectors (United Methodist COs) who registered their position with the church during the Vietnam War. Statements provided by these individuals yield insight into four areas of inquiry: (1) the sources and factors that contributed to the formation of the CO ethic; (2) the processes that yielded the pacifist stance; (3) these Methodists' patterns of ethical formulation, viewed in the light of wider Christian moral discourse; and (4) the various means the COs used to implement their pacifist ethic. Conclusions from these four areas of inquiry suggest something of the church's role in the ways the individuals have developed, articulated, and implemented their pacifism.

A DESCRIPTION OF THE CASE MATERIAL

The legacy of the CO in United Methodism has been a story of dissenters adopting a position that the majority of Methodists have valued but not supported. Traditionally the United Methodist Church has espoused a just-war ethic. That stance has let it support the government's war efforts while maintaining that war itself is an affront to both God and humanity. Therefore the United Methodist CO has had to stand not only against the call for combatant service but also against the church's endorsement of each military campaign. As one Methodist scholar has noted, this has led to instances where the espousal of pacifism "was as suspect as treason."[1]

From 1936 through the present day, the United Methodists' Board of Church and Society has invited COs among the church's members to record their convictions with the denomination by completing a registration card. This act has served two distinct yet complementary purposes. First, registration has located the individual within a religious tradition that affirmed the CO option. Second, completing the card has also enabled the board to establish a network of communication between the denomination's COs and its offices. However, the resources and programs offered to COs by their local churches and annual conferences have not been standardized from one locale to another. It is impossible to estimate the number of United Methodist COs who sought guidance and support from other sources because they did not know what their own denomination offered.[2]

The present study covers registration materials filed between January 1, 1964, and December 31, 1973—that is, during the key decade of the Vietnam War. During that period 641 registrants filed cards. Of those cards 491 were deemed eligible and worthy of extensive study.[3] Of the 491 only 2 were from women. The majority of the cards (66.5 percent, or 327 cases) were filed during the three years from 1968 to 1970, when military action was greatest.

The mean age of the study population is impossible to determine. The first two editions of the card (both used prior to 1968) did not ask the registrant to list a date of birth but simply requested the registrant to check an appropriate age range. The 251 registrants who used the third edition of the document (after 1968) were asked for birth date. If all cases are included, regardless of the potential for conscription and actual combatant service, the mean age for the post-1968 registrants is 20.1 years.[4]

All three editions of the card asked the persons to define their current occupational or educational involvement. Of the 491, 77.8 percent, or 382, labeled themselves students. Not counting the 72 individuals not yet through high school, the total number of United Methodist COs who were involved in some form of higher education was 310, or 63.1 percent of the 491. A 1978 book by Lawrence M. Baskir and William A. Strauss, attorneys who assisted COs in Vietnam War times, states that higher education became the "main sanctuary" for those who wished to avoid the draft.[5] If we take that claim seriously, the high percentage of United

Methodist COs enrolled in college and graduate schools raises some interesting questions. Fifty-six of the registrants were employed in a variety of occupations in the private and public sectors. There were case materials from twelve young men who were serving in the armed forces. Six individuals who filed statements were in some form of ministry, and four registrants indicated they were working in volunteer service organizations such as VISTA or the Peace Corps. Thirty-one COs reported that they were unemployed.

FORMATIVE FACTORS IN THE DEVELOPMENT OF CONSCIENTIOUS OBJECTION

In a survey entitled *Principles of Christian Theology,* John Macquarrie has delineated six sources of Christian theology and reflection, six formative factors that work in the development of an individual's religious convictions. Macquarrie's six are Scripture, tradition, experience, culture, revelation, and reason.[6] Judging from registrants' own replies, we must add another factor: family. I have organized the case information around those seven factors.

Of the 491 cases 412 (83.9 percent) contain some reference to a biblical text or a theme attributed to Scriptures. Registrants mentioned sixty-five specific texts, with the Sixth Commandment (Exod. 20:13) cited most frequently, by eighty-nine persons. Sixty-four registrants cited the Great Commandment (Matt. 22:34–40), and fifty-three cited "love your enemies" (Matt. 5:44). As for the citing of themes rather than texts, often the references were ambiguous, their ambiguity heightened by casual weaving of thematic strands into a tapestry of biblical images. Despite the ambiguity, however, four themes were quite clear: the origin and value of existence, the loving nature of God, the unity of the human family, and the divine right of judgment.

In the survey of formative factors, the term *tradition* carries a double meaning. In the broadest sense tradition may be defined as the history of the church as it has attempted to interpret the content of primordial revelation in a particular context. Thirty-five individuals cited a specific event, historical figure, author, or book that had been instrumental in the formation of their convictions. Also deserving examination is the role of the United Methodist Church as a formative factor in the development of the United Methodist COs' positions. A total of 183 individuals named their denomination as a formative factor. Seventy-three acknowledged that the "teachings" of the church on pacifism, warfare, discipleship, or related issues were influential in their decision-making process. Others offered a variety of vague statements about their connections to their local congregations: "I was raised a Methodist," "I grew up in the church," "My family always attended worship," and "The church has always been a big part of my life." For thirty-four registrants, Sunday school was a forum in which students, as one registrant put it, "learned the fundamentals and principles of Methodism, read the Scriptures and learned about God's Creation."[7] References to youth fellowship, confirmation, worship, Bible study, church camp, vacation Bible school, and prayer meetings were similarly vague, providing little information on the mechanics of ethical formation. In addition to the programmatic resources of the church, the counsel of pastors and Sunday school teachers was mentioned by thirty-six individuals.

The heading of "experience" denotes those apparently mundane incidents through which 127 registrants were enabled to reevaluate their moral convictions. Thirty registrants made reference to an academic course of study or the collegiate context as a wellspring of new ideas and insights. Twenty-two registrants found their experience in the armed forces to be a factor in their application for the CO exemption. Sixteen registrants found the specter of the draft to be so unsettling that they cited the contemplation of induction as a motive for moral decision. An influential experience in the lives of twenty-one registrants was the chance to meet people from other cultural settings, both in the United States and abroad. The encounter with other COs and with veterans was a formative experience in the lives of fifteen registrants, and nine claimed that they were influenced by their contact with "peace churches." Fourteen registrants recalled specific experiences in their lives that became significant in later years as they pondered the possibility of participation in war. Many of these accounts dealt with the registrant's first encounter with violence or death: "When I was a little kid I use to play war with the other boys around the neighborhood. We would hunt each other with toy guns and sticks. I only came to realize what I was doing [in] my first year of high school when I went shooting out in the woods with some friends and we started hunting each other and I almost killed one of the guys. I think now of how many other boys are doing the same thing around the world."[8]

Of the 491 cases studied, 118 individuals included some mention of parents, family, or home training as an integral element in the formation of their conviction. Phrases such as "the Christian attitude of my parents" and "the insight and support of my family" indicated that fa-

milial influence was communicated in a variety of ways. Twenty registrants claimed that they were influenced by the example and counsel of
a parent or family member who was a CO. Others referred to a "passive
approach to conflict" or a "nonviolent" style of parenting that proved
to be inspirational in their ethical reflection.

Given the social upheaval that rocked America during the Vietnam
War years, it is surprising that only a relatively small number of United
Methodist COs made any mention of the cultural milieu in which they
pondered their moral obligations. Fifty-one registrants referred to international incidents, political and literary figures, Eastern philosophies
and religions, popular films and songs, and a host of other components
in their descriptions of the cultural sources of their conviction. Notice-
ably absent from this list were references to controversial events that
occurred within the execution of the war itself (e.g., the 1968 My Lai
massacre), references to incidents on the domestic front (e.g., Woodstock
and the Kent State incident), and references to individuals who figured
prominently in the popular antiwar movement (e.g., Tom Hayden).

Sixty-three registrants made reference to what they considered to be
a personal revelatory event that directly affected the course of their ethical reflections. In most cases the self-disclosure of the divine came
through a devotional or spiritual exercise. Twenty-nine registrants indicated that prayer was instrumental in the shaping of their moral
framework. Seven registrants made reference to regular Bible study as
a source of their ethical reflection. *Contemplation* was a term ten registrants used to identify an activity that led to the CO position. The witness of one's conscience under the influence of the Holy Spirit was cited by nine registrants as being an essential source of ethical reflection:
"It is also my belief that God, as the Holy Spirit, pervades the very being of those who have accepted him and guides each one by individual
conscience. I believe that the Holy Spirit (as conscience) directs my actions and that I am responsible to act according to my conscience. I feel
that participating in war would be turning away from the Holy Spirit
within me."[9]

Eight registrants reported that their CO position resulted from what
could be described only as a conversion experience. These statements
invariably drew a direct connection between personal salvation and the
call for a radical pacifist obedience to Christ. The fact that most of these
accounts were sparse or vague may attest to either the ineffable character of these encounters or the relatively young age of the registrants.

Only one case, submitted by a graduate student, offered a defense that was primarily speculative in nature, promoting an argument based on a metaphysic drawn from both experience and rational abstraction.

THE FORMATIVE PROCESS OF CONSCIENTIOUS OBJECTION

The invitation to "describe the process by which you became a conscientious objector to war" addressed the process of ethical formation. Three distinct patterns can be discerned in the resulting descriptions. In the first the presence of a formative process was explicitly denied. The CO conviction was described as an essential part of the registrant's conscience that had remained unchanged since birth. This assertion appeared in twenty-six cases. It is impossible to identify or infer the method by which these registrants came to an awareness of their convictions. Some of these individuals believed themselves to be the bearers of, or respondents to, a special invitation to peaceful living.[10]

The second group of narratives described the gradual development of the CO position. The emphasis in these 222 accounts was on the moral sojourn that provided the resources for the conscious construction of the CO stance. Unlike the previously cited cases, these statements reported that an initial sense of ignorance, indifference, or uncertainty had been gradually replaced by a well-reasoned and deeply held ethical conviction. One hundred and twenty-seven individuals located the beginning of this process in their childhood experience. These cases trace the development of the CO ethic back to the registrant's earliest recollections. Invariably the registrants saw their conviction as a product of their participation in the family or the church. Ninety-five registrants reported that their pacifism was a later development. Their CO conviction resulted from a gradual and subtle process that they considered to be linked to their internal personal, spiritual, and ethical maturation. Therefore pacifism was perceived to be a product of the registrant's moral inquiry rather than an external principle that had been assimilated.

The third and most common pattern was found in the accounts of 243 individuals who described their CO conviction as a response to some provocation or challenge. In each of these cases a specific event or experience either changed the content of the registrant's ethical reflection or provided a definitive validation of the CO position. These challenges were perceived at three levels within the consciousness of the registrant: intellectual, emotional, and spiritual.

One hundred and ninety-six individuals indicated that some experience, usually no longer than two years prior to registration, had challenged their epistemological framework in such a way as to affirm the validity of the pacifist option. Although the college context was the setting for many of these intellectual challenges, the publications of peace organizations and antiwar authors, the witness of pacifist friends and clergy, seminars sponsored by religious and secular fellowships, and the popular expressions of cultural unrest that marked the Vietnam era also played roles in the intellectual debate that produced the CO conviction.

Thirty-three registrants utilized explicitly affective arguments as the basis for the CO claim. In the context of this project, the phrase "affective argument" refers to statements that reported the registrant's emotions or "gut" reactions to an experience as undergirding the construction of the CO conviction. Expressions of profound sadness at the inability of nations to "get along with each other" were often accompanied by disgust at the horrors and brutality of war. Other respondents offered interpretations of a love ethic rooted in the experience of divine agape. In every instance these challenges elicited powerful responses that were often difficult to articulate but unquestionably sincere.

The third type of challenge may be classified as "spiritual" in nature and content. Fourteen registrants reported an encounter with the teachings or person of Christ that led them to confess a pacifist ethic: "My recent conversion has enabled me to re-evaluate my pacifism. I am convinced that it is God's will for me to be a CO and thus not cooperate with the immoral military system and war. The atrocities of Vietnam made the situation immediate."[11] Many of these references were somewhat vague with respect to the chronological placement of the encounter, and few provided insight into the process of moral decision making.

THE MORAL PATTERNS OF CONSCIENTIOUS OBJECTION

In his study *A Survey of Christian Ethics,* Edward L. Long Jr. suggests that the patterns evident in the development of Christian ethical thought can be arranged according to three motifs that have been prominent in the formulation of Christian ethical positions. This approach provides an analytical tool that can locate the registrants' statements within the moral patterns of the Christian tradition.

Long begins with a description of the prescriptive motif, noting that most religious traditions have developed detailed and practical prescriptions for conduct.[12] A total of 247 cases presented arguments that were built exclusively on injunctions that required little or no interpretation. "Thou shalt not kill" is the classic example. In these cases the CO often equated the will of God revealed in both religious law and the Gospels with the confession of a pacifist ethic.

The use of reason in the development of ethical norms is considered under Long's second category of formulative motifs.[13] Unlike the prescriptive motif, the process of deliberation involves a creative project in which the agent constructs an ethical stance from the raw materials of experience and the ideals suggested by an accepted system of values. The deliberative motif was the dominant formulative pattern in 122 cases. Within this collection seven major themes were identified as distinctive confessions: life is a gracious gift, creation reflects a divine design, all humanity is a unity, all humanity bears the "imago Dei," conscience is a facet of that divine stamp, waging war usurps God right to judge, and war presumes the right to take life.

In addition to these assertions, two significant pragmatic concerns were evident. The first can be labeled "the futility of war." Thirty-five registrants echoed the sentiments expressed in the following statement: "I believe that war is inconclusive and unnecessary and wasteful. . . . I believe that violence grossly debases man's moral character and social capabilities. I am personally disgusted with the whole U.S.A. concept of counter-revolution being based on military rather than economic aid."[14] Closely related to the pragmatic rejection of war was the appeal to other more preferable options. Fifteen registrants expressed their desire to see governments pursue nonmilitary solutions because these options served a greater utilitarian interest.

In defining his third motif, the relational ethic, Long outlined what amounts to a two-step process of confrontation and application. In the first step the individual is confronted by a compelling and inspiring source of moral authority that may evoke a number of responses. In the Christian context disciples respond to the call of Christ, a call that redefines all relationships. The second step brings this new perspective into contact with the particularities of context and relationships, challenging the convert to apply these new insights to the ongoing task of ethical decision making. As each new experience is encountered and interpreted, the moral agent must decide which course of action is most appropriate or responsible, given the situation.[15]

Sixty-one registrants advanced arguments that reflected the relational pattern. These statements can be divided into two broad categories: agape-based and *koinonia*-based positions. The first category contains forty-four statements that emphasized the character of the registrant's response to God's loving initiative in Christ. In each of these cases the registrant's experience of divine love provided a guide for the development of an ethic that included pacifism. Agape was also used as a criterion for the evaluation of ethical choices.

The second category is described by the concept of the "*koinonia* ethic*." This approach, articulated by Paul Lehmann, among others, has suggested that the primary response to the divine initiative is not exclusively an inquiry into the prescriptions of agape but rather an attempt to discern the nature of God's ongoing and creative activity in the fellowship of the faithful.[16] Actions are evaluated by the manner in which they promote those qualities evident in God's relationship to the human community in general and to the *koinonia* in particular: forgiveness, justice, and reconciliation.

This community-based approach was evident in the writing of seventeen registrants. The following example of the approach suggests the character of this community-based pacifism. The statement is provided by a twenty-five-year-old member of the Peace Corps. His mention of the term *koinonia* is unique:

> God, through Christ, is doing all that is possible to bring man to mature human actions. I have accepted a place in the historical community of Christ, the KOINONIA. My decisions are not bound by the laws of the church, rather by understanding with free conscience, and by what will bring about the greatest amount of human maturity.
>
> I recognize that all within the KOINONIA have not made the same decision as I have. Yet, I feel that if the KOINONIA is to speak to all mankind that I must stand as I do, conscientiously opposed to war in any form and opposed to government service in war-related activities.[17]

It is interesting to note that issues that might be regarded as foreign to the CO debate (such as poverty and economic responsibility, race relations, or inequities in civil rights) were most often mentioned in those cases that promoted an ethic based on the *koinonia* concept.

Sixty-one cases reflected a synthesis of two or more motifs. As Long has noted in his study, these modified forms allow for greater flexibility in the development of an ethical position.[18]

THE IMPLEMENTATION OF THE CO ETHIC

Each registrant was asked, "What specifically are you doing for peace?" The responses often came in the form of a list, citing the various organizations and peace-related activities in which the CO had participated. The general descriptive headings used to classify these endeavors have arisen out of the case material.

The most common peace-related activity identified by the registrants was some form of political involvement. One hundred and seventeen individuals indicated that their request for a CO status was a means of working for peace. Twenty-four individuals lent their support to a variety of legislative reforms or aided the campaign efforts of candidates who promoted antiwar platforms. An additional twenty-two registrants petitioned incumbent political leaders to adopt strategies that would bring about an end to the war. Participation in antiwar demonstrations and peace rallies was an activity cited by thirty-nine registrants.

Voluntary affiliation was another form of implementation. Twenty-eight registrants cited their involvement in some aspect of the church, and ninety-four COs appealed to their affiliation with a number of organizations dedicated to the ideals of peace and nonviolence. An additional thirty-two registrants mentioned some form of service rendered to a particular organization as a method of implementing their convictions.

One hundred and seventy-one registrants reported a variety of activities that shared a singular intent: the proclamation of an alternative ethic. In some of these cases the thrust of this proclamation was prophetic. In other statements the COs' witness bore an evangelistic emphasis. Another group of statements were clearly pastoral in tone, depicting the CO as a counselor or guide to those who were struggling with the implications of pacifism. Twelve individuals expressed their conscientious objection through preaching or public speaking in various settings.

Recognizing, as one twenty-two-year-old college student commented, that "peace cannot be legislated," eighty-eight COs implemented their conviction by devoting themselves to the incarnation of peace in their lives.[19] What distinguished these cases from those that witnessed to an alternative ethic was the absence of a pedagogical or prophetic motive for this activity. There was no sense that discipleship was a call to exemplary living for the sake of social change. The desire to imitate Christ out of obedience to his call for discipleship was, at least in the minds of these registrants, an essentially private and spiritual endeavor.

Thirty registrants claimed that prayer or meditation was a means by which their convictions were implemented. Praying to God for the establishment of world peace or the kingdom of God was both a personal devotion activity and a strategy for social reconstruction. Fasting for peace, Bible study, and recording one's opposition to war in a journal were activities that received a single notation.

Another approach to the implementation of the CO ethic may be described as one of preparation. A total of thirty-one registrants reported that they were currently preparing themselves to join the pursuit of peace at some future time. Many of the COs saw their present activities and career aspirations as a tool that would allow them to use their talents more effectively at a later time.

CONCLUSION

The cases record 491 odysseys that share a common historical and ethical intersection: the espousal of conscientious objection during the Vietnam War era. The cases do not, however, support sweeping generalizations regarding the background, orientation, and temperament of the registrants. Many statements simply did not provide sufficient data to support this form of conjecture.

The empirical and typological information reported in this project, however, provides a unique insight into the development of the pacifist ethic within a tradition that affirms both the liberty of conscience and the just-war tradition. Support for the pacifist minority has been expressed in the official pronouncements of the church but seldom promoted by the programmatic agencies of the denomination. If the case material examined here is a valid indicator of ethical formulation among United Methodist COs, it is also apparent that although the denomination made few direct contributions to the development of pacifism among its membership, the ministry and fellowship of the local church were significant features in the emergence of pacifism in United Methodist youth.

If the United Methodist Church continues to endorse the CO option, it bears a responsibility to its members, clergy, and the ministry of the local church. With regard to the formative sources of ethical discourse, the denomination should develop curriculum and programs that identify those options that have been sanctioned by the church and that equip disciples to offer effective critique of the values that foster this diversity. This pedagogical approach would enable United Methodists to appreciate the diversity of their ethical heritage and the complexity of the church's response to the issues raised by war.

The description of the process of ethical reflection suggests that such an educational emphasis should be incorporated into the denomination's publications and programs at all age levels. The impact of early religious training both at home and in the church suggests the need for resources that appreciate the complex moral choices young Christians must make. Even those individuals who developed their CO claims later in adolescence admitted the importance of early religious instruction as a resource for their later reexamination of their convictions. In addition, a directory should be compiled that would identify pacifist clergy and laity who have expressed an interest in assisting potential COs. Youth must have access to resources and perspectives that might not be readily available to them through the ministry of their congregation.

The church's responsibility in assisting the CO to implement the pacifist conviction is difficult to define. Many registrants did little to involve themselves in peace-related activities beyond declaring their pacifist stance and the pursuit of a peaceful lifestyle. There was no evidence that the registrants were dissatisfied with the programs offered by the church during the Vietnam War era. In other words, registrants did not typically view the church as a vehicle for social change with regard to the issues of war and peace. They therefore did not look to the denomination to provide opportunities for involvement in the peace movement.

The testimony of the COs appears to confirm what the church has explicitly stated: the United Methodist Church is not a peace church. Nevertheless, the accounts of these United Methodist COs bring to light a concern that must be placed on the agendas of the denomination's programmatic and episcopal offices. These men and women have described a process of moral reflection that minimized the role of the national church in the formation and implementation of the registrants' moral stance. Depending on one's appraisal of the role of the institutional church in the process of personal ethical reflection, this assessment is either a challenge to the denomination's leadership or a confirmation of the essentially personal nature of moral development. In any event, it is a reality that demands further study.

NOTES

1. Walter G. Muelder, *Methodism and Society in the Twentieth Century* (Nashville: Abingdon, 1961), 81.

2. I was not made aware of the denominational resources available to persons such as I, even though I consulted extensively with my local pastor. Obviously the local pastor is the main link in any communications network within United Methodism's connectional system. In my opinion, the pattern I experienced continues to be an inherent weakness in the structure of the denomination.

3. Three criteria were used in assessing the case materials. First, the information on the cards had to be legible. Secondly, only those cases that contained responses to all questions were considered to be eligible. Finally, a judgment was required regarding the adequacy of a number of vague or incomplete responses.

4. For a full description of the demographic material, as well as an extensive analytical treatment of the COs' statements, see Stanley Ronald Parks, "The United Methodist Conscientious Objector in the Vietnam War Era: A Study of Ethical Formulation and Implementation" (Ph.D. diss., Drew University, 1992).

5. Lawrence M. Baskir and William A. Strauss, *Chance and Circumstance* (New York: Knopf, 1978), 36.

6. John Macquarrie, *Principles of Christian Theology* (New York: Scribner's, 1977), 4.

7. Case 87. I assigned the case numbers; the board's archives lack any organizational scheme. The purpose of assigning case numbers to the individuals was to simplify the classification of the material. Since these records are not available to the general public, and the references are cited in accordance with my own scheme, inquiries into the source material must be directed to me and cleared through the office of the General Board. Quotations from the case material are recorded verbatim in the text of this study for the purpose of preserving the authenticity of the statements.

8. Case 39.

9. Case 280.

10. The assertion that a number of registrants viewed themselves as prophetic voices for peace in a warring world is borne out by the manner in which these individuals implemented their CO convictions. The idea of being chosen for the special task of teaching or witnessing to God's will was not foreign to many of the registrants.

11. Case 373.

12. Edward L. Long Jr., *A Survey of Christian Ethics* (New York: Oxford University Press, 1967), 73.

13. Ibid., 45.

14. Case 229.

15. Long, *Survey of Christian Ethics*, 61.

16. Paul Lehmann, "The Foundation and Pattern of Christian Behavior," in John A. Hutchinson, ed., *Christian Faith and Social Action*, 93–116 (New York: Scribner's, 1953).

17. Case 105.

18. Long, *Survey of Christian Ethics*, 102.

19. Case 298.

13

𝔾

PACIFISM, JUST WAR, AND REALISM

A Response to William R. Marty and S. Ronald Parks

𝔾

Ted Koontz

First, a general comment. I am struck by how different the moods and impulses of various pacifists have been.[1] The contrast between those in the revivalist, "restorationist" movements described in our various denominational histories and the liberal Protestant pacifists ("engaged pacifists") described by Charles Chatfield is stark. Also, moods vary considerably across various stories. In most of the "sectarian" accounts we seem to have stories about the loss of pacifist commitment—of decline of pacifist sentiment and acculturation into a more bellicose American mainstream. By contrast Chatfield's story seems to be one of growing power and influence on the part of "engaged pacifists," with pacifism increasingly shaping not only the consciousness of isolated groups but also the whole ethos in which American policy, indeed world politics, is molded. I wonder how we may account for this difference in mood. And I wonder how accurate these portrayals are, or must be.

What is the path of sectarian pacifist groups? Is it inevitably toward denominationalism, toward joining the mainstream, toward the acceptance of war as a Christian moral option? Whether inevitable or not, that movement certainly seems evident in the stories we have encountered. Certainly it is part of the experience of the historic peace churches (HPCs). In fact the HPCs have also been far from unanimous in holding to pacifism against acculturating influences. That is true despite the way they (or we, since I am a Mennonite) have gotten off very easily in this volume, even being held up as examples of groups that have not gone the way of other originally pacifist groups. If we recall the percentages of conscientious objectors from the HPCs in World War II, we of the HPCs will want to make our claims to uniqueness with some modesty. Moreover, at least among Mennonites, the forces of acculturation are much stronger now than they were during World War II—although they have not, at least not yet, resulted in dramatic declines in measurable pacifist commitment.[2]

So some HPC people, or at least some Mennonites (I know less about the other HPCs), are on this acculturation path. Moreover, some of us are on another path: from "sectarian" pacifism to the kind of pacifism that Chatfield describes. Although some Mennonites may be moving toward more acceptance of war, there are also quite a few of us moving in the direction of a liberal, engaged pacifism. Perhaps we can say that Mennonites are being acculturated into two different American mainstreams (although that is still a vast oversimplification). One stream is conservative, nationalistic, and militaristic in orientation, or at least more accepting of military service. The other is liberal, internationalist, and sympathetic to revolutionary movements seeking justice. The latter offers an engaged pacifism that seeks social transformation. If I must choose between the two streams, I clearly prefer the liberal, justice-oriented one. Yet I am not entirely happy with either alternative. I reject the more nationalistic and militaristic stream for reasons that are obvious, given my pacifist commitment; the second also makes me uncomfortable, however, especially for two reasons. First, I do not trust its staying power when the sailing gets rough—when the next Hitler arises. Second, I think any *Christian* pacifist commitment must be deeply rooted theologically and ecclesiologically. I fear that the roots of the liberal, engaged sort of pacifism are all too shallow.

Now to Parks's and Marty's statements. I appreciate very much the information that Ronald Parks offers on pacifist Methodists in the Vietnam era. It helps us go beyond simple impressions based on anecdotes and lets us hear the Methodist COs speak for themselves. His report also reflects a careful sorting and analysis of the data, using helpful analytical tools that allow us to view some important issues in a systematic way. I have no objections or serious questions about what Parks has done.

One point worth noting is that CO convictions are often responses to challenge or to some context that *forces* reflection. Not only CO decisions but many other moral decisions come that way. This raises the question, which in fact Parks raises, of what the church might do to help youth think about the issues of war and peace and make considered judgments about them. What kind of challenges can we present to youth so that they feel forced to reflect on these issues and begin seriously to do so?

Two larger questions might give us a broader picture than Parks intended in his report. The questions are meant not as criticism but as a request for explanation and expansion. First, how many Methodist COs were there during the Vietnam era, and what percentage of Methodist draftees were COs? How do these numbers compare with the numbers in other wars for Methodists? In other words, were Methodists becoming more pacifistic or less? Also, how did the numbers compare with numbers from other groups?

A second question, given the type of resistance there was to the war during the Vietnam period, concerns quality rather than quantity. Were there many Methodist *selective* conscientious objectors, people saying that some wars may be justified, but this particular war is not? Does Parks have any data on this? A different but related question is whether he can tell us anything about how Methodist COs fit either into the activist-engaged pacifist strand or into the more sectarian strand. What kind of sensibility did they have? A bit of that sensibility came through in what Parks described, but I would be interested in hearing how those United Methodist sensibilities fit into the categories that inform this book's focus.

Turning to William Marty's contribution, I feel torn. I am a Mennonite and a professor in a Mennonite seminary—sort of a "theologian" (if defined broadly enough) out of that sectarian pacifist tradition. I also am a child of the anti–Vietnam War peace movement, so that in some important respects I have inherited the liberal pacifist impulse. I am also a student of just-war theorists, having worked with Michael Walzer and James Johnson in graduate school and in postgraduate work. I hold a Ph.D. in international relations from a program that was essentially "realist" in orientation (Harvard, where I studied mainly with Stanley Hoffmann). With that mixture, how do I respond to the challenge of a William Marty—or to the seemingly incompatible pictures of liberal pacifism (or engaged pacifism) drawn by Marty on the one hand and Chatfield on the other? It is hard to imagine more diverse interpretations. Are we talking about the same people? The same movement? The same time?

Although I do not live exclusively in any of the worlds I have described, I have come to orient myself fundamentally toward my Mennonite faith commitment. I will not attempt to define what that means here. Just so you can locate me on your mental maps, however, be advised that for me the Mennonite tradition does not require the kind of global or total withdrawal from society and from responsibility for the world that Marty wants to require of all consistent pacifists. On that point, by the way, he is in good company, Reinhold Niebuhr being only the most prominent of those who stand with him.

Some general responses to Marty's contribution follow. I find it to be a powerful restatement of the classical criticisms of liberal pacifism. I agree with Marty that the policy prescriptions in the Western countries in the interwar years, particularly after the rise of Hitler, were generally wrong as means to head off war. I agree also with his generally pessimistic view of world politics. I expect that power and the threat of power (including military force and war), even if they are not inherent or permanent features of international politics, are at least ones we will live with for quite some time. Despite these points of agreement, I find Marty's remarks to be too global and too little nuanced as criticism of the orientation reflected by the interwar liberal pacifists during this period. I disagree with what I think is an implied *general* superiority of "realism" over "liberal pacifism" as a total orientation toward the way in which one ought to see world politics and to operate in the global context. I find "realism"[3] to be adequate as a general frame of reference for understanding some phenomena in international relations but inadequate for understanding others. I find it to yield helpful policy advice in some circumstances and advice that is downright disastrous in others.

In short, I fear that a generally or totally realist orientation toward foreign policy gets us in trouble at least as often as does an orientation that is generally or totally based on an "interdependence" model—which is roughly what I see the liberal pacifists of the interwar years holding. Although Marty rightly criticizes some shortcomings of some liberal pacifists during those years, I think it important to keep in mind that he chose the easiest case to make against liberal pacifism and for realism. Few dare to question the evil of Hitler's ambition or even to argue that nonviolent means could have stopped him. It is true: there was no clear pacifist answer to Hitler. But we do not always face a Hitler. The point is, if we act like we are facing a Hitler when we are not, we also may blunder into a war that we might have avoided. Realism, too, may lead to wars, including "unnecessary" wars.[4] At least it is clear that the failings of liberal pacifist prescriptions are not the sole culprit in history, since this "hybrid" pacifism was newly invented or at least newly influential between the wars. Whose policy prescriptions led to the world's wars, including its "unnecessary" ones, before the 1930s? Realists would be a likely group to suspect.[5]

I was troubled also by the rather large moral mandate to protect the innocent that I heard implied in part of Professor Marty's argument. The world is full of injustice and innocent suffering. I am not sure what is implied by the horror stories of the Soviet Union, China, and Cambodia. I agree that they are horrible, particularly since I have visited both Cambodia and China and heard personal horror stories firsthand. But what is the policy recommendation? Does the argument imply that we should have fought the Soviets immediately after World War II? Or that we should not have given up in China when we did? Or that we should have reinvaded Cambodia? Is there any end to the military interventions that might be justified implicitly by the argument that Marty has offered? More generally, are we morally required to correct all the wrongs in the world using all possible military and other means at our disposal? Furthermore, all nations do not see injustice and innocent suffering in the same way. If we claim the right to judge the injustices of others by our standards and the right to correct them, not only morally but through military means, are we willing to grant others the same right?

Who are we to judge the relative evils of the world? Are others entitled to judge (and correct) our evils in a similar way? I see a policy that not only becomes difficult to implement—a policy both exhausting and dangerous—but also can move subtly to a kind of crusading where we take it on ourselves to make sure that things turn out right all around the world. I suspect Professor Marty does not intend this, but I sense some need to limit the argument more carefully at this point.

Next, a comment on typologies of war and peace. I have noted that pacifists need to be separated into different groups if the typologies are to help to describe reality. There also are more nonpacifist positions on war and peace than we have dealt with thus far, however. I think recognizing that fact is significant for our evaluations of nonpacifist alternatives.

Bainton, as Marty notes, separated out the crusade, or holy war, from just war. Marty, however, throughout his statement, refers to just war and realism as if they belong together. I find that problematic. Speaking that way obscures some important issues.

As Marty rightly reminds us, just-war theory starts with the argument that there is a moral responsibility growing out of Christian love to defend the innocent from unjust attack. It also holds that there are various *moral* constraints, not only pragmatic ones, on the conduct of warfare. War should be fought, for example, so as to protect the innocent, including innocent civilians in the enemy country. The constraints are built into calculations of costs and benefits, calculations that just-war thought allows and indeed requires.

Another significant feature of just-war thought is that when we calculate costs and benefits, we are required to calculate the *overall* costs and benefits, not only the costs and benefits to us. That is, just-war theory is a "universalistic" moral perspective. It does not consider only our good or our interests.

This view, it seems to me, stands in sharp contrast to yet another Christian and secular nonpacifist view of the relation of ethics to war and peace. The view I have in mind is not pacifist, just-war, or crusade, yet it is the operative ethic on which the overwhelming majority of Christians in most times and most places have made most decisions about war and peace. It is the view that Christians should simply give their rulers a blank check and obey them.[6] This view does not have Christians exercising personal moral judgments about warfare, asking about costs and benefits, or imposing moral constraints on its conduct. Rather, it has Christians doing what they are told. A point that Stanley Hauerwas has made about the operative ethic in the United States is right: "When the President says 'Go fight!' we say 'Yes, Sir!'" I believe that this attitude has been typical not only of the American Christian ethic toward war and peace but also throughout Christian history. Indeed just-war theory, inasmuch as it emphasizes that a war is just only if conducted by a legitimate authority, may tend to encourage such a view.

Closely related to this is the view that we often call realism. If ordinary citizens are simply to obey rulers, then on what substantive grounds should rulers decide issues of war and peace? The answer from a realist framework is typically, "From a realistic assessment of national interests." Note that the calculation is not made on the basis of the defense of innocents, as in just-war thought, nor is it based on a weighing of the costs and benefits for everyone affected by the war. Within this perspective, as it has been outlined by most political theorists, there is no serious room for moral qualms or considerations. This view is best reflected in one of the most ancient documents articulating it. Thucydides wrote that "we both alike know that into the discussion of human affairs the question of justice only enters where there is equal power to enforce it, and *the powerful exact what they can, and the weak grant what they must.*"[7] This essentially is the view reflected also in Machiavelli, in Hobbes and Clausewitz, and in Morgenthau and Kissinger.

This view sometimes seeks to justify its lack of restraint in war by arguing that "war is hell," so that the greatest mercy in war is to end it quickly using all means possible. There can be no limitation of evil in hell, and there can be no moral constraints on war once it is underway; such constraints might make the war longer or more costly to us. The only moral consideration is to win the war as quickly and cheaply—for us—as possible. This is the gist of General Sherman's justification of his march across the South. It was he who said, "War is hell!" The "moral" argument behind this statement is that because I am getting the war over more quickly, I am justified in burning cities and crops and otherwise attacking necessities of life for civilians in order to force surrender of soldiers. In other words, effectiveness is the only criterion; and our community is the community that counts, not the global community.[8]

This realism strikes me as a moral view significantly different from classic just-war theory. We should untangle them analytically because they *are* quite different. Also, we should untangle them because one—just-war theory—is far more attractive morally to Christians than the other. Nevertheless, I think that realism is able to offer both the more consistent critique of pacifism and the more accurate picture of how nations often act, although it is harder to justify in Christian ethical terms. We should untangle these views from each other also because in conflating the two, the opponent of pacifism has the best of both worlds. On the one hand one can seem to be arguing a plausible Christian moral position, while on the other hand one can seem to be giving a hard-headed analysis of the world in which evil must be resisted by almost any amount of force necessary.

If we see the difference between so-called realism and just-war thought, however, we see that nonpacifists also confront hard choices. For example, if one goes with just-war theory, one will confront the same awkward situation that pacifists face, although at a different point: there will sometimes be cases where one will be unable to defend innocents using morally acceptable means—morally acceptable according to just-war thinking itself, quite apart from a pacifist view. That is, there are acts and policies that just-war principles also prohibit—for instance, the torture or murder of prisoners once they have been captured and disarmed, even though doing so may sometimes be necessary to win the "just" war and thereby defend the innocent victims of aggression. In contrast, because realism focuses on effectively winning wars, it may allow such actions and even require them if they make prosecution of the war more effective.

Another way to say this is to note that just-war policies may not always be able to prevent harm to innocents without collapsing into realism. (Often even the maximum amount of available force is not able to prevent such harm.) It seems that *all* moral views that do not reduce finally to pure consequentialism come to a point where one must "withdraw"—if we want to use that word—or else surrender. All such moral views thus must sometimes fail to ensure justice. The problem is not unique to pacifism. If we become aware of this difference between just-war thought and realism, and if we are honest, we will come to see that the debate is not only between pacifists who must choose between naïveté and irrelevance and nonpacifists who choose to show love by defending the innocents. Nonpacifists too have to decide sometimes whether a war that is justified in terms of its end must be "lost" because it cannot be prosecuted within morally acceptable bounds. Or, conversely, they must decide whether to give up those bounds and accept realism, which is to reject their own moral criteria.

All this is not to deny that there is power in Professor Marty's realist critique of a sometimes overly optimistic pacifist idealism. It is only to insist that there are problems with alternative views. I think these problems are at least as significant as the problems with liberal pacifism.

A final problem lies in what seems to be a demand that pacifists accept full responsibility for historical outcomes or else get off the playing field entirely. Some of my remarks thus far speak to this point. I think that just-war theorists, if they are serious, also decline to accept full responsibility. They too will not do just anything possible to ensure the "right" outcomes. Sometimes they also will have to get off the playing field—or else stop being just-war theorists.

My basic concern is this: if I may put the question so boldly, does the demand to accept full responsibility for historical outcomes amount to a lack of faith in God? This way of putting the question implies that such a demand does indeed represent a lack of faith in God—an implication I believe to be true. Of course to say that we do not need to—indeed, that we dare not—accept full responsibility for history's outcomes does not mean that we should refuse to do what we can *morally* do to ensure the right outcomes (assuming we know what the right outcomes are, an assumption we should make very modestly). But it does mean that there is no imperative to do what we believe to be morally wrong in order to ensure the triumph of the right. Whether pacifist or believers in just war, virtually all Christians believe that at certain points they must rely on God's providence and grace. Such reliance is not a matter of choice; they simply must have such trust. They conclude that there simply are many evils that we physically *cannot* overcome, no matter what means we might try to use. If there are lots of evils out there that we cannot overcome (and thus do not feel compelled to overcome), why then should we feel compelled to use means that we feel are inherently immoral?

It is surely true, as Professor Marty reminds us, that nonviolence does not ensure the survival of the innocent. He observes several times that nonviolence or pacifism, or at least neutrality, does not always work. But neither does war or violence always work. War does not always work even if a nation employs all available means without constraint. Simply put, the good guys sometimes lose. Indeed they often lose—unlike the case Professor Marty describes. Nothing ensures the victory of right—whether through nonviolent means or through either just or realist war. History simply is not wholly in any one party's hands.

For Christians that is not necessarily cause for despair, for their faith assures them that history is in God's hands. This assurance surely cannot be taken to mean that humans need not do what they morally can do to promote "right" outcomes. On the other hand, the assurance is not a promise that the right (as humans see the right) will always triumph. Nor does it promise an end to suffering, even the suffering of innocents. Nevertheless, Christians through the centuries have believed that even in suffering and through the seeming triumph of evil, God is present. They have believed that the God who triumphed over evil through innocent suffering and death on the cross triumphs in history, even while evil humans still kill innocent ones. With that faith, some Christians decide that they need not join those who hurt and kill in order to help their God.

NOTES

1. In my own work I prefer to reserve the term *pacifist* for those who hold, minimally (their claim can be and often is broader), that it is *morally* wrong for *them* to participate *directly* in killing in *war*. I differentiate this from what I call "abolitionism," which I use to refer to those who have a strong desire for peace or an aversion to war but who are not necessarily committed to personal nonparticipation in all wars. Abolitionism stresses the moral mandate to abolish war by setting up a world system that will make war obsolete. By these definitions, so-called liberal pacifists often have been abolitionists rather than pacifists (although some have been both—the terms are not mutually

exclusive). I recognize that historically the term *pacifism* has meant something closer to what I call "abolitionism" than to what I call "pacifism," but I believe the term *pacifism* has come to mean essentially what I have outlined here, perhaps largely because of the tendency to identify pacifism with conscientious objection.

2. For a recent study of "modernization" among Mennonites, see J. Howard Kauffman and Leo Drieger, *The Mennonite Mosaic: Identity and Modernization* (Scottdale, Pa.: Herald, 1991).

3. Properly, from my perspective, the word *realism* should always be in quotation marks. It stands for a particular school of thought that claims to interpret international politics by describing it simply the way it is, "realistically" rather than "idealistically" or "moralistically," but there also are other plausible frameworks for describing international politics. To allow the name *realism* to stand without noting that it is an interpretive framework, an argument, instead of literally a description of reality, is to prejudice the argument in its favor. For the sake of style, however, I will not use quotation marks around the term from here on.

It is worth noting also that there are "softer" versions of realism than the one I describe here. The one described here best expresses realism's fundamental logic, however. Softer realisms do not have a coherent logic of their own but rather are parasitic on other moral perspectives—perspectives that in fact realism undermines over the long term. A current expression of a soft realism is that of David Mapel in his "Realism and the Ethics of War and Peace," in Terry Nardin, ed., *The Ethics of War and Peace*, 54–77 (Princeton, N.J.: Princeton University Press, 1996).

4. I place *unnecessary* in quotation marks because no wars are strictly necessary. They are always necessary only because some other end has been determined to be more important than the avoidance of war. The phrase "unnecessary wars" thus refers to wars that are unnecessary even for the achievement of the other end for which war is a means.

5. It might be argued that realists have sought not peace but rather something like justice (or if my account of what realists want is right, national interest) and that it is thus unfair to accuse them of failing to do what they did not set out to do. If we value peace, however, we may still wish to evaluate their policies by the value we attach to peace. Even if we do not, it is by no means clear that "innocents," whom Marty is concerned that liberal pacifists have failed to protect, have been better protected, generally, by the prescriptions of the realists.

6. John H. Yoder has helped me to see this most clearly; see his *Christian Attitudes toward War, Peace, and Revolution: A Companion to Bainton* (available from the Associated Mennonite Biblical Seminary Peace Studies Program, 3003 Benham Ave., Elkhart, Ind. 46517), 81–93.

7. Thucydides, *The History of the Peloponesian War,* excerpted in Melvin Small and J. David Singer, eds., *International War: Anthology and Study Guide* (Homewood, Ill.: Dorsey, 1985), 129; emphasis added.

8. I owe much of my understanding of the contrast of realism and just-war thought to Michael Walzer; see especially "Against 'Realism,'" chap. 1 of his *Just and Unjust Wars* (New York: Basic, 1977).

PART 5

❧

CATHOLICS, CHRISTIAN REFORMED

❧

14

🙏

HARDER THAN WAR

Roman Catholic Peacemaking in Twentieth-Century America

🙏

Patricia McNeal

For the American Catholic community, support for pacifism is something rather new. In the Catholic tradition the pacifism of the primitive Christian church, like other features of the radical gospel, largely disappeared with the age of Constantine. Not until the twentieth century, in their attempt to address contemporary issues of war and peace, did American Catholics rediscover this heritage. In the century's early decades some Catholics spoke out against war, but rather than being outright pacifists, they based their opposition on the just-war doctrine. This doctrine remained the dominant Catholic position on war until the 1930s and early 1940s, when a few Catholics began to appeal to the gospel tradition of pacifism as a way to oppose war in the modern age. Since about World War II outright pacifism has broadened among Catholics, not only in America but worldwide. Institutionally a key event was the Second Vatican Council in 1962. Since then, although the whole Catholic church has not become pacifist, there has emerged within it an approval of pacifist dissent. Through the work of various persons and organizations, the American Catholic church has become a force for peace.

• • •

The person most responsible for this shift toward pacifism was Dorothy Day. She was the first American Catholic to challenge the normative just-war teaching, and eventually she became the Catholic in the United States most identified with pacifism. Perhaps because she was a convert to Catholicism, she did not initially confront the just-war tradition or offer an intellectual critique; she merely proclaimed her pacifism.[1] Nonetheless her proclamation was powerful. As George Weigel has put it, "Dorothy Day was the single greatest influence on the transformation of American Catholic thought on the moral problem of war and peace since Vatican II."[2]

For Dorothy Day to reach the dual position of Catholic and pacifist was a long journey. Ironically, the journey did not even begin until she had firmly formed herself as a radical. Only after she had explored every radical position and participated in a variety of radical causes did Day begin her long and lonely journey as a radical who was also Catholic and pacifist. In her autobiography, *The Long Loneliness,* Day reflected on her pacifism during World War I and cryptically wrote, "I was pacifist in what I considered an imperialist war though not pacifist as a revolutionist."[3]

Around World War I Day had brief moments when she experienced religion, yet she decided that comfort received from religion was a sign of weakness.[4] Then on March 3, 1927, she gave birth to a daughter, Tamar, and later she told how the birth of her child compelled her to become a Catholic. "No human creature," she wrote in her autobiography, "could receive or contain so vast a flood of love and joy as I felt after the birth of my child." The experience brought her "the need to worship and adore." All her radical experience and her "whole makeup," she continued, led her "to want to associate myself with others, with the masses, in praising and adoring God. Without even looking into the claims of the Catholic Church, I was willing to admit that for me she was the one true church."[5]

Day was baptized a Catholic on December 28, 1927. Three years later she still did not personally know one Catholic lay person.[6] This all changed when Peter Maurin, a French peasant and thinker whose spirit and ideas would dominate the rest of her life, appeared at her door. Together they founded the Catholic Worker movement.[7]

Maurin's message, whether oral or written, was essentially that of Catholic radicalism. His radical ideal was rooted not in the material world but in the realm of the spirit. His goals would be achieved at the end of time—with the Second Coming of Christ. He combined this eschatological view of history with Christian personalism, an outlook that maintains the primacy of Christian love and couples it with a view of freedom that involves belief in the individual's capacity to turn from tyranny of sense toward the spirit. According to Maurin, embracing personalism required suffering. Maurin saw personalism expressed in individuals who embraced voluntary poverty and who, at the cost of personal sacrifice, daily performed the works of mercy proclaimed in the sayings of Jesus known as the Beatitudes.[8] Personalism—rather than political analysis, with which she had become disillusioned—appealed greatly to Dorothy Day.

For Day, war was the absolute opposite of active love, the antithesis of the radical Christian vision she had embraced. Having been opposed to war before her conversion to Catholicism, she now clearly saw that the gospel message was peace. For Day, the only alternative to violence was nonviolence—or what she called Catholic pacifism. She emphasized the individual, not the state, and refused to cooperate with the state in any way on the issue of war. In her pacifism she brought together the personalism and anarchism of the Catholic Worker ideal of love. Day rooted that pacifism in a matrix of personalism, which called for a heightened sense of personal responsibility for one's neighbors and involvement in struggles for justice on their behalf. In this sense her Catholicism enhanced her long-held pacifism and put it in a revolutionary context.[9] As historian Mel Piehl stated, "after 1945, it was the issue of pacifism that most effectively represented the Catholic Worker's gospel idealism."[10]

As editor of the *Catholic Worker,* Day announced that pacifism was the paper's position. She believed the Catholic Worker movement was a total way of life and that consistency with the Catholic Worker ideal during a time of war demanded a pacifist response. As early as October 1933 the newspaper stated that it would send delegates to the United States Congress against War—and that they would be representing "Catholic Pacifism."[11] Since in American history this was the first such collective statement from a group of Catholics, Day and her colleagues must have known that they represented scarcely anyone except themselves.

Catholic Worker pacifism derived from Dorothy Day's personal commitment. In 1935 Paul Hanley Furfey was able to elaborate Day's basic conviction about Catholic pacifism to make a Catholic case against war. Furfey was a priest and educator from the Catholic University of America and a friend of the movement. In an article he wrote for the *Catholic Worker* in 1935, he anticipated the theological rationale that would eventually form the basis of Catholic Worker pacifism. He based the antiwar case on the gospel counsel of perfection. The article offered an imaginary debate between Christ and a patriot. In that debate Furfey based the theological principle for pacifism not on the just-war theory but on the Christian's calling to a kingdom of love and peace, which takes precedence over one's calling to obey the state. He urged abandonment of the "Constantinian Compromise," that is, the church's fourth-century accommodation with the war-making state, calling instead for a return to the eschatological pacifist vision of the early saints and church fathers.[12] This was the first American Catholic statement that reflected a pacifism based on the gospel message of peace. With it the American Catholic peace movement was born.[13]

Nonetheless, Catholic pacifism did not become a central issue of the Catholic Worker movement until the Spanish Civil War, 1936–39. In July 1936, after that war erupted, Day's *Catholic Worker* proclaimed pacifism and neutrality. Ironically, the issue of pacifism was overshadowed by anticommunism. American Catholics as a whole used the war as a rallying point for strongly anticommunist views. They grew angry at Day— not because of her pacifism and refusal to take sides in the war, however, but because she refused to support Franco against the communists. The pacifist Catholic counter-opinion that Day attempted to offer provoked the strongest reaction against the Catholic Worker movement since its inception.[14]

Adding to its troubles, by World War II the Catholic Worker movement faced dissension within. This time the cause of the dissension was Catholic pacifism itself. The heart of the movement was Dorothy Day, who was located in New York City, where she had begun the *Catholic Worker* and was selling it for a penny a copy. On New York's Mott Street she also had opened a "house of hospitality," where she and her co-workers administered corporal works of mercy and held roundtable discussions between intellectuals and members of the working classes. She also had begun a farm commune in Easton, Pennsylvania. As the Catholic Worker movement spread beyond New York, it came more and more to be defined by its New York–based newspaper, houses of hospitality, and a fascination with the supposed simplicity of the rural life. However, a Catholic Worker–affiliated Chicago house of hospitality began publishing its own newspaper, the *Chicago Catholic Worker,* with John Cogley as editor. That paper rejected pacifism. Also at the St. Francis House of Hospitality in Seattle, movement personnel stopped distributing the New York paper because they found it to be filled almost entirely with pacifism; instead they distributed the *Chicago Catholic Worker.*[15]

In June 1940 Day sent a letter to all individuals in the movement concerning the issue of pacifism. Day acknowledged, as author William Miller has summarized, that some members of Catholic Worker groups throughout the country did not stand with the New York leaders on this issue and that neither the New York paper, letters, nor personal conversations had changed their views. But, she said, they "wish still to be associated with us, to perform the corporal works of mercy." That, she said, was all right, but what was not all right was that some "had taken it on themselves to suppress the paper." Such persons, she thought, would have to cut their ties with the movement.[16] By the end of 1942 sixteen of the houses, or one-half of them, had been closed.[17] Although there were many reasons for the decline of the movement during World War II, Day admitted in the May 1942 issue of the *Catholic Worker* that she was being accused of splitting the movement from top to bottom by her pacifism.

As the war progressed, the issue that troubled Catholic Workers more than any other was the military draft. Dorothy Day's pacifism made her advocate total resistance to the draft. The individual, she thought, should not cooperate in any way with the U.S. government's Selective Service System. In May 1943 she printed a statement, set off in a box, in the *Catholic Worker* urging men not to register for the draft. The government chose to ignore this legal offense, but Catholic church authorities did not; they thought that Dorothy Day and the *Catholic Worker* "had gone too far." The authorities called her to the New York chancery and told her, "Dorothy you must stand corrected."[18]

Up to that time church authorities had not challenged Day on conscription. As early as July 1940 she had testified before the House Military Affairs Committee that conscription was contrary to the teachings of the church. Monsignor Michael J. Ready also testified, however, and he gave the official position of the Catholic hierarchy's main concern. That concern was merely to preserve draft exemption for, in Ready's words, "students for the priesthood and those under vows to serve the works of religion."[19] By contrast, Day said she was speaking for Catholic lay people. Senator Burke, one of the bill's sponsors, asked her whether the clause granting exemption from combat for any member of a "religious sect whose creed or principles forbid its members to participate in war in any form" would protect lay Catholics. Replied Day: "It does not protect Catholics, no, it may protect the Quakers, the Mennonites, the Dunkards, but not Catholics. . . . There is nothing in the Catholic Creed which would entitle us to that exemption. It does not deal with Catholics."[20]

Two hundred and twenty-three Catholics are known to have been conscientious objectors during World War II. Sixty-one of them were sentenced from eighteen months to five years in prison, whereas 135 were legally recognized as COs and assigned to Civilian Public Service (CPS) camps. Dorothy Day petitioned for a Catholic camp, and the government assigned Catholic COs to a forestry camp in New Hampshire, first located at Stoddard and later moved to Warner. Eventually the camp was closed because of financial difficulty, at which point the National Service Board for Religious Objectors (NSBRO)—an organization formed by various churches to look out for the interests of the COs—willingly accepted the financing of the men. According to NSBRO records Mennonites absorbed $5,975.34 of the expenses for the Catholic COs, and Quakers absorbed $32,707.31.[21] Gordon Zahn, in a thorough account of the Catholic COs in the CPS camps given in his book *Another Part of War: The Camp Simon Story,* contended that what enabled Day to reach out and assist all men regardless of their degree of resistance was her respect for the individual—the heart of Christian personalism. Zahn believed that the Catholic COs were indeed able to offer a corporate witness against the war.[22]

• • •

By June 1948 the Catholic peace movement had almost completely dissolved. Little remained to show for it except the *Catholic Worker,* the Catholic peace movement's principal benefactor throughout the war period. From World War II until Vatican II in 1962 the paper alone kept the Catholic pacifist witness alive and drew some Catholics toward nonviolence as a means of social protest. According to Mel Piehl, during the 1950s Robert Ludlow, writing for the *Catholic Worker,* was "the first Catholic pacifist to understand and to appropriate the Gandhian theory of nonviolence as a comprehensive method of religious peacemaking." Piehl thought that Ludlow was "the first to see Catholic pacifism not simply as the witness of a small minority to the counsels of perfection, but as the forerunner of a possible historic shift in the whole Catholic Church's attitude toward war."[23] Piehl was partly correct: Ludlow did provide the theory. Nonetheless, the revival of the Catholic Worker movement's peace witness during the 1950s must be attributed far more to Ammon Hennacy, an American radical from the Midwest.

Ammon Hennacy began his "one-man revolution" in 1950, just when most peace action was receding into oblivion. He joined the Catholic Worker movement and gave seven years of his life to it. According to

Hennacy's most recent biographer, Patrick Coy, "Hennacy crusaded for one great human value, freedom." He was attracted to Day, and as with hers, the bases of his belief were personal responsibility and a heart full of compassion that did not participate in government or depend on it to correct social injustice. Hennacy also embraced poverty and led a life of hard physical labor, mainly to avert cooperation with evil institutions and remain true to his vision. He joined the Catholic Worker movement and was baptized a Catholic not because of any deep reflection but because he admired Dorothy Day and got what he called a "crush" on her.[24] Unfortunately in the end he could not remain in the Catholic church, for he was unable to forgive the church for what he perceived as its marriage to corruption and tyranny.[25]

In 1950 Hennacy had begun practicing civil disobedience in Phoenix, Arizona, by fasting and picketing a tax office for five days. His twin purposes were to show penance for the dropping of the bomb on Hiroshima and to protest money being spent on bombs and troops in Korea. In 1954 Hennacy, Day, and a few other Catholic Workers refused to take shelter during New York City's annual air-raid drill, participation in which was required by the Civil Defense Act. On June 15, 1955, Hennacy, Day, and five Catholic Workers were joined in a similar protest by twenty-three others, mainly members of the War Resisters League and the Fellowship of Reconciliation. The following year they repeated their performance and were sentenced to five days in jail. Every year thereafter a dozen or more practitioners of nonviolent resistance appeared, committed civil disobedience, and served prison sentences for it. On May 3, 1960, approximately two thousand students and adults throughout New York City resisted the yearly drill.[26] It was the largest direct action demonstration to date in the United States against nuclear warfare. This demonstration marked the new strategy the American peace movement would use in the 1960s. The tactic of calling together massive numbers of individuals to commit civil disobedience to change the U.S. government's public policy was a form of nonviolent resistance already being used successfully by the civil rights movement.[27]

On January 2, 1961, Hennacy left the Catholic Worker movement to make his home in Salt Lake City. Although Ammon Hennacy did not make a lasting impression on the Roman Catholic church in the United States, he did leave his mark on the Catholic Worker movement. By his undaunted actions he had introduced to the movement the way of nonviolent resistance. Ludlow had said that Gandhian nonviolence and Catholic Worker pacifism were compatible, but Hennacy had demonstrated how to fuse the two and how to apply massive tactics of nonviolence to the issue of peace in America. As a result practitioners of nonviolence were not left waiting for the state to apply moral principles to nuclear issues; they helped to initiate change in public policy. No longer were they just pacifists saying no to war; they were posting actions for peace. They considered themselves to be peacemakers.[28]

Day, however, envisioned the Catholic Worker movement as being much broader than the peace movement was. Her priorities included concern for the poor and oppressed, civil rights, and labor. For her, the issues of justice and peace were inseparable. Nonviolent tactics could be used to bring the gospel message not only to issues of war and peace but to all questions of social injustice. Day remained faithful to Maurin's broad vision, but she also incorporated Hennacy's vision into the Catholic Worker movement. Describing the difference between Ammon Hennacy and Peter Maurin, she wrote, "Ammon is deep and narrow, but Peter was so broad that he took in all the life of man, body, soul and mind."[29]

By the early 1960s it became clear to many Catholic Workers that the peace issue was of such significance that there should be a Catholic group solely dedicated to peace. One idea was to reactivate PAX, a group formed within the Catholic Worker movement during World War II to support Catholic conscientious objectors; another possibility was to form a Catholic peace fellowship under the auspices of the Fellowship of Reconciliation (FOR). The latter idea lost out because of the old Catholic suspicion of Protestants. As one *Catholic Worker* editor put it at the time, "All they want to do is use you."[30] Although Protestant and Catholic pacifists had achieved a high level of cooperation during the late 1950s, Catholic Workers wanted to maintain their own identity. Self-consciously Catholic yet critical of the existing militaristic and capitalistic American system, they were cautious about encroachments of other groups, even other Catholic groups. Stressing autonomy, they reactivated PAX.[31]

Eileen Egan, a close friend of Dorothy Day, was mainly responsible for the organization, while Gordon Zahn worked closely with her. PAX was affiliated with PAX in England, whose most prominent member was Archbishop Thomas D. Roberts. The archbishop stressed the need for autonomy, especially freedom—above all, financial freedom—from hierarchical control. Because of financial difficulties PAX grew slowly, but it was able to publish a valuable quarterly magazine called *Peace,* which it began in 1963 to observe an annual peace mass in commemoration of Hiroshima; to conduct monthly meetings; and to sponsor an annual conference at the Catholic Worker farm in Tivoli, New York. Founders of PAX proclaimed no official position, although they themselves were pacifists. Moreover, PAX devoted most of its energy not to individuals directly but to lobbying for peace within the institutional church.[32]

• • •

The main reason for PAX's emphasis on the institutional church was the Second Vatican Council. In the year of PAX's founding, 1962, more than 2,400 bishops had assembled in Rome for that solemn event. Before convening them, Pope John XXIII had issued what became a world-renowned encyclical on peace, *Pacem in Terris*. The encyclical set the tone for the council's discussions about war. In it John XXIII condemned not just nuclear war but all war in the nuclear age. By repudiating the suitability of using war to restore violated rights, he implicitly rejected, or at least undermined, the theory of the just war. *Pacem in Terris* heralded a new approach to warfare and a revolution in the meaning of Catholic peacemaking. At the Second Vatican Council just-war doctrine and pacifism collided. By 1964 the cold war, the possibility of a nuclear holocaust, and the pope's encyclical on peace had suggested to a number of bishops throughout the world that a just war was no longer possible.[33]

The pacifist branch of the American Catholic peace movement took a direct approach to the council's proceedings. In 1964 some members of the Catholic Worker movement and of PAX went to Rome in hopes of encouraging the council fathers to condemn nuclear weapons and affirm the right of conscientious objection. At the council these peacemakers offered two types of peace witness. The first type was presented by a Dorothy Day–led group of women who fasted, prayed, and discussed the issues with the members of the hierarchy—an intensely personal and spiritual type of witness.[34] The other type was made by three members of PAX who acted as a political lobby: Eileen Egan and Gordon Zahn, along with a young lay theologian and close friend of philosopher Thomas Merton named James Douglass. The three worked tirelessly to produce a positive statement condemning nuclear warfare and affirming conscientious objection.

The final statement at Vatican II did condemn "total war"—although it remained silent on the morality of deterrence, refusing to pass judgment on the intentions of nations that possessed nuclear weapons. The peace lobby was more successful on conscientious objection. The council affirmed it. Its final text on conscientious objection clearly upheld the

rights and duties of individual conscience and recommended legal provision for those who resist military commands. It also dropped the negative statement that presumed the duty of a person to obey lawful authority until the injustice of its commands was clear.[35]

The peace lobbyists had wanted to shut the door on the just-war
doctrine on grounds that it was not a viable ethic for modern warfare.
They could shut the door only partially, however. The development of
nuclear warfare and the cold war had influenced the council fathers
enough that they tried to reevaluate the traditional just-war doctrine in
which they had been trained, but not enough to move them to a new
ethic. At best, the council fathers opened the way for a new ethic—an
ethic of peace on the affirmation of the dignity of personhood, the
Gospels, and nonviolence.[36]

• • •

As a result of the Second Vatican Council, Catholics acquired the authority to dissent. Consequently some began to challenge not only the
authoritative statements of their church but also the policies of their
government.[37] At Vatican II the bishops elevated not only peace but also
social justice to top priority. Thus they continued the Catholic tradition
of linking justice with peace. In the 1960s, as social changes swept across
the land, this tradition had a profound impact on American Catholics.
The civil rights movement, the birth of a women's movement, and a
mounting concern with poverty and urban blight caught up many Catholics who were committed to establishing a just order in America.[38] Involvement in these domestic, nonviolent struggles for social justice in
American society became a stepping stone for many American Catholics to move into the peace movement, especially as the United States
escalated its role in Southeast Asia.

Within the array of social justice activities, activists made the Catholic connection between justice and peace. As the Vietnam War escalated,
they also gave both direct and indirect support to the American Catholic peace movement. Many Catholics remained committed to a single
issue such as race or community organizing and supported the peace
movement only indirectly. Other Catholics moved from their social justice work into the peace movement. Some integrated the two. Some
Catholics made no connection between their religion and society's problems and left the church—most notably Mario Savio, leader of Berkeley's Free Speech movement; Tom Hayden, the author of the "Port Huron Statement," which launched the Students for a Democratic Society;

and Timothy Leary, who urged use of the drug LSD as a sacrament in the counterculture of the 1960s.[39] On the other hand Jack Kerouac, an important "beat" novelist and counterculture guru, could not abandon his Catholicity.[40] Beyond a doubt, the impact of social changes in American society and the changes among Catholics after the Second Vatican Council were causing identity crises among American Catholics. Catholics were rethinking the meaning of their faith within American society and were becoming visible and vocal in their criticism of American injustices.

Meanwhile some Catholic activists revived the idea of a peace fellowship under the auspices of FOR. In 1964 they organized the Catholic Peace Fellowship (CPF)—the first Catholic peace group to be organized on an ecumenical basis. The main CPF founders were two priests, Daniel Berrigan and his brother Philip, and Catholic Workers Tom Cornell and Jim Forest. In 1968, with an unprecedented action of burning draft files at Catonsville, Maryland, the Berrigans became the leading peace figures in the Catholic peace movement. From 1933 to 1968 Catholics had moved from a marginal status in the American peace movement to a position of central importance.[41]

By the late 1960s the Berrigan brothers, the *Catholic Worker*, PAX, the CPF, campus groups, and thousands of Catholic individuals were responding to the peace call of Vatican II. By 1969, 2,494 Catholics were among the 34,255 individuals classified as conscientious objectors. In absolute numbers the Catholic church had more COs than did any other religious body.[42] By November 1968 most of the American bishops had moved toward neutrality on the war, and in that month they issued a pastoral statement entitled *Human Life in Our Day*.[43] For the first time in U.S. history the American Catholic hierarchy declared that conscientious objectors, even selective conscientious objectors, have a basis for their position in modern Catholic teaching. According to a later Gallup poll report, when the Vietnam War began Catholics "were more hawkish than other Americans"; "when it ended, they were more dovish. And they have remained that way for a generation."[44] Finally, in November 1971 the bishops condemned the Vietnam War as unjust. Their collective statement, entitled "Resolution on Southeast Asia," concluded that "at this point in history, it seems clear to us that whatever good we hope to achieve through continued involvement in this war is now outweighed by the destruction of human life and moral values it inflicts." And so, the bishops said, their conviction was "that the speedy ending of this war is a moral imperative of the highest priority."[45] Although the bishops were late in their condemnation, it was the first time in history that a national hierarchy had condemned the war efforts of its own nation.

With the end of U.S. involvement in Vietnam the Catholic peace movement (like the American peace movement in general) entered a period of less action, although later it would regroup on the nuclear issue. Despite this slowdown, the shift in official Catholic thought away from the just-war tradition and toward acceptance of pacifism and non-violence as legitimate Catholic alternatives left more American Catholics concerned about peace than ever before. Moreover, Catholic peace-makers continued with a twofold campaign: to stop the U.S. government from pursuing its militaristic policies and its nuclear weaponry and to convert the American Catholic church to a pacifist and nonviolent position. The campaigns took many forms. The Berrigans founded a movement called "Plowshares," which used direct-action demonstrations against nuclear weapons. The *Catholic Worker* and the CPF continued in their pacifism and opposition to the draft. In 1972 PAX formed a new group, Pax Christi USA, affiliated with Pax Christi International.[46]

The organization of Pax Christi USA was one of the most important developments in the post-Vietnam phase of the Catholic peace movement. Founded by Eileen Egan, Gordon Zahn, Joseph Fahey, Dorothy Day, and others, the new organization set out to make the Catholic church an instrument of positive peacemaking by educating and converting individual Catholics to peace. Two bishops, Carroll T. Dozier of Memphis and Thomas J. Gumbleton of Detroit, agreed to act as moderators. Although attempting to maintain a balance among all segments of the Catholic peace movement, Pax Christi USA was primarily pacifist in orientation, and all members were nuclear pacifists. In 1992 its membership peaked at 12,000 (91 of them bishops), with nearly 500 groups in religious communities, 300 local groups, and 125 peace parishes.[47]

The conversion of the American Catholic church into a force for peace is nowhere more clear than in the direction that the National Conference of Catholic Bishops (NCCB) had taken since 1970. More than any other individual within the administration of the NCCB, J. Bryan Hehir may deserve credit for this achievement. Hehir worked hard in the "Call to Action" conference held in Detroit in 1976. The conferees proclaimed a nuclear pacifist position; going even beyond condemning the *use* of nuclear weapons, they condemned their production and possession.[48] In 1978 and 1979 Hehir worked diligently to draft a statement that the bishops then issued in support of the Strategic Arms Limitation Treaty. His greatest achievement was work he did on the 1983 pastoral letter that the American Catholic bishops issued: *The Challenge of Peace: God's Promise and Our Response.* This letter stunned people by its bold advocacy of peace. Nonetheless it also disappointed members of the American Catholic peace movement, for it abandoned a nuclear pacifist position to give qualified assent to deterrence as a legitimate policy of the U.S. government.[49] Still, members were gratified to see their position as peacemakers affirmed officially for the first time.[50] Never before in the history of Catholicism had the bishops proclaimed pacifism and active nonviolence to be a means of Christian action in the service of the nation, just as valid as participation in military defense.

Since the publication of *The Challenge of Peace,* the American Catholic peace movement has continued its religious witness and quests for a new theology of peace. Since 1983 members of the peace movement have worked within a church that recognizes the legitimacy of their positions. Pacifists, nuclear pacifists, practitioners of gospel nonviolence and nonviolent resistance, conscientious objectors, and selective conscientious objectors are now at home in the Roman Catholic church.

NOTES

1. Patricia McNeal, *Harder Than War: Catholic Peacemaking in Twentieth Century America* (New Brunswick, N.J.: Rutgers University Press, 1992), 29–48.

2. George Weigel, *Tranquillitas Ordinis* (New York: Oxford University Press, 1987), 149.

3. Dorothy Day, *The Long Loneliness* (New York: Harper and Row, 1952), 87.

4. Eileen Egan, "Dorothy Day: Pilgrim of Peace," in Patrick G. Coy, ed., *A Revolution of the Heart: Essays on the Catholic Worker,* 69–133 (Philadelphia: Temple University Press, 1988), 49–50.

5. Day, *The Long Loneliness,* 139.

6. Ibid., 166.

7. Robert Coles, *Dorothy Day: A Radical Devotion* (Reading, Mass: Addison-Wesley, 1987), 71.

8. The best source on Peter Maurin is Marc H. Ellis, *Peter Maurin: Prophet in the Twentieth Century* (New York: Paulist, 1981). My summary in this paragraph also draws heavily on William Miller, *A Harsh and Dreadful Love: Dorothy Day and the Catholic Worker Movement* (New York: Liveright, 1973), 56.

9. Egan, "Dorothy Day," 73.

10. Mel Piehl, *Breaking Bread: The Catholic Worker and the Origin of Catholic Radicalism in America* (Philadelphia: Temple University Press, 1982), 198.

11. *Catholic Worker,* Oct., 1933.

12. McNeal, *Harder Than War,* 38.

13. Ibid.

14. A complete study of American Catholics' reaction to the Spanish Civil War is found in the works of J. David Valaik: "American Catholic Dissenters and the Spanish Civil War," *Catholic Historical Review* 53 (Jan. 1968): 537–46; and "Catholics, Neutrality and the Spanish Embargo, 1937–1939," *The Journal of American History* 54 (June 1967): 73–85.

15. McNeal, *Harder Than War*, 42.

16. Day quoted in Miller, *A Harsh and Dreadful Love*, 168.

17. Egan, "Dorothy Day," 73.

18. Piehl, *Breaking Bread*, 198. Perhaps the interpretation here is too beneficent toward church authorities.

19. Ready quoted in U.S. Congress, House Committee on Military Affairs, Report of the Hearings anent H.R. 10132, July 30, 1940, pp. 299–323.

20. Burke and Day quoted in Egan, "Dorothy Day," 79.

21. NSBRO papers, box A-44, Swarthmore College Peace Collection.

22. Gordon Zahn, *Another Part of War: The Camp Simon Story* (Amherst: University of Massachusetts Press, 1979), 251–52.

23. Piehl, *Breaking Bread*, 205.

24. Miller, *A Harsh and Dreadful Love*, 279.

25. Patrick G. Coy, "The One-Person Revolution of Ammon Hennacy," in Coy, ed., *A Revolution of the Heart*, 134–61.

26. *Catholic Worker*, June 1960.

27. For the best description of the demonstration, see Lawrence S. Wittner, *Rebels against War: The American Peace Movement 1941–1960* (New York: Columbia University Press, 1969), 265.

28. McNeal, *Harder Than War*, 93.

29. Dorothy Day, as quoted in Miller, *A Harsh and Dreadful Love*, 266.

30. James H. Forest, "No Longer Alone: The Catholic Peace Movement," in Thomas E. Quigley, ed., *American Catholics and Vietnam*, 134–73 (Grand Rapids, Mich.: Eerdmans, 1968), 144.

31. McNeal, *Harder Than War*, 94–95.

32. Ibid.

33. Ibid., 95–96.

34. A text of a leaflet issued to explain the purpose of the fast is found in "Appeal to Rome," *Reconciliation Quarterly* 40 (Fourth Quarter 1964): 612–14.

35. *Pastoral Constitution on the Church in the Modern World* (Huntington, Ind.: Our Sunday Visitor, 1968), 85–86.

36. Ibid.

37. Jay P. Dolan, *The American Catholic Experience: A History from Colonial Times to the Present* (New York: Doubleday, 1985), 426.

38. Ibid., 420–48.

39. James Terence Fisher, *The Catholic Counterculture in America 1933–1962* (Chapel Hill: University of North Carolina Press, 1989), 205–48.

40. Ibid.

41. McNeal, *Harder Than War*, 173–76.

42. "1970: A Year of Concern for all CO's," *The Reporter for Conscience's Sake,* Jan. 27, 1970, p. 2.

43. *Human Life in Our Day* (Washington, D.C.: U.S. Catholic Conference, 1968), pars. 98 and 99.

44. George Gallup Jr. and Jim Costelli, *The American Catholic People: Their Beliefs, Practices and Values* (New York: Doubleday, 1987), 82.

45. "Resolution on Southeast Asia," par. 13, as quoted in Marvin Bordelon, "The Bishops and Just War," *America,* Jan. 8, 1972, p. 17.

46. McNeal, *Harder Than War*, 230.

47. Patricia Scharber Lefevere, "Pax Christi Marks 20th Year," *National Catholic Reporter,* Aug. 28, 1992, pp. 37, 8.

48. Hehir has explained his nuclear pacifist position in J. Bryan Hehir, "The New Nuclear Debate: Political and Ethical Considerations," in Robert A. Gessert and J. Bryan Hehir, *The New Nuclear Debate,* 35–76 (New York: Council on Religion and International Affairs, 1976).

49. Hehir abandoned his nuclear pacifist position because of deterrence. See J. Bryan Hehir, "Moral Issues in Deterrence Policy," in Douglas MacLean, ed., *The Security Gamble Deterrence Dilemmas in the Nuclear Age,* 53–71 (Totowa, N.J.: Rowman and Allanheld, 1984).

50. *The Challenge of Peace: God's Promise and Our Response* (Washington, D.C.: United States Catholic Conference, 1983), par. 333.

15

꼿ㄹ

JUST-WAR THOUGHT AND NATIONALIST BEHAVIOR

The Case of the Christian Reformed Church

꼿ㄹ

Ronald A. Wells

The question underlying the work of this volume, as I understand it, is to ask whether and to what extent the various churches of the United States (other than the "historic peace churches") contributed to thought and behavior on matters of war and peace. In asking this question, those of us outside the historic peace churches acknowledge with gratitude the faithfulness of, for example, Quakers and Mennonites in clearly standing for peace and nonresistance. Their courage and costly faithfulness is an encouragement to all. It is a further encouragement that by helping to produce this book, editor Schlabach, a peace-church scholar, has promoted dialogue with those Christian communities for whom ethical decisions about war have not been as clear and unambiguous as they have been for the peace churches. This sort of dialogue, long overdue, must be good for all Christian churches.

The aim of this essay is to illuminate aspects of the larger question by discussing one of the churches in the Calvinist expression of Protestantism, the Dutch Reformed church, now the Christian Reformed church (CRC). First I briefly review the theory about the church and the world that we of the CRC take as given. Then I concentrate on the CRC's experience as an immigrant church, focusing on two traditions of thought within it. Finally I explicate the CRC's official pronouncements in limiting the scope of justifiable participation in war. In the conclusion, invoking Reinhold Niebuhr, I ask whether good theory is enough to overcome the seductions of nationalist ideology.

The various churches discussed in this volume, except the Methodists, are denominations or sects that George M. Marsden, following R. Laurence Moore, calls "outsider" groups.[1] By that term he means to give a functional, not normative, judgment. The historical "insiders" were Congregationalists, Presbyterians, Episcopalians, most Methodists, and some Baptists—in short, those religious groups that either formed, or were heirs to, the evangelical mainline of American Protestantism. Quite rightly the revivalistic workings of these groups have been called "the central mode of this culture's search for cultural identity."[2] Indeed one scholar has written that "the story of American Evangelicalism is the story of America itself in the years 1800–1900."[3]

Insider religion assumed a cultural mandate that outsider religion did not. Central to that cultural mandate was—and is—the question of the degree to which the New England Puritan vision of "the city on the hill" could actually be translated into making America be the righteous, even "redeemer," nation.[4] Since insiders' struggles concerning general cultural leadership differed from those of outsiders, insiders are likely to have been more sorely vexed by questions of war and peace than were those who saw their groups' historic missions as lying outside the corridors of cultural power. The former had to relate ethical choices to the use of power, whereas the latter, largely eschewing the seductions of cultural power, could be more consistent and clear about their witness in time of war. This tension was particularly great for churches in the Calvinist tradition whose ideology in New England was to establish, as one scholar has put it, "the origins of the American self."[5]

Calvinist thinking about war and peace, or about the church and the state, has always turned on a prior discussion about the tension between "the community of faith" and "the world." This has been true from the Reformation to the present. It is not mere chauvinism for a Calvinist to claim that debates among Calvinists were more crucial than those that emerged from other branches of sixteenth-century Protestantism. As historian Crane Brinton reminded us in his inimitable way, "Calvinism is the center of Protestantism."[6] Anyone who imagines this to be an enviable position should recall that Brinton saw Protestantism as an inherently unstable movement, as it tried to reconcile the history of the church with Renaissance-humanist assertions of biblical literacy and private conscience. In Brinton's words: "The Calvinist would not let sinners sin freely, if he could help it, even though in strict logic it might be maintained that God obviously intended the sinner to sin. Where they were in power, the Calvinists censored, forbade, banished and punished behavior they thought sinful. In this they were clearly in their own minds

God's agents, doing God's work. In practice, these firm believers in the inability of human effort to change anything were among the most ardent of workers toward getting men to change their behavior."[7] But it was not always clear what Calvinists wanted to change from or to in human behavior. This lack of clarity was due to the inherent instability of Protestantism and to the ambiguity of viewpoint that naturally inheres in a position that is self-consciously centrist on the issues of church and state and on issues of the faithful community and the world.

There are other positions on this question that came out of other expressions of sixteenth-century Protestantism: using shorthand terminology for present purposes, I will call the "right wing of Protestantism" (e.g., Lutheran) "medieval" and call the "left wing of Protestantism" (e.g., Mennonites) "modern." The right wing of the Reformation is sometimes called the "magisterial Reformation" because, in its view, the church is part of a social order in which the princes and the magistrates have an obligation to institute and maintain right religion. This is a type of Protestant medievalism in which religion and society are aspects of a coherent whole. Luther's image is helpful here: he believed that God's intentions are like a sword God wields. The sword has two edges, the church and the state, and both move together to accomplish God's will. In this view it is almost inconceivable that there could be any conflict between the twin purposes of God. Thus when Lutherans and similarly Anglicans thought about societal issues, they typically emphasized bringing the church and the state into harmony.

The Anabaptist and "free church" expressions of Protestantism are on the opposite end of the Protestant spectrum. I call them "modern" here because they founded their identities on the separation of church and society. Although some of them were "quietist" (accepting social matters as given because genuine reality was spiritual and otherworldly), others were "activists" (especially the historic peace churches, which courageously confronted the power of the principalities). The common conviction among all Anabaptist and free church people (sometimes known as the "Radical Reformation") was that the community of faith *never* coincides with the state or any other secular definition. Since their societal thinking emphasized the separation between religious and political institutions, they made little positive contribution to a discussion to find the right relationship to those civic institutions that they saw as normatively separate.

The middle ground of the Protestant continuum is relatively more ambiguous than either the magisterial option or the radical one. The

Calvinists neither dissociated religion and society nor said they were the same. To them, the church was to be neither dependent on the state for origin and support nor separate from it in the doing of God's "kingdom service." Perhaps because of this ambiguous and ambivalent position, there was a great deal of creative political thinking among Calvinists as to just what the relationship of religion and society is or ought to be. For the Calvinist, the Lutheran assertion that state power is God's power begs the question of evil governments and how to evaluate them. Similarly the Anabaptists' eschewing of power at all levels of society seemed to the Calvinist to be a simple and perhaps devious attempt to avoid the responsibilities of power in the service of God.

In the religious wars and the various other conflicts of the sixteenth and seventeenth centuries, the Calvinists made many mistakes in the uses of power: for instance, the conspiracy of Amboise in 1560, when Huguenots tried to kidnap King Francis II of France, or Cromwell's using the vengeful sword of the Lord at Drogheda in Ireland in 1640. Despite such outrages they developed interesting theories, drawing from Calvin, about appropriate resistance to tyrannical authority. Thus we may still read the pamphlets of François Hotman (1573), Theodore Beza (1574), and Phillippe Mornay (1579) with profit, as well as the writings of Calvin himself. In his great work, *The Institutes of the Christian Religion* (1536), Calvin built a carefully reasoned system that he intended to guide Christian living and believing for all laypeople. As to the state, and particularly to the issues surrounding war, he laid out the carefully strictured occasions on which Christians may participate in the use of state power and those on which they should oppose it. For example, he wrote:

> Kings and people must sometimes take up arms to execute such public vengeance. On this basis we may judge wars lawful which are so undertaken. For if power has been given them to preserve the tranquility of their dominion, to restrain the seditious stirrings of restless men, to help those forcibly oppressed, to punish evil deeds—can they use it more opportunely than to check the fury of one who disturbs both the repose of private individuals and the common tranquility of all, who raises seditious tumults, and by whom violent oppressions and vile misdeeds are perpetrated? If they ought to be the guardians and defenders of the laws, they should also overthrow the efforts of all whose offenses corrupt the discipline of the laws. Indeed, if they rightly punish those robbers whose harmful acts have affected only a few, will they allow a whole county to be afflicted and devastated by robberies with impunity? For it makes no

difference whether it be a king or the lowest of the common folk who invades a foreign county in which he has no right, and harries it as an enemy. All such must, equally, be considered as robbers and punished accordingly. Therefore, both natural equity and the nature of the office dictate that princes must be armed not only to restrain the misdeeds of private individuals by judicial punishment, but also to defend by war the dominions entrusted to their safekeeping, if at any time they are under enemy attack. And the Holy Spirit declares such wars to be lawful by many testimonies of Scripture. But if anyone object against me that in the New Testament there exists no testimony or example which teaches that war is a thing lawful for Christians, I answer first that the reason for waging war which existed of old still persists today; and that, on the other hand, there is no reason that bars magistrates from defending their subjects. Secondly, I say that an express declaration of this matter is not to be sought in the writings of the apostles; for their purpose is not to fashion a civil government, but to establish the spiritual Kingdom of Christ. Finally, that it is there shown in passing that Christ by his coming has changed nothing in this respect.[8]

Now a critic might quickly and rightly say that this is not a clear call to Christian action; rather, it is a logical exercise in indirect argument. Just so. For Calvinists, there can be no Lutheran conferring of sacrality on the state and its actions, and neither can Calvinists accept that the state is, *mutatis mutandis,* secular and therefore outside the scope of religious thought and action. There are certain conditions in which the state can act Christianly and others when it cannot. Therefore the position is unstable, like the center of Protestantism itself. The Lutherans and Anabaptists at least had theoretical clarity on their polar opposite ends, thus giving believers in the two communities Archimedian reference points. There was not, nor could there be, a Calvinist Archimedes to give that orientation point that would forever settle the questions of the relationship of faithful communities to the nations or states in which they found themselves.

It is with this self-conscious theological baggage that Dutch Calvinists emigrated to the New World. As Oscar Handlin wrote in his insightful book *The Uprooted,* the history of emigration is a history of alienation and its consequences.[9] Emigration is, in a substantial sense, a deviant behavior. A person or group has to be alienated from a homeland to leave behind the familiar, the natural ties of hearth and home, and embark on a voyage overseas; this is especially true of people in the

nineteenth century, when emigration typically meant permanent separation. The migration of the Dutch Reformed to America—notwithstanding some of their own fileopietistic protestations—fits the main
contours of migration from Europe. Conditions in the sending country had to be right, as did those in the receiving country. Thus Dutch
Calvinist migration beginning in the 1840s was an uprooting of people
from the countryside for much the same reasons that Germans and Irish
migrated at the same time. A significant finding has emerged from social history's investigations, however. Although the Dutch emigrated for
the same socioeconomic reasons as did other Europeans, there was a
considerable overrepresentation of a subgroup of Dutch Calvinists, the
Seceders of 1834. Historians cannot demonstrate that the desire for religious liberty was the key factor in the Seceders' migration, but the fact
that their secession from the state church had made them religious outsiders had a great deal to do with their patterns of adjustment to, and
ambivalence toward, the America they came to find.[10]

All immigrant churches in the nineteenth century were outsiders, in
the sense I am using the term. Their peoples came for a variety of reasons, mostly from the countrysides of Europe. Most, although not all,
were psychologically unprepared for the rigors of the new culture, dominated by both market economy and sociopolitical liberty. The churches became major rallying points for collective identity, and for some, as
historian Oscar Handlin has suggested, religion became a way of life.[11]
This is precisely what happened for the Dutch Calvinist emigrants who
followed a leader named Albertus Van Raalte to western Michigan. The
crisis of cultural identity was not long in coming. Van Raalte wanted his
"*kolonie*" to succeed in the New World, but without his people changing their religious orientation. He advocated amalgamating with the
Dutch Reformed church that had been in America since the seventeenth
century, when New York was New Amsterdam. By the 1840s, however,
the Dutch Reformed church had become an American denomination,
in all affective meanings of that term. They spoke English and used the
hymns of the New England and evangelical mainline churches; with
their northern European roots, they had become insiders. For the newer immigrants this constituted one too many bridges to cross. If they
would acculturate to America, they would do so on their own terms
rather than on terms that would lead to assimilation.[12] In 1857, after an
initial affiliation with the older church as advocated by Van Raalte, a
seceder element established the Christian Reformed church. By 1880 the
Seceding church back in the motherland endorsed the action and rec-

ommended that new emigrants affiliate with the CRC. Thus the new CRC grew steadily through the immigration that continued to World War I.

One hundred years later we can see that the CRC's attempt to hold off America was always doomed. By 1990 the CRC had become a member of the National Association of Evangelicals, and its college, via the Christian College Coalition, was one of the flagship schools of conservative evangelicalism's presence in American higher education. In a certain way the situation was always destined to be so. The ethos of the secession of 1834 in Holland and of the church's founding in 1857 was deeply pietistic. Never mind that those Dutch Calvinists would rail against Methodism's shallow, even pelagian, theology of free will and free grace; their great-grandchildren would be found next to Methodists and Baptists at Billy Graham rallies, singing "Just As I Am" as reverently as anyone.

Nonetheless, there is a certain way that the theological rigor of the CRC set its people apart from their more pragmatic ecclesiastical neighbors. Unlike many in the mainline (i.e., evangelical) churches, these were people who took their theology seriously and demanded a truly learned clergy. In the years leading up to World War I the leaders of the CRC sometimes even offered trenchant criticism of nationalism's shallow character. By the eve of the war the battle against America was clearly being lost, but a minority among the CRC followed the lead of Dutch religious-political leader Abraham Kuyper (1837–1920). Like Kuyper, this minority, often called "neo-Calvinists," wanted an entire reinterpretation of religion and politics on the basis of "antithesis." (Thus Kuyperian neo-Calvinists are also called "Antitheticals.") As historian James D. Bratt has written, the neo-Calvinists operated not so much "from hostility to America in particular but from hostility to 'the world' in general. America happened to be the world at hand."[13] In the early years of this century there were not enough neo-Calvinists around to stay the tide of the acculturation being pushed by the majority. They became vital to the story by the 1920s, however, when everything changed. For example, while John Van Lonkhuysen of the neo-Calvinists saw the danger of Billy Sunday's fundamentalist evangelicalism both for church and society, the editor of the denominational weekly, Henry Beets, used *The Banner* to celebrate Sunday's western Michigan crusade.[14]

Beets was a key figure in the CRC's taking its place as an American denomination. Under him *The Banner* expressed the movement from secessionist piety to Calvinist triumphalism. "Our great and peculiar duty and calling," Beets editorialized in 1907, is "to become more and more what God in his providence in the past had designed us to be as a Calvinistic people." In that endeavor Beets thought that Calvinists "had no right to be benevolently assimilated." Instead he viewed "Christian isolation" as "a duty." Nevertheless he wanted such isolation to last only long enough "to develop ourselves quietly and without undue haste, to become firmly settled as to our principles." He hoped that in time his people would be "prepared enough, strong enough, to cast us with body and soul and all our previous Calvinism as a world-and-life view as well as a religious system, into the arena of American religious and political and social life."[15]

With such views stated in the CRC's magazine, the longer the church was in America, the less tenable was the ambivalence toward the culture. Moreover, as Calvinists, the CRC people were honorary heirs to New England Puritanism. Thus, if they proved their loyalty to America, they could become authentic insiders; being so would allow them in turn to leaven the loaf of the larger culture and move it in a direction oriented toward God's kingdom. Then World War I produced a language and identity crisis for the CRC.

The crisis was not on the issues of peace and war but on CRC's own issues; nonetheless the war escalated the crisis. It cowed the few neo-Calvinists, the most outspoken of whom was Herman Hoeksema, minister in Holland, Michigan. One issue was flags in CRC sanctuaries. Hoeksema said that he might allow the flag in the church on other occasions, but not during worship services. He insisted that when the people of God met, they met as a transnational assembly, in sympathy with Christians the world over. He hoped that the church would not be co-opted into mere service to the nation.[16] Other neo-Calvinists were intimidated into silence during the war both by physical threats from other Americans and by the superpatriotism of some of their fellow church members—the so-called progressivist faction—who saw the war as the occasion to get the church finally and fully into American culture. The zenith (or the nadir) of this, seen again in the issue of the flag, came in 1918 when editor Beets had the following poem published in *The Banner*:[17]

Here's to the Red of it—
There's not a thread of it,
No, nor a shred of it
In all the spread of it
From foot to head,

But heroes bled for it,
Faced steel and lead for it,
Precious blood shed for it,
Bathing it Red.

Here's to the White of it—
Thrilled by the sight of it,
Who knows the right of it
But feels the might of it
Through day and night?
Womanhood's care for it
Made manhood dare for it,
Purity's prayer for it
Keeps it so White.

Here's to the Blue of it—
Beauteous view of it,
Heavenly hue of it,
Star-spangled hue of it,
Constant and true,
States stand supreme for it,
Diadems gleam for it,
Liberty's beam for it
Brightens the Blue.

Here's to the Whole of it
Stars, stripes and pole of it,
Body and soul of it,
On to the goal of it
Carry it through.
Home or abroad for it,
Unsheath the sword for it,
Fight in accord for it
Red, White and Blue.

Even the historiography of the CRC is a victim of the debate over
World War I. In a book published in 1973 Henry Zwaanstra, professor
of American church history at Calvin Theological Seminary, presented
the war as an end of an era that brought a complete victory for the progressive, Americanist faction. But James D. Bratt, professor of American religious history at Calvin College, has dissented. Bratt conceded the
progressivist victory in the war, but he interpreted the war not as the

end but as the beginning of an era, a new era that by its end saw the defeat of the progressivists and their Americanism.[18] There is indeed merit in both interpretations. Zwaanstra was correct in that the progressive-assimilationist majority of the leadership had put the CRC on the road to becoming an American insider denomination during a period of relative calm, 1920–60. By guarding confessional orthodoxy in Calvin College and Seminary and by encouraging American-style evangelical piety in the homes and schools, the progressives eased the CRC into its comfortable position in American life. The movement to the suburbs accompanied the arrival of Dutch ethnics into the great American middle class, which coincided in its bourgeois pieties with the civil religion of the era.

Bratt, however, seems to have the better inclination—although if defeat came to the progressives, it was a long time coming. Perhaps *defeat* is the wrong word; perhaps *pluralism* best describes the situation after 1970. The new migration into Canada after World War II changed the theological climate in the CRC just as the cultural explosion of the 1960s was about to rearrange all our analytical categories. The post–World War II immigrants were overwhelmingly of the Kuyperian or neo-Calvinist persuasion. The progressive-Americanist hegemony in the CRC had not eliminated their neo-Calvinism, so they had a heritage on which to build as they challenged the CRC leaders. By 1970 the cultural ferment in America had caused even the most complacent of the pietist and confessional wing of the CRC to realize that Bob Dylan was right: the children were no longer under their parents' control, and the times, they were a-changing. But their method (orthodox confessionalism) and intent (stability) gave the progressive Americanists little room to move.

The neo-Calvinists, coming unexpectedly from the left, outflanked the moderate political orientation of the progressives. Young leaders of the Antitheticals, reflecting cultural affinities for the university style of the 1960s, were very energetic; moreover they were very sure of their principles and of the historical rightness of their position. In the words of Bratt: "They had stood firm and the world came round to meet them. Marx's dialectics met Kuyper's; the West stood at the crisis. . . . Liberalism was the culprit; Christianity's syntheses therewith (which among 'conservatives' took the form of bourgeois pieties) the problem; and institutional introversion was the church's pathetic response."[19]

The most ear-shattering of the Antitheticals' several thunderbolts was a book written by some Canadian young Turks in 1970, a book that frontally assaulted the accomplishments of CRC leadership over the previous two generations. It pictured the progressivist-pietist group as secure in a kind of pious but unengaging orthodoxy that had left the church merely secure among the American bourgeoisie. The CRC, the young Canadians said, had gone "awhoring after that great American Bitch: The Democratic Way of Life."[20] The rhetoric and tactics of the neo-Calvinists (sometimes called Dooyeweerdians because of their intellectual debt to Dutch legal philosopher Herman Dooyeweerd) offended many CRC people, but pietist and confessional elements could scarcely match their intellectual rigor. Whatever the intrinsic merits of their often-overstated positions, their voices signaled that Kuyper was definitely back in Calvinist circles.

Out of the general ferment of the 1960s and the presence of the energetic neo-Calvinists came a rethinking of a number of supposed verities—a rethinking aided by the agonizing presence in American culture of the Vietnam War. It is not that the repositioning of the neo-Calvinists in CRC discourse led ineluctably to a vitally important synodical pronouncement on war in 1977. Yet their presence and their common cause with some now-chastened members and some new members of the progressives issued in that truly remarkable report. The report's title was "Ethical Decisions about War."[21] The 1973 annual Synod of the Christian Reformed Church had appointed a special committee "to provide the church's membership with guidelines for making ethical decisions about war." Although the synod accepted that the Indochina war gave immediate poignancy to the study, they also believed that the guidelines finally to be issued would have a "lasting impact on the CRC's stance on warfare. The impact would be as much for giving pastoral aid to conscientious objectors as for the ways in which the church, as a corporate body, might act in times of war."[22] In 1977 "Ethical Decisions" was presented and accepted.

The report was too long and too carefully argued for inclusion here in any detail; nevertheless it contained certain elements that deserve attention. Of great significance was the hermeneutic the committee applied to Scripture. Although they accepted the basic Protestant principle that Holy Scripture should be the final authority, the members were averse to both exegetical details and prooftexts. They began with the disarming disclaimer that "if the teachings of the Word of God on the Christian's involvement in war were as clear as some responses [to a survey sent out to churches] alleged, the subject would not have torn and troubled the church down through the centuries, and the Synod would not have appointed a committee to make this study." Further, the committee set forth an underlying premise about revelation that, one supposes, may have surprised the clergy who preach every Sunday. It took the position that God's revelation in the Bible unfolds more fully as it goes along. "Each new divine disclosure," the committee declaimed, "is richer and clearer than those made earlier, reaching a climax in the full and perfect revelation when God speaks in his Son."[23] The notion of progressive revelation, although not novel in Reformed circles, set the tone for the committee's evaluation of biblical material. Thus, although the writers insisted on their scriptural orthodoxy, they gave a certain camber to their argument that cannot have pleased the CRC's biblical literalists. They would not, the report insisted, "scrap or explain away these troublesome passages about the war-like God of the Old Testament." At the same time, however, their biblical contextualization required them to observe that no modern nation stands today in the same relation to God as did Israel of old. That special relation now obtains between God in Christ and the church, and the church—as church—should never, as a corporate body, engage in earthly, physical warfare. The biblical analysis of progressive revelation in the report went even further, however. The writers referred to John Calvin's idea that God accommodates humankind in Scripture as he does existentially. When the spirit of God comes to us—in Reformed doctrine we never choose the spirit—God never insists on total change right away but brings us along. God may allow some hardness of heart early on in our walk as God's people, but not later. Consequently, as to warfare and the Bible, the report presented an astonishing section that declared, "It does seem that by the time Jesus Christ our Lord preaches his Sermon on the Mount we are in a new moral atmosphere from that of the bloody war and total destruction we find, for example, in some passages of Samuel."[24]

"Ethical Decisions" went on further to point out that wars displease God because they always represent a massive failure to implement God's law of love. Moreover, war is evil not only in its taking of human life but also in the way it devalues the whole quality of human life. To this, the report insisted:

God's response to this massive evil—as well as to all other evils—was to send, at last, his own Son as a personal Word of reconciliation and peace. In the new age of peace, God's plan for reconciling human beings to him and to each other has been ushered in by Christ and is now entrusted to those who bear his name and act as his body. Following both the teaching ("Blessed are the peacemakers, for they shall be called sons of God") and the example of our Lord, we who claim his name must live peaceably ourselves, furnishing to the world conspicuous examples of peace-loving, harmonious living, and must also privately and publicly denounce war and strive to prevent it by prayer, by redressing the grievances of oppressed people, by prophetic calls to peace, by urging the faithful exercise of diplomacy, by entering the political arena ourselves, and by strong appeals to all in high places to resolve tensions by peaceful means. Christians must be *reconcilers*.[25]

Pacifist readers of these words might take heart that a Reformed denomination had finally seen the light. Alas, not quite so. The report continued with a careful analysis on what might (unfairly) be called "situation ethics." It conceded that there are certain times and places in which the biblical revelation about love and reconciliation may be disobeyed—indeed must be—in order that a greater good might result. The report dismissed militarism quickly and summarily but also said that it had to part ways with the "often tempting" position of pacifist brothers and sisters.[26]

The report then gave a long explication of classic just-war theories that, because they are well known, need not be repeated here—other than to observe that the reporters sincerely insisted that just-war theory in no way obliges a Christian to think that any war will be just; the theory merely allows for that possibility in extreme cases, while insisting that the cases be indeed extreme. Perhaps sensing the tendency of their own arguments, toward the end of their work the writers reasserted that "obviously, most of the reasons for waging war are Christianly impermissible and considerably outside the kingdom of God. Christians," they thought, will "readily recognize that most reasons for going to war are wrong."[27] Also, although the writers accepted the government of the state as a gift of God for the good order of society, they advised that the loyalty the Christian gives to any given state is always in tension and is conditional, resting on the state's ability to conform to what God intends.[28]

Further, the report broke new ground in Reformed thinking on the conscience, insisting that neither the state nor the church should bind or constrain the conscience of a believer on the matter of participation in war. The report was not fully individualistic, however, for it reminded readers that the work of the individual conscience ought always to be referenced against the collective conscience of the church—just as, for example, an individual reading of Holy Scripture must always be referenced against the collective wisdom of the community of faith.

Thus, the report concluded, in times of particular wars the church should convene a special assembly at which the standards of God would be applied to the current situation. This will be necessary because all future wars cannot now be declared acceptable or unacceptable. When a war occurs, if such a solemn assembly can reach agreement, then the church should make a prophetic witness to its nation on the morality of that conflict. If it cannot reach agreement—as will often be the case—then the church must support those persons who conscientiously object to the war and also pray for those who side with the nation's demands. Importantly, both are enjoined not to be triumphalist in denouncing or reproving the other, so as not "to threaten that loving Christian communion which is expressive of the covenant of grace."[29]

The report of 1977, "Ethical Decisions about War," is a landmark in the social teaching of the Christian Reformed Church. The CRC could never again descend to the nadir of earlier years when its pacifist members were attacked and cowed in times of national crisis. The report makes a pacifist response to war *a*—although not *the*—legitimate stance for Reformed Christians, and it draws the strictures ever more tightly around the situations in which participation in war would be acceptable. The historic peace churches may not find the statement to go far enough, but they must accept that one Reformed denomination, in its official guise, has moved far closer to them than could have been imagined a half-century ago when all the world went to war for the second time in this century.

In the end, it is fair to ask what impact "Ethical Decisions about War" has had on the life of the CRC. The answer is not clear. That the military draft has been eliminated as a fact of life is important here. Were young people to be required to serve a period of military service, one might have expected quite a few to choose conscientious objection. Without that fact, however, we have little way to test the long-standing effect.

The Gulf War of 1991 presented the first real test. The sorry conclusion is that the CRC failed its own test. Despite the fact that the guidelines of 1977 specifically called for a special assembly to discuss a given war, the church called none between the time of Iraq's invasion of Kuwait in August until the allied bombers rained death on Baghdad in January. Moreover, the editor of *The Banner* showed himself to be a worthy successor of Henry Beets. Galen Meyer actually invoked the guidelines of 1977 to write an editorial declaring the Gulf War to be "just"—to the strong protest of many in the CRC, including myself.[30]

As I discussed the Gulf War with colleagues at Calvin College, and especially with students, the following question frequently came up: what good is it to have a good position on war if, when the test comes, it does not issue in good behavior? I did not have an adequate answer to that question then, nor do I now. As a historian I see that the acceptance of "Ethical Decisions" by the synod of 1977 did not signal a broad and deep acceptance of its contents by the people of the CRC. It was the creature of a faction within a pluralistic church. Although that faction is present and accounted for throughout the church, it is probably over-represented in the church's intelligentsia. The neo-Calvinists and their Kuyperian allies among the chastened progressives, to use James Bratt's terms, still have an important—but not a determinative—role in the CRC. The pietist and confessional elements, moving toward mainstream evangelicalism, believe that they represent the rank and file of the CRC, and in that they are correct.

This story may also be true of the other denominations represented in this volume. Whether we are committed pacifists or Niebuhrian re-alists, we are outsiders in our denominations. Perhaps that accounts for the fact that a follower of Menno Simons, who was a permanent out-sider, has graciously invited us to contribute to this volume.

NOTES

1. George M. Marsden, *Religion and American Culture* (New York: Harcourt, Brace, Jovanovich, 1990); R. Laurence Moore, *Religious Outsiders in the Making of America* (New York: Oxford University Press, 1986).

2. Perry Miller, *The Life of the Mind in America* (New York: Harcourt, Brace and World, 1965), 7.

3. William McLoughlin, ed., *The American Evangelicals* (New York: Harper and Row, 1968), 1.

4. George M. Marsden, Mark A. Noll, Nathan O. Hatch, *The Search for Christian America* (Colorado Springs, Co.: Helmers and Howard, 1989); Ronald A. Wells, "Religion in American National Life: What Went Wrong?" *The Mennonite Quarterly Review* 65 (Apr. 1991): 117–27.

5. Sacvan Bercovitch, *The Puritan Origins of the American Self* (New Haven: Yale University Press, 1975).

6. Crane Brinton, *The Shaping of Modern Thought* (Englewood Cliffs, N.J.: Prentice-Hall, 1963), 71.

7. Ibid., 75.

8. John Calvin, *Institutes of the Christian Religion,* trans. and ed. Ford Lewis Battles (Grand Rapids, Mich.: Eerdmans, 1973 [1536]), 213–14.

9. Oscar Handlin, *The Uprooted* (Boston: Little, Brown, 1951), 3.

10. The best guide to the transit of culture among the Dutch Calvinists is the definitive effort of James D. Bratt, *Dutch Calvinism in Modern America: A History of A Conservative Subculture* (Grand Rapids, Mich.: Eerdmans, 1984), from which much of the material to follow is freely drawn.

11. Handlin, *The Uprooted,* 117–43.

12. Milton Gordon's typology is very helpful here; see Milton M. Gordon, *Assimilation in American Life* (New York: Oxford University Press, 1964), esp. 84–131.

13. Bratt, *Dutch Calvinism,* 51.

14. "Billy Sunday: A Near-by View," *The Banner,* Sept. 28, 1961, pp. 608–10.

15. H. Beets, "Not Ashamed of the Basis of 1857," *The Banner,* Apr. 11, 1907, pp. 184–85.

16. Bratt, *Dutch Calvinism,* 88–104.

17. "A Toast to the Flag," *The Banner,* Feb. 28, 1918, cover.

18. Henry Zwaanstra, *Reformed Thought and Experience: A Study of the Christian Reformed Church and Its American Environment* (Kampen, The Netherlands: J. H. Kok, 1973), 316–22; Bratt, *Dutch Calvinism,* 259.

19. Bratt, *Dutch Calvinism,* 209.

20. Hendrik Hart, James Olthuis, Calvin Seerveld, and Bernard Zylstra, *Out of Concern for the Church* (Toronto: Wedge, 1970), 32–33.

21. "Ethical Decisions about War," *Acts of Synod,* Christian Reformed Church (Grand Rapids, Mich.: CRC Publications, 1977), 550–74.

22. Ibid., 550.

23. Ibid., 551.

24. Ibid., 556.

25. Ibid., 558.

26. Ibid., 561.

27. Ibid.

28. Ibid., 572.

29. Ibid.

30. Galen Meyer, "A Tragic War for a Just Cause," *The Banner,* Mar. 11, 1991.

16

࿇

ETHICAL ISSUES FOR PACIFISTS AND
HISTORIANS OF PACIFISM

*A Response to Patricia McNeal and Ronald A. Wells
and Questions for Future Research*

࿇

Charles Chatfield

In their essays Patricia McNeal and Ronald Wells have opened new agendas. McNeal offers a story, a narrative, the larger version of which is in her book. That is a public service because the Catholic peace movement can absorb its past into the future only from the framework of narrative. McNeal's story is also an inestimable favor to scholarship, for only from narrative can scholars begin their analytical work. Her story correctly stresses the interactive process of validation. Other historians need to follow her example of coupling story line with institutional analysis. Questions about the role of churches as they challenge and validate social currents and trends should be part of other inquiries into pacifist history. Moreover, if we could know more of the international dimensions of McNeal's story, we could better appreciate the global connections of all expressions of pacifism.

Ronald Wells offers a case study of rigorous thinking. His also is a story, an exceptionally clear story, of a collective attempt to define an ethic of peace. In his essay Wells took hard thinking and made it gentle, personal. His effort is most commendable, especially since he cast analytical ethics as an engaging narrative.

. . .

Another engaging story is that of a Czechoslovakian named Premsyl Pitter (1895–1976). Of the many pacifists of the interwar period, Pitter was extraordinary. In World War I he had found himself drafted into the Austrian army. There he began to wonder why he, a Czech, was fighting for the empire that repressed his own land. Indeed, why was he fighting at all? At some point he fell in with an old Italian who converted him to Christian pacifism. After the war Pitter returned to Czechoslovakia, where with a bit of seminary education he became an evangelist. He also developed a sort of settlement house where he took in orphaned children and educated them, and he was at the core of the Czech Fellowship of Reconciliation. Then came World War II.

Early in that war, as the Germans drove toward Prague, Pitter took into his home Jewish children whose parents were being carted off to extermination camps. After the war, when German parents were being persecuted, he took in German children. Then, as Czechoslovakia became a communist satellite, he realized that he had several bad choices. The state demanded that he educate the children in the ideology it prescribed. If he refused to do so, he might end up in Siberia. Alternatively, instead of staying and refusing, he might try to get out of the country. He did escape, finding refuge in Switzerland, where he worked with Czech refugees.

I once had a lengthy personal interview with Pitter at his home near Zurich, and toward the end of it I asked him how, as a committed and absolute pacifist, he had felt during the closing years of the war. What were his feelings when he heard about Allied victories bringing down the German empire whose repression he knew firsthand?

Pitter replied, "Well, on the one hand I knew that every battle, every victory, was won with violence and carried the seeds of a new violence; but on the other hand those victories were, in a way, a blessing, a good thing."

"Was that not something of a dilemma?" I pressed him. He looked at me as though I were the most naive child that he had ever taken into his school. And he replied simply, "Charles, life *is dilemma.*"

Indeed, life is dilemma. Life is a story of choosing.

. . .

People who have taken pacifist positions within denominations, sects, and communities in this country have faced a number of dilemmas.

Whether they knew it or not, they were acting out their own choices. On behalf of pacifists, historians have begun to explore a number of the ethical questions they faced. Some important ones are the following:

1. How do pacifists, as a minority, establish or maintain their ethic within a religious community when that community is in the process of being assimilated into a larger, fundamentally nonpacifist culture?

2. How does a minority generate an institutional base within its community, denomination, or church from which to transmit and validate an ethical tradition that in every instance is a matter of individual choice? How do pacifists validate both an ethical principle and the right and necessity of making individual choices?

3. On what, after all, do pacifists ground their witness? Almost invariably, in this book's chapters, the answer comes from a gospel base. Whether occupying an evangelical, a pentecostal, a social-gospel, or a Catholic framework, religious pacifists have reached back to Scripture, as though searching for a kind of compass. On what should pacifism be grounded? On what is it based?

4. Where do we pacifists find the collective story or narrative in which to locate the pacifist ethic? This question is exciting because it has so many contexts, especially for pacifists without a peace church heritage. Perhaps pacifists return to the Bible precisely because the Bible at least offers a story: principle validated in experience.

5. How do pacifists validate an ethical principle when their society and maybe even their own denomination rejects it? How can pacifists persuade society to validate pacifism as an ethical option? Further, in a society with a penchant for voluntary associations as agents of change, what does it mean to build from an individualized ethic to a cultural one or to one that has cultural relevance? As peace activist A. J. Muste liked to paraphrase the theologian Martin Buber, "Pacifism is to drive a normative plowshare into the hard soil of reality."

6. How do pacifists defend an alternative ethic, their commitment and ethic of commitment, against social repression? Conversely, how do they defend a pacifist tradition (in the sense of conscientious objection or refusal to serve in the military) in the absence of conscription?

7. Finally, how do pacifists mobilize political resources to challenge national purpose? And how do they do so without being triumphal in mood or arbitrary in judgment?

Those are a few of the questions raised by the essays in this book. There is, however, another set of questions and challenges arising out of dilemmas that face historians. On behalf of the historians of pacifism this book's essays raise and explore questions such as the following:

1. How can historians find a language to both *distinguish* and *relate* various problems of pacifism and peace advocacy throughout changing historical and social contexts? Can they relate or compare the history of pacifism in the technical sense (absolute pacifism) to the kind of pacifism that some have called "positive" peace or "positive" pacifism— that is, essentially, peace advocacy?

2. How far can historians take pacifism as a phenomenon in history without assuming that it is normative? Is it even worthwhile to describe pacifism as a historical phenomenon without establishing its ethical basis and its political applications? In other words, is the study of pacifism in history worthwhile if academicians have not established its normative value for themselves? Can they treat it simply as a historical story? If historians do not interact with pacifism and let it engage them, can they treat the subject authentically?

3. Out of what did pacifism arise? What was the relationship between theological understanding and religious commitment, between a social ethic and ethnicity or other social and cultural characteristics, between the principle affirmed and the immediate historical context?

4. How does pacifism's decline in some traditions relate to its growth and change in others? Is there some calculation of utility, some sort of cost-price model to help historians think about pacifism's transformation? Is change simply a process of assimilation that dissolves one form of pacifism but incorporates another, validates it, and makes it operative?

5. If such transformation is a process of cultural assimilation, there are other questions about the same process. Can we describe authentic cases of such assimilation without losing the inner springs of the pacifist witness? How can we avoid becoming fixated on the narrative? What exactly has happened when pacifist traditions have undergone assimilation? To what extent did the larger culture absorb them?

6. Can historians produce meaningful accounts of pacifism or peace advocacy in the United States without a comprehensive and comparative understanding of pacifism in other political cultures? This book explores some of the same issues that are under discussion in Europe. In North America the exploration involves different cultural communities within one nation. In Europe historians explore pacifism in terms of the differences among national cultures.

7. More particularly, how can historians take what they themselves are hearing, observing, and feeling within specific religious traditions and relate it to the ecumenical revolution of the twentieth century? Ecumenism is a major twentieth-century revolution in thought, not in the United States alone, but globally. Somehow historians must integrate the study of pacifism—of attitudes toward war, peace, and social justice—with the history of this twentieth-century revolution in thought.

The ecumenical revolution came alongside other cultural revolutions. It grew from at least the missionary, the social-gospel, and the evangelical movements. Each of those movements represented a field of cooperation, and the three each evolved into a movement at about the time of World War I. Wartime experience heightened the social consciousness of ecumenism enormously. Subsequently the ecumenical approach was transformed from a search for minimal common denominators into a dialogue about differences. How does that ecumenical movement relate to the history of religious institutions, to life within the nation and its culture, and to the process of dialogue over social issues, including pacifism?

8. The final query is difficult to articulate. The overall history of the twentieth century has a kind of superstructure. In images more than in tight logic, there seems to be a mental superstructure for the twentieth century, a paradigm or blueprint from which historians have built up the century's history. That history is the story of wars, revolutions, and holocausts.

In the next century, however, historians very likely will look back and see a very strong substructure in the twentieth century. This substructure is a revolution in attitudes, institutions, human interactions, communications, and sensitivities. It is global interdependence, planetary consciousness, and international organization. It is a conflict-resolving process. Very probably the peace movements and in fact pacifism itself are parts of such a revolution, which includes changes in just-war (or justified-war) thinking about war and peace. How do today's historians do justice to this revolutionary substructure of the twentieth century? How do they recover and *restore* it without ignoring or mitigating the harsh reality of that superstructure of wars, revolutions, and holocausts?

These questions, sometimes unstated, run through this book. Premsyl Pitter saw life as dilemma. Insofar as pacifism affirms life, it too is dilemma. Therefore, pacifism affirms choice. Historians of pacifism must couch the living dilemmas of pacifists in stories of life choices. The chapters of this book offer challenging questions for more chapters in the history of pacifism.

CONTRIBUTORS

C. LEONARD ALLEN teaches theology and ethics at Abilene Christian University, Abilene, Texas. He is the author of *The Cruciform Church: Becoming a Cross-Shaped People in a Secular World* (1990) and other works. He also serves as pastor of Abilene Mission Church of Christ.

JAY BEAMAN, trained in sociology at Iowa State University and now teaching sociology at George Fox College, Newberg, Oregon, wrote on Pentecostals and pacifism as part of his work for an M.Div. degree at North American Baptist Seminary. The published version of his master's thesis is *Pentecostal Pacifism: The Origin, Development, and Rejection of Pacifist Belief among the Pentecostals* (1989).

MICHAEL W. CASEY, a professor of communication at Pepperdine University, Malibu, California, has published *Saddlebags, City Streets, and Cyberspace: A History of Preaching in the Churches of Christ* (1995). He has written also on the Churches of Christ and pacifism, with articles in *The Mennonite Quarterly Review* (1992) and *Restoration Quarterly* (1993).

CHARLES CHATFIELD is a professor of history at Wittenberg University, Wittenberg, Ohio, and surely a dean among historians of pacifism. Among numerous other titles his writings include *For Peace and Justice: Pacifism in America, 1914–1941* (1971), *An American Ordeal: The Antiwar Movement of the Vietnam Era* (with Charles DeBenedetti, 1990), *The American Peace Movement: Ideals and Activism* (1992), and *Peace/Mir: An Anthology of Historic Alternatives to War* (with Ruzanna Ilukhina, 1994).

MURRAY W. DEMPSTER is the vice president for academic affairs and a professor of social ethics at Southern California College, Costa Mesa, California. He is the coauthor of *Salt and Light: Evangelical Political Thought in Modern America* (1989), coeditor of *Called & Empowered: Global Mission in Pentecostal Perspective* (1991), author of a number of scholarly articles on social ethics, and editor of *PNEUMA: The Journal of the Society for Pentecostal Studies*.

RICHARD T. HUGHES is Distinguished Professor of Religion at Pepperdine University. He is the author of, among other writings, *Reviving the Ancient Faith: The Story of Churches of Christ in America* (1996), coauthor of *Illusions of Innocence: Protestant Primitivism in America, 1630–1875* (1988), and editor of *The American Quest for the Primitive Church* (1988) and *The Primitive Church in the Modern World* (1995).

WILLIAM E. JUHNKE, a history professor and the occupant of the F. Henry Edwards Chair of Religious Studies at a Reorganized Latter Day Saints (RLDS) school, Graceland College, at Lamoni, Iowa, has published in *Restoration Studies VI* (1995) on the subject of the RLDS becoming a peace church. He has also contributed to the book *Nonviolent America: History through the Eyes of Peace* (1993), edited by Louise Hawkley and James C. Juhnke.

GEORGE R. KNIGHT has been on the faculty of Andrews University, Berrien Springs, Michigan, since 1976—since 1985 as professor of church history. He has been a research editor for *The Journal of Adventist Education* (1980–1991), the editor of *Andrews University Seminary Studies* (1988–1991), and the director of Andrews University Press (1992–1995). In addition to writing numerous articles and reviews on church history, theology, and educational foundations, he has authored or edited many books. Among them are *Millennial Fever and the End of the World: A Study of Millerite Adventism* (1993), *Anticipating the Advent: A Brief History of Seventh-day Adventism* (1993), *Philosophy and Education: An Introduction in Christian Perspective* (1980, 1989), and *Myths in Adventism* (1985).

TED KOONTZ, trained in international relations, is a professor of ethics and peace studies at the Associated Mennonite Biblical Seminary in Elkhart, Indiana. He has taught at Silliman University Divinity School in the Philippines and served on the staff of the Mennonite Central Committee's Peace Section. Among his various publications a recent one is "Christian Nonviolence: An Interpretation," in Terry Nardin, ed., *The Ethics of War and Peace* (1996).

THEODORE KORNWEIBEL JR., a professor of African-American history at San Diego State University in California, is the author of *No Crystal Stair: Black Life and "The Messenger," 1917–1928* (1975) and the editor of *In Search of the Promised Land: Essays in Black Urban History* (1981) and a microfilm collection entitled *Federal Surveillance of Afro-Americans (1917–1925): The First World War, the Red Scare, and the Garvey Movement* (1985). He has a book in preparation on the U.S. government's campaigns against black militancy, 1918–25.

PATRICIA MCNEAL is an associate professor and the director of the Women's Studies Program at Indiana University South Bend. Over the past decades she has published many articles on Catholic conscientious objection, Catholic peace organizations, the Catholic pacifist and social activist Dorothy Day, and the Catholic peace movement generally. She has been a visiting fellow at the Institute for International Peace Studies at the University of Notre Dame and is the author of *Harder Than War: Catholic Peacemaking in Twentieth Century America* (1992).

WILLIAM R. MARTY, a professor of political science, teaches at the University of Memphis in Tennessee and is also the associate editor of the *Journal of Interdisciplinary Studies*. He has written more than two dozen articles and essays on the relationships between reason, revealed religion, and political or social life.

S. RONALD PARKS, trained at Lancaster Theological Seminary (M.Div) and Drew University (Ph.D.), is the pastor of the Everett Extended Ministry of the United Methodist Church in Everett, Pennsylvania. His essay in this book grows out of his doctoral dissertation on the ethical formation of United Methodist conscientious objectors during the Vietnam War. At present he is continuing such research with United Methodist case studies from the Persian Gulf conflict.

THERON F. SCHLABACH is a history professor at Goshen College, Goshen, Indiana, who is currently in residence as a senior fellow of the Young Center for the Study of Anabaptist and Pietist Groups, at Elizabethtown College, Elizabethtown, Pennsylvania. He is the editor or editor-in-chief of two Mennonite history book series and of other projects and has been an editor of *The Mennonite Quarterly Review*. His own books include two on American social welfare history, plus *Gospel versus Gospel: Missions and the Mennonite Church, 1863–1944* (1980) and *Peace, Faith, Nation: Mennonites and Amish in Nineteenth-Century America* (1988).

SHIRLEY HERSHEY SHOWALTER, president-elect of Goshen College, Goshen, Indiana, has written numerous articles on interdisciplinary topics in journals ranging from *Quaker History* and *The Mennonite Quarterly Review* to *The Chronicle of Higher Education*. In 1995–96 she was a visiting scholar at the University of North Carolina, developing a project on contemplation, imagination, and teaching.

MERLE D. STREGE, a professor of historical theology at Anderson University, Anderson, Indiana, is a member of the Wesleyan/Holiness Movement Study Project and is the official historian of the Church of God (Anderson, Indiana). He has written *Tell Me the Tale: Historical Reflections on the Church of God (Anderson)* (1991) and *Tell Me Another Tale: Further Reflections on the Church of God (Anderson)* (1993) and has edited *Baptism and Church: A Believers' Church Vision* (1986).

GRANT UNDERWOOD is a professor of religion at Brigham Young University–Hawaii and has written extensively on Mormonism, a principal example being *The Millenarian World of Early Mormonism* (1993). He and his wife, Sheree, "work for peace" in a family of nine that includes two sets of twin girls.

RONALD A. WELLS is a professor of history at Calvin College, Grand Rapids, Michigan, and the director of the Calvin Center for Christian Scholarship. He has been the editor of two periodicals, *Fides et Historia* and *The Reformed Journal.* He also is the author or editor of seven books, including *History through the Eyes of Faith* (1989) and *The Wars of America: Christian Views* (1991).

INDEX